DRIVING TOURS
GERMANY

Macmillan • USA

CONTENTS

Written by Adi Kraus
Copy editors: Emma Stanford, Dilys Jones

Edited, designed, produced and distributed by AA Publishing, Norfolk House, Priestley Road, Basingstoke RG24 9NY.

© The Automobile Association 1992
Reprinted 1994

Maps © The Automobile Association 1992

All rights reserved. No part of this publication may be reproduced, stored in a retrieval system, or transmitted in any form or by any means – electronic, mechanical, photocopying, recording or otherwise – unless the written permission of the publishers has been given beforehand.

Typesetting: Servis Filmsetting Ltd, Manchester

Colour reproduction: Scantrans P.T.E., Singapore

Printed and bound in Italy by Printers S.R.L., Trento

The contents of this publication are believed correct at the time of printing. Nevertheless, the publishers cannot accept responsibility for errors or omissions, or for changes in details given.

Every effort has been made to ensure accuracy in this guide. However, things do change and we would welcome any information to help keep the book up to date.

Published by AA Publishing

Published in the United States by Macmillan Travel.
   Prentice Hall
   Macmillan Company,
   15 Columbus Circle,
New York, NY 10023.

Macmillan is a registered trademark of Macmillan Inc.

ISBN 0-13-220427-4

Cataloging-in-Publication Data is available from the Library of Congress

Title page: *Landshut fortress, Bernkastel*

Above: *Loreley Rock, St Goarshausen*

Right: *Freiburg's Rathaus*

Introduction **4–7**

Route map of Germany **6–7**

The Northern Lowlands & the East **8–29**

Tour 1 Northern Ports & Two Seas **10–13**
Tour 2 The Royal Connection **14–17**
Tour 3 Old & New Capital of Germany **18–21**
Tour 4 The Upper Elbe, Rocks & Castles **22–25**
Tour 5 Towns & Forests of Thuringia **26–29**

The German Midlands **30–47**

Tour 6 The Harz Mountains & Forests **32–35**
Tour 7 East & West of the Weser **36–39**
Tour 8 Nature Parks & Fairy Tales **40–43**
Tour 9 Dams, Lakes & Woods **44–47**

Bavaria **48–81**

Tour 10 Franconia & its Historic Towns **50–53**
Tour 11 Around Nürnberg & Regensburg **54–57**
Tour 12 The Danube & Bavarian Forest **58–61**
Tour 13 Around Lake Chiem & Berchtesgaden **62–65**
Tour 14 The Bavarian Lakes **66–69**
Tour 15 The Alps South of München **70–73**
Tour 16 Bavarian Swabia **74–77**
Tour 17 The Alps East of Lindau **78–81**

Baden-Württemberg **82–95**

Tour 18 Lakes & Shores of Konstanz **84–87**
Tour 19 The Southern Black Forest **88–91**
Tour 20 Spas & the Northern Black Forest **92–95**

The Five River Valleys 96–117
Tour 21 The Tranquil Saar Valley **98–101**
Tour 22 The Enchanting Mosel Valley **102–105**
Tour 23 The Romantic Neckar **106–109**
Tour 24 The River Main & East of the Rhine **110–113**
Tour 25 Along the Left Bank of the Rhine **114–117**
Index **118–120**

INTRODUCTION

This book is not only a practical guide for the independent traveller, but is also invaluable for those who would like to know more about the country.

It is divided into 5 regions, each containing between 3 and 8 tours. The tours start and finish in major towns and cities which we consider to be the best centres for exploration. Each tour has details of the most interesting places to visit en route. Side panels cater for special interests and requirements and cover a range of categories – for those whose interest is in history, wildlife or walking, and those who have children. There are also panels which highlight scenic stretches of road along the route and which give details of special events, gastronomic specialities, crafts and customs. These are cross-referred back to the main text.

The simple route directions are accompanied by an easy-to-use map of the tour and there are addresses of local tourist information centres in the towns en route as well as in the start town.

Simple charts show how far it is from one town to the next in kilometres and miles. These can help you to decide where to take a break and stop overnight, for example. (All distances quoted are approximate.)

Before setting off it is advisable to check with the information centre at the start of the tour for recommendations on where to break your journey and for additional information on what to see and do, and when best to visit.

TOURIST OFFICES

Australia – Lufthansa House, 12th Floor, 143 Macquerie Street, Sydney 2000 (*tel*: (02) 221 1008).
Canada – 175 Bloor Street East, North Tower, 6th Floor, Toronto, Ontario M4W 3R8 (*tel*: (416) 968 1570).
UK – Nightingale House, 65 Curzon Street, London W1Y 7PE (*tel*: (071) 495 3990).
US – 747 Third Avenue, 33rd Floor, New York, NY 10017 (*tel*: (212) 308 3300); 104S Michigan Avenue, Suite 600, Chicago, Illinois 60603–5978 (*tel*: (312) 782 8557); 444 South Flower Street, Suite 2230, Los Angeles CA 90017 (*tel*: (213) 688 7332).

ENTRY REGULATIONS
A valid passport is required by EC nationals and those of Australia, Canada, New Zealand and the US. Nationals of other countries must have a visa.

CUSTOMS REGULATIONS
Visitors from non-EC countries can take in 200 cigarettes or 50 cigars or 250 grams of tobacco, a litre of spirits and two litres of wine without paying duty. Visitors from EC countries can take in 300 cigarettes, or 75 cigars or 400 grams of tobacco, 1.5 litres of spirits and 5 litres of still wine. There are no currency restrictions.

EMERGENCY TELEPHONE NUMBERS
Police and Ambulance 110
Fire 112

CREDIT CARDS
Eurocheques are welcomed but credit cards are not much used in Germany; only the major cards are known and accepted in good hotels, shops, banks and top restaurants.

HEALTH
No vaccinations are needed to enter Germany. Citizens of other EC countries are entitled to free medical treatment, on production of Form E111 or

Berchtesgaden in Bavaria, surrounded by some of Germany's grandest mountain scenery

INTRODUCTION 5

The Rhine, European trade artery and river of tales and legends

equivalent form. You must obtain this before leaving home, from your main post office. It is wise to take out travel insurance as well, in case of accident or illness.

CURRENCY
There are 100 pfennigs (Pf) in 1 Deutsche Mark (DM). Coins: 1, 2, 5, 10, 50Pf and DM1, 2, 5. Notes: DM 5, 10, 20, 50, 100, 500, 1000.

BANKS
Banks are open Monday to Friday 08.30–13.00 hrs and 14.30–16.00 hrs (17.30 hrs on Thursdays). Exchange offices of the Deutsche-Verkehrs-Kredit-Bank are located at main railway stations, and road and rail frontier crossing points. Generally they are open from early morning until late at night.

TIME
Germany is one hour ahead of Greenwich Mean Time (GMT) in winter and two hours ahead in summer.

POST OFFICES
Post offices are generally open Monday–Friday from 08.00–18.00 hrs, Saturdays till 12.00 hrs. Poste restante mail is issued on presentation of an identity card passport. Money orders telegraphed from abroad are cashed in DM. Post boxes are bright yellow.

ELECTRICITY
220 volts on a continental two-pin plug.

INTRODUCTION

TELEPHONES

International calls can be made from public telephone kiosks showing a black receiver in a green square. They take DM1, 2 and 5 coins. Cheap rates operate during the weekend and Monday to Friday 20.00–08.00 hrs. Cardphones can also be used for telephoning abroad.

MOTORING

Accidents

As a general rule you are required to call the police when individuals have been injured or considerable damage has been caused. Failure to give aid to anyone injured will render you liable to a fine.

Documents

You must have a valid driving licence, passport, third party insurance and vehicle registration document. Anyone remaining in Germany for more than a year must have a German driving licence. Presentation of the foreign driving licence is usually sufficient for the issue of a German permit.

Car hire

Car hire is available at most airports, main railway stations and in larger towns. You must be over 21 and have driven for at least a year.

Breakdowns

If your car breaks down, try to move it to the side of the road so that it does

USEFUL WORDS

The following is a list of useful words and phrases.
English German
yes ja
no nein
please bitte
good morning/day guten Morgen/Tag
goodbye auf Wiedersehen
excuse me entschuldigen Sie bitte
how are you? wie geht es Ihnen?
very well, thanks; and you? danke, gut; und Ihnen?
do you speak English? sprechen Sie Englisch?
I don't understand Ich verstehe nicht
my name is . . . Ich heisse . . .
where? wo?
when? wann?
today heute
yesterday gestern
where is . . . ? wo ist . . . ?
open offen
closed geschlossen
good gut
bad schlecht
big gross
small klein
expensive teuer
cheap billig
how much does it cost? wieviel kostet es?
Monday, Tuesday, Wednesday, Thursday, Friday, Saturday, Sunday Montag, Dienstag, Mittwoch, Donnerstag, Freitag, Samstag, Sonntag
1 to 10 eins, zwei, drei, vier, funf, sechs, sieben, acht, neun, zehn

PUBLIC HOLIDAYS

1 January – New Year's Day
Good Friday; Easter Monday and Ascension Day – variable dates
1 May – Labour Day
3 October – Day of Unity
3rd Wednesday in November – Day of Prayer and Repentance
24 December (pm), 25 and 26 December – Christmas

INTRODUCTION 7

not obstruct traffic flow. A warning triangle and hazard lights, if fitted, must be used.

The motoring club ADAC operates a breakdown service. Assistance is given free of charge; only the cost of materials has to be reimbursed. In the event of a breakdown on a motorway a patrol can be summoned from an emergency telephone. A small arrow on the marker posts on the verges indicates the direction of the nearest one. When calling, ask specifically for 'Strassenwachthilfe' (road service assistance).

In the Altstadt of Limburg in Hessen. Its half-timbered houses typify the medieval German town

Driving conditions
Drive on the right, pass on the left. There are on-the-spot fines for speeding and other offences.

Speed limits
On motorways (recommended only) 130kph (81mph); outside built-up areas 100kph (62mph); and in built-up areas 50kph (31mph). Traffic regulations are strictly enforced, particularly in relation to speeding and use of alcohol.

At present, different limits are still in force in what was East Germany: 100kph (62mph) on motorways; 80kph (50mph) on main roads; and 50kph (31mph) in towns.

Route directions
Throughout the book the following abbreviations are used for German roads:
 A – Autobahnen
 B – Bundestrasse (federal/national roads)*

* figures only on maps as B roads are numbered only.

CONSULATES

Australia (embassy) – Godesberger Allee 105–7, 5300 Bonn 2 (*tel:* (228) 81030).
Canada – Europa-Center, 1000 Berlin 30 (*tel:* 261 1161).
UK – Uhlandstrasse 7, 1000 Berlin 12 (*tel:* 309 5292).
US – Clayallee 170, Berlin 33 (*tel:* 832 4087).

THE NORTHERN LOWLANDS & THE EAST

The North German plain covers a wide area from Holland in the west to Poland in the east. Many rivers and lakes provide attractive breaks in what otherwise would be an unexciting landscape. Proceeding from the south, the central region is covered by moorlands, which at some 20km (13 miles) from the coast give way to marshes. The North Sea tides raise and lower the normal water level by 2 to 3.5m (7–11 feet), and high sea shipping is possible both on the River Elbe up to 100km (60 miles) from the North Sea coast, and 70km (42 miles) up the River Weser. Dykes protect low-lying lands from flooding at high tides.

The Baltic Sea coast offers quite a different scene. Sand dunes form the coastal strips, up to 100m (300 feet) high, in some places even higher, and seaside resorts enjoying sandy beaches have developed. The winds are less strong than on the North Sea, but you still need protection against them on the beach.

Further south, Saxony and Thuringia are hill country, far removed from the effects of the northern seas. Extensive woodlands, mostly unspoilt by mass tourism, offer a relaxing atmosphere away from the big towns. Its underdeveloped tourist industry will soon provide more opportunities for holidays and relaxation for the hard-pressed urban population.

The livelihood of the people on the northern shores is provided by the sea, with shipbuilding and a large fishing industry as the main employers. A special dialect, called plattdeutsch (or platt) is spoken here, especially in the ports, and is not easily understood by outsiders, even German-speakers.

Berlin has been proclaimed as the capital of a united Germany and its economy is supported by a fair amount of local industry. However, the massive discrepancies between the wealth and know-how of the heavily subsidised western sectors and formerly communist East Berlin, which was not ever exposed to market forces, has left economic and social divisions which will take many years to balance out.

Saxony used to be one of Germany's prime industrial centres, but the recent years have seen serious neglect in the modernisation of its plants and machinery. It will take a major investment programme to bring local industry into the 1990s, but judging by Saxony's previous industrial record, before communist control, one can only assume that it will soon regain its rightful place at the top of the economic pile.

Tour 1

There is 'water, water everywhere' on this tour of Germany's northern tip. From Hamburg, on the Elbe estuary, the route takes a break on the island town of Ratzeburg, in the middle of a lake, before crossing into what used to be East Germany, and Schwerin, the 'Town of the Seven Lakes'. Then it's up to the Baltic Sea and the once-powerful ports of the Hanseatic League before heading northwest from Lübeck to Kiel via an agglomeration of lakes called the 'Holsteinische Schweiz' (Switzerland of Holstein) in an attempt to convey their scenic beauty. The mighty River Elbe, and its extensive estuary, provides a natural border to the south, and guides the way back to Hamburg.

Tour 2

Starting in Bremen, another historic and prosperous German port, this tour journeys in an area where the clearest German is spoken, and a strong link between the Hanoverian and English crowns was forged in the 18th century. Industry and commerce are happily balanced here with old traditions and notable reminders of the past. A fascinating detour into the vast tracts of the heathland known as the Lüneburger Heide, rounds off this tour. Wildlife and flora flourish in this carefully protected environment, where, in certain defined areas, the car becomes off-limits and horse-drawn carts provide the only transport.

THE NORTHERN LOWLANDS & THE EAST

Tour 3
Although unified in name, it will take some time before the very real social and economic wall is finally torn down in Berlin. At present, there are still 'Ossis' trying to make ends meet in the east, and the prosperous 'Wessis' living it up in West Berlin. Life is never dull in the western sector, where plenty of bars and nightclubs do not close until the early hours of the morning. During the day the scene changes, and this is the time to venture through the Brandenburg Gate on to Unter den Linden for a stroll down Berlin's memory lane. This was the old heart of Berlin, and there is tangible evidence of its former power and prestige in many of the important buildings and the art treasures of its magnificent museums.

Tour 4
From the world of business and politics, this tour travels from the bustling environs of Leipzig, via the delicate porcelain of Meissen to a resurrected town. The job of restoring Dresden is not quite finished yet, but the work so far has been little short of miraculous. One of the great highlights here is the priceless Zwinger collections of art treasures and porcelain displayed in a baroque palace. Further on, there are startling natural wonders in the form of bizarre rock formations; and the tour ends with a visit to the famous World War II POW camp, Colditz.

Above: Die Bastei (the Bastion), set above the Elbe near Bad Schandau, calls for a good head for heights

Tour 5
A passing acquaintance with German literature really brings this tour alive. The itinerary starts in Weimar, a historic cultural centre which was once home to the artist Lucas Cranach, and the poets Goethe and Schiller. Then the route continues on to Jena, cradle of 18th-century German philosophy and 19th-century scientific discovery, to Eisenach, where Martin Luther translated the New Testament between 1521 and 1522. Later, still, the beautifully, unspoilt Forests of Thuringia provide much needed relaxation, as they must have done for past generations of great thinkers.

Left: The Renaissance Rathaus of Celle, one of the architectural delights of this Niedersachsen town

2/3 days – 550km (341 miles)

NORTHERN PORTS & TWO SEAS

Hamburg • Ahrensburg • Ratzeburg • Schwerin
Wismar • Lübeck • Kiel • Rendsburg • Hamburg

Hamburg has twice suffered the effects of large-scale destruction. First a fire in 1842, and then as a result of bombing during World War II, but its historic buildings have been carefully restored.

Look out for the six spires piercing the horizon. They belong to the churches of *St Michaelis*, *St Nikolai* (one of the tallest in Germany), *St Petri*, *St Katherinen*, *St Jakobi* and to the *Rathausturm* (Town Hall Tower). The central attraction is the *Rathaus* (Town Hall) and the *Rathausmarkt* (market), which was redesigned after the fire of 1842. *Hauptkircke St Michaelis* was founded in 1751 and is noted for its tower, *Der Michel*, the popular emblem of the town.

Hamburg's famous entertainment district, *St Pauli*, lies just north of the Elbe, southwest of the city centre. For a real bird's eye view of Hamburg, check out the sights from 270m (890 feet) up the *Fernsehturm* (television tower).

Visitors to historic Lübeck can take a walking tour guided by a colourful town official

[i] Burchardstrasse 14

From Hamburg take the B75 northeast for 21km (13 miles) to Ahrensburg.

Ahrensburg, Schleswig-Holstein

1 Built around 1595, the moated castle of Ahrensburg lies north of the town and was reopened to the public in 1955, after complete renovation. Today it is in excellent condition and its cosy interior has remained largely unchanged over the centuries. The façade consists of three sections with gabled roofs, flanked by two towers, all in late-Renaissance style. Valuable furniture and paintings adorn the interior.

[i] Stadtverwaltung

Continue on the B75 to Bad Oldesloe, then take the B208 southeast for 50km (31 miles) to Ratzeburg.

Ratzeburg, Schleswig-Holstein

2 Three dams and bridges connect the island town of Ratzeburg with the mainland. An **observation tower** on the embankment offers particularly attractive views of the town and its surroundings. The magnificent **Dom** (cathedral) is one of the largest and oldest Romanesque church buildings in northern Germany. Built of bricks, it was founded in 1154 by Heinrich der Löwe (Henry the Lion), and stands on the northern part of the island. Ancient paintings can be seen in the cloister while the High Altar is decorated by an illustration of the *Crucifixion*. Do not miss the chapel of the south transept which is furnished with beautiful ornaments finished in old gold. Near the cathedral, the *Herrenhaus* (Gentlemen's House) was erected for the dukes of Mecklenburg and now houses a local museum.

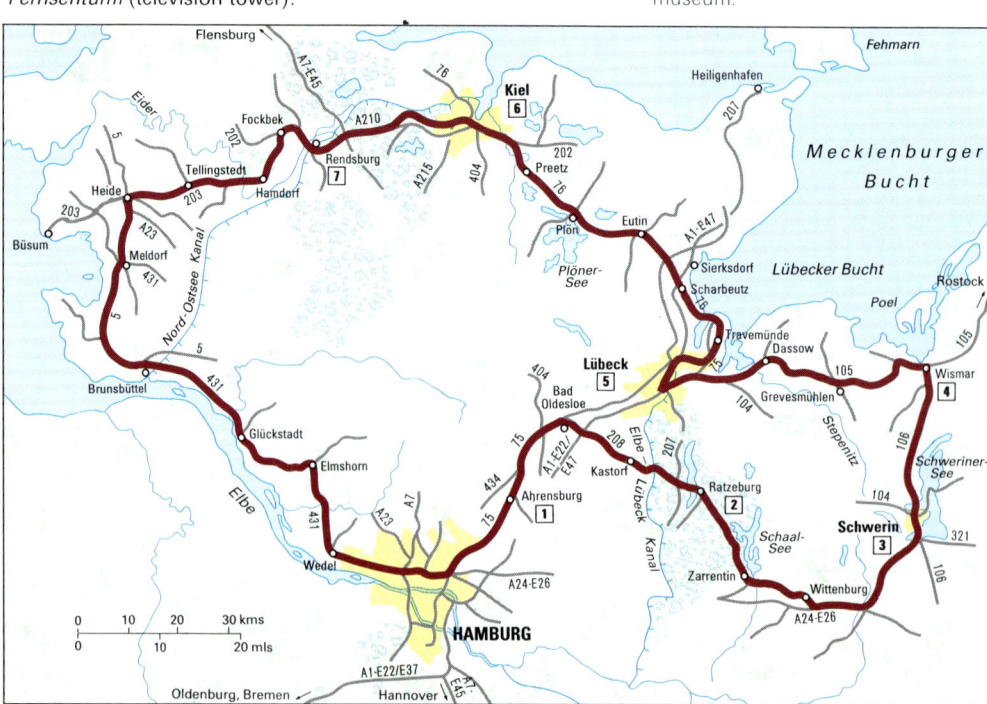

[i] Alte Wache, Am Markt 9

*Drive southeast via Zarrentin and Wittenburg to the **A24**, then continue east on the **A24** to the Hagenow exit and turn north to Schwerin, 64km (40 miles).*

Schwerin, Mecklenburg-Vorpommern

3 Also called the 'Town of the Seven Lakes', Schwerin was founded by the Saxon duke, Heinrich der Löwe (Henry the Lion) in 1160. After he had defeated the Slavonic tribe of the Obotriten (Abodrites), Heinrich expelled their leader, Duke Niklot, from his castle on the **Schlossinsel** (Castle Island), founded the County of Schwerin in 1167 and started to rebuild the **castle**. In 1358, Albrecht II bought Schwerin, and from then on the castle, with few interruptions, became the residence of the dukes of Mecklenburg until the demise of the German monarchy in 1918.

Today, the castle is the handiwork of several architects and builders, notably Gottfried Semper and Adolph Demmler. The latter was heavily influenced by the French-style elegance of Château Chambord in the Loire Valley. The surrounding gardens are planted with many exotic trees, and brilliant lawns, interspersed by ponds. There is also an **Orangerie**, lined with colonnades which transforms the inner courtyard into a romantic setting for evening concerts and recitals. The interior of the castle is beautifully appointed with inlaid parquet floors, highly polished wood-panelled walls and gilded beams supporting the ceilings. Highlights include the Throne Room, the Ancestor's Gallery, the Smoking Room and the Equerry's Chamber. Overlooking the Burgsee (Castle Lake), one wing houses a history museum exhibiting articles dating back to the Stone Age; and the Renaissance-style **Schlosskapelle** (chapel) built between 1560 and 1563 is lavishly decorated.

In the old town, which is situated between two lakes, the **Pfaffenteich** and the **Burgsee**, the historic streets and squares have been recently and thoroughly restored, including the market square and the **Rathaus** (town hall), a part of which dates back to the 14th century. The Court Architect, Demmler, added its new neo-Gothic façade in 1835. The **State Museum**, a model of late classicism, received Italian Renaissance ornaments to improve its modest façade. The exhibits include many paintings by Flemish, Dutch, German and French masters of the 17th and 19th centuries. The **Dom** (cathedral) was built between the 13th and early 15th centuries. Especially noteworthy are the Gothic Altar of the Cross, brass tomb plates and the Gothic font.

[i] Markt 11

*Take the **B106** north for 31km (19 miles) to Wismar.*

RECOMMENDED WALKS

3 *Schwerin, Mecklenburg-Vorpommern* At Schwerin there is a pleasant walk along the **Schweriner See** and the **Schlosspark**.

5 *Lübeck, Schleswig-Holstein* About 1.5km (1 mile) north of Lübeck is the **Brodtener Steilufer**, a 4km (2½-mile) long cliff, with fine views over the sea, and a golf course.

SCENIC ROUTES

Between Lübeck and Kiel, the route passes through the picturesque **Holsteinische Schweiz** (Swiss Holstein) region. Take the main road from Lübeck to Travemünde, and then the **B76** via Eutin to enjoy the delights of this popular lakeland holiday destination.

The castle at Schwerin, a Loire château on a German lake

SPECIAL TO...

4 *Wismar, Mecklenburg-Vorpommern* The curiously named **Baumhaus** (Tree House) in Wismar's old harbour is the point from which ships' movements were monitored. At night a tree was placed across the harbour to prevent ships entering or leaving.

5 *Lübeck, Schleswig-Holstein.* The **Sommerspiele** festivities at Eutin, between Lübeck and Kiel, offer annual open-air theatre performances in the **Schlosspark** (castle grounds) every July and August. Composer Karl Maria von Weber's opera *Der Freischütz* is always on the programme here, in honour of his position as the town's most famous son.

FOR HISTORY BUFFS

5 *Lübeck, Schleswig-Holstein* The **Buddenbrookhaus** in Lübeck, at Mengstrasse 4, was owned by the well-known novelist Thomas Mann's family from 1841 to 1891. Built in 1758, it is named after one of Mann's most famous novels, *Buddenbrooks*, which describes the decline of a wealthy Lübeck family. He was awarded the Nobel Prize for Literature in 1929.

Wismar, Mecklenburg-Vorpommern

4 The Baltic seaport of Wismar is protected from the open sea by the island of **Poel**. First mentioned as *Aqua Wissemara*, it was probably founded by the nearby town of Lübeck. In 1259, the ports of Wismar, Lübeck and Rostock on the Baltic Sea formed a pact against pirates, which later developed into the all-powerful Hanseatic League. The Swedish Crown owned the town from 1648 to 1803, and then mortgaged it to Mecklenburg. It was 1903 before Wismar was truly returned to the province of Mecklenburg.

Views over the large market square are dominated by the **Wasserkunst**, a grandiose Dutch Renaissance-style former pumping station, which supplied the town with fresh water. Around the square, there are a number of attractive, carefully restored old houses with gabled roofs, plus an historic residence called 'The Old Swede' dating from 1380 – the oldest in Wismar.

i Bohrstrasse 5a

*Take the **B105** west for 53km (33 miles) to Lübeck.*

Lübeck, Schleswig-Holstein

5 Back into what was West Germany before unification, Lübeck is a major port on the Baltic Sea, and also the northern end of the important Elbe-Lübeck Kanal, which carries the Elbe river traffic out into the Baltic.

The town was founded in 1143 by Count Adolf I of Holstein, and became a Free Imperial City in 1226. It was the capital of the Hanseatic League, the association of ports and towns on the Baltic and North Sea coasts founded in the mid-14th century, and later joined by many other German cities further south. The object of the association was primarily to safeguard and control shipping in the region, but it was also a powerful trading entity, and guarded its neutrality with great care.

From the 16th century, Lübeck declined in importance with the gradual dissolution of the Hanseatic alliance. By the 19th century, the town had to endure French rule which, together with competition from other ports, seriously affected the fortunes of the city. However, the opening of the Elbe-Lübeck Kanal prompted a rush of industrialisation, and the recent fall of the East German frontier will surely attract better fortunes. Lübeck does a good trade in red wine, even producing its own *Rotspon* label. Hanseatic merchants first brought back marzipan from the Orient and, with a couple of improvements, it has become one of Lübeck's gourmet specialities.

The outline of the city is basically oval-shaped and surrounded by water. The entrance from the west is mighty **Holstentor**, the old city gate with its twin towers, completed in 1477, and recognised as the emblem of the town. Modern traffic passes by on either side and above the entry portal is a Latin inscription which translates to read 'Unity inside, peace outside'.

Beyond the Holsten gate, there is a fine vista of red brick-built churches and slim spires, and it is a short walk to the imposing **Rathaus** (Town Hall) which stands in the market square and is one of the most grandiose in Germany. Building commenced when Emperor Friedrich II granted Lübeck the status of a Free Imperial city in 1226. A close inspection reveals several styles, the oldest part being the Gothic south façade, followed by the Renaissance-style Neues Gemach annexe. A tour of the

The port of Lübeck, whose prosperity has rested on trade since the days of the Hanseatic League

TOUR 1

interior includes the wine cellars, which together with the Admiral's Room and the Brautgemach (Bridal Suite) should not be missed.

A stroll through the city is highly recommended. Stop off to see 13th-century **St Marienkirche** (St Mary's Church), the prototype for many of the typical brick-built churches scattered around the Baltic area. It has a memorial chapel whose bell crashed down during the air bombardments of 1942. There are several other fine churches in the Old Town, and the **Dom** (cathedral) houses Bernt Notke's superb 1477 *Triumpkreuz* (Triumphal Cross). One of Lübeck's finest restaurants occupies the **Shabbelhaus** on Mengstrasse, an old merchant's house painstakingly restored to its original design after having been completely destroyed during World War II.

[i] Breite Strasse 75

*From Lübeck follow the **B75** north via Travemünde to Scharbeutz and continue on the **B76**, via Eutin, to Kiel, 81km (50 miles).*

Kiel, Schleswig-Holstein

6 Kiel is the main ferry port for traffic to Scandinavia and a favourite destination for cruise ships. The North Sea–Baltic or Kiel Canal from Brunsbüttel ends here, near the point where the Elbe reaches the North Sea. The busiest canal in the world, it is 97km (60 miles) long and ships take between seven and nine hours to pass from one end to the other.

The yachting world knows Kiel for its annual June regattas, and the **Hindenburg Ufer** (quay) is a good spot from which to view all the port activities.

[i] Sophienblatt 30

*Take the **A210** west for 37km (23 miles) to Rendsburg.*

Renaissance doorway in the market square at Wismar

Rendsburg, Schleswig-Holstein

7 Rendsburg lies between the River Elbe and the important Kiel Canal with its Altstadt (Old Town) situated on an island in the Eider. The **Altes Rathaus** (Old Town Hall) is a timber-framed building dating back to 1566. Near by is the 13th-century **Marienkirche** (St Mary's), its interior decorated with valuable 14th-century wall paintings and a splendid 1649 baroque altar.

But it is Rendsburg's technical achievements which are of greatest interest, such as the railway bridge spanning the Kiel Canal at a height of 42m (137 feet), avoiding any obstruction to the funnels of passing ships. A suspended transporter ferry runs underneath the railway lines for passengers and cars. The 1,280m (mile) long **Kanaltunnel** passes 20m (66 feet) beneath the canal and carries road traffic with an escalator tunnel (the longest in Europe) running parallel for pedestrians.

[i] Rathaus

*Take the **B203** to Heide, then the **B5** to Brunsbüttel and continue on the **B431** to Hamburg, 213km (132 miles).*

Hamburg – Ahrensburg **21 (13)**
Ahrensburg – Ratzeburg **50 (31)**
Ratzeburg – Schwerin **64 (40)**
Schwerin – Wismar **31 (19)**
Wismar – Lübeck **53 (33)**
Lübeck – Kiel **81 (50)**
Kiel – Rendsburg **37 (23)**
Rendsburg – Hamburg **213 (132)**

BACK TO NATURE

5 *Lübeck, Schleswig-Holstein*
At **Heiligenhafen** (from Lübeck take the **A1** (**Oldenburg**)/**B207**), there is the **Graswarder nature reserve and bird sanctuary**, offering daily tours between April and September, to see large colonies of breedings birds, including several species of terns and black-headed gulls.

Keep a lookout for white storks. These large white and black birds have big red bills. They feed in the marshes and fields and sometimes nest on rooftops.

FOR CHILDREN

5 *Lübeck, Schleswig-Holstein*
Not far north of Lübeck, **Hansa Park** at **Sierksdorf** is easily reached by taking the **A1** and turning right at the Eutin exit for Sierksdorf. This excellent fun park offers a great variety of exciting entertainment from shows like 'Panther of Padishah' and the 'Acapulco Diver' to dolphin and sealion performances. There is also the 'Metro-Liner' which promises the 'fastest train' experience for those determined to travel at speed, and many fun fair rides for the whole family in the pleasantly arranged landscaped gardens.

2/3 days – 484km (300 miles)

THE ROYAL CONNECTION

Bremen • Hannover • Braunschweig • Wolfsburg
Wienhausen • Celle • Lüneburger Heide • Bremen

Bremen, like Hamburg, is an independent federal state, together with its port of Bremerhaven, some 57km (35 miles) further down the River Weser. The heart of the ancient city is the market square, surrounded by beautifully kept old and modern buildings. In front of the *Rathaus* (Town Hall) the statue of Roland was erected in 1404 as a symbol of civic justice and strength.

Close by stands the *Dom* (St Peter's Cathedral) with its two 98m (320-foot) high towers. Dating back to the 11th century, it illustrates the development of medieval architecture from Romanesque to late-Gothic, though much of the structure was rebuilt at the end of the last century.

Der Schnoor, in the eastern part of the old town near the Weser, is a typical fishermen's quarter of narrow streets with picturesque 15th- to 19th-century cottages, now adapted to house crafts and antique shops or restaurants.

SCENIC ROUTES

The stretch of road between Wolfsburg and Gifhorn, (B188) is one of the loveliest sections of the **Deutsche Ferienstrasse** (German Holiday Road). One of Europe's finest natural preserves, the Lüneburger Heide offers a wealth of magnificent views and native wildlife. Away from the highways, on the route from Bispingen to Ehrhorn, it is hard to believe that the great industrial cities of the north are less than an hour's drive in all directions.

SPECIAL TO...

1 *Hannover, Niedersachsen*
The annual **Hannover Trade Fair** in April is the largest of its kind in the world, and transforms the city into a buzzing cosmpolitan arena. There are a host of special events planned alongside the main exhibitions, and Hannover really lets its hair down.

[i] Hillmannplatz 6

*From Bremen head southeast to Verden, via Achim, turn south on to the **B215** to Leese and continue south on the **B441** to Hannover, 140km (87 miles).*

Hannover, Niedersachsen

1 Hannover (Hanover in English) is the capital of the province of Niedersachsen (Lower Saxony). Its position and transport links have made it an important industrial and trading centre on the busy east–west Mittelland Kanal.

Despite industrialisation, the city's legacy of green open spaces interspersed with lakes lends credence to its claim to be the Grossstadt im Grünen (the Green Capital).

Written records first mention a market place called *vicus Hanovere* in 1150. Heinrich der Löwe (Henry the Lion) gave it city status, and a treaty in 1495 brought Hannover under the rule of the Calenberg family, whereupon Duke Georg von Calenberg moved his residence here. Hannover flourished under Kurfürst (Elector) Ernst August. In 1658 the Duke married Princess Palatine Sophia, a granddaughter of James I. Their son,

Detail from the ornately carved façade of Bremen's Rathaus. Its confident style reflects Bremen's history as Germany's oldest port and a city of free merchants

George Ludwig, later succeeded to the English throne as George I, forming a union between the Hanoverian and the English crowns which lasted up until the Victorian era.

During the 19th century, the city enjoyed a further golden age of economic and cultural growth. Fashionable architect/builder George Ludwig Laves founded the **Opera House**, and created plans for the future outline of the city.

To explore the most interesting sights, start on the quayside by the River Leine at the **Beginenturm**, a sturdy round stone tower which stands on the spot of the original settlement. Next, the 14th-century **Marktkirche** (Market Church) is a Gothic brick-built structure which succeeded a Romanesque church first mentioned in 1238. On the market square, the late Gothic **Altes Rathaus** (Old Town Hall) dates from the first half of the 15th century, and has been beautifully restored.

Kramerstrasse leads off the square and its historic timber-framed houses are some of the few remaining examples of Old Hanover, most of which was destroyed by bombing during World War II. Not far from the Friedrichswall, the early 20th-century **Neue Rathaus** building is unmistakably Prussian. Erected during the Wilhelmina era, this grandiose neo-Gothic edifice sports an enormous dome, rather out of proportion with the rest of the building. A lift provides easy access to the top and a view over the town.

The **Herrenhausen Garten**, in the grounds of **Herrenhausen Castle**, is regarded as one of the finest gardens in Europe. Laid out in 1714, it consists of four quite different and separate sections. The oldest section is French-influenced, with flowered borders and allegorical statues positioned in the corners; while the **Berggarten** (mountain garden) is of specialist interest on account of the variety and rarity of its species. Do not miss the greenhouses which contain a wealth of orchids, cacti and other tropical flowers; and there is a mausoleum dedicated to the House of Hannover in the northern part of the garden which contains the sarcophagus of King George I of England.

Hannover can offer a choice of interesting museums including the excellent **Kestner-Museum** which exhibits 5,000 years of Egyptian, Greek and Roman antiquities, plus European decorative art – ceramics and Art Nouveau silverware. The **Niedersächsiche Landesmuseum** (Museum of Lower Saxony) has a historical department dealing with the evolution of man in the area, among other exhibitions, and the **Sprengel Museum of 20th-century Art** is situated in the attractive Maschsee Park.

[i] Ernst August Platz 8

*Take the **B65** east for 66km (41 miles) to Braunschweig (Brunswick).*

TOUR 2

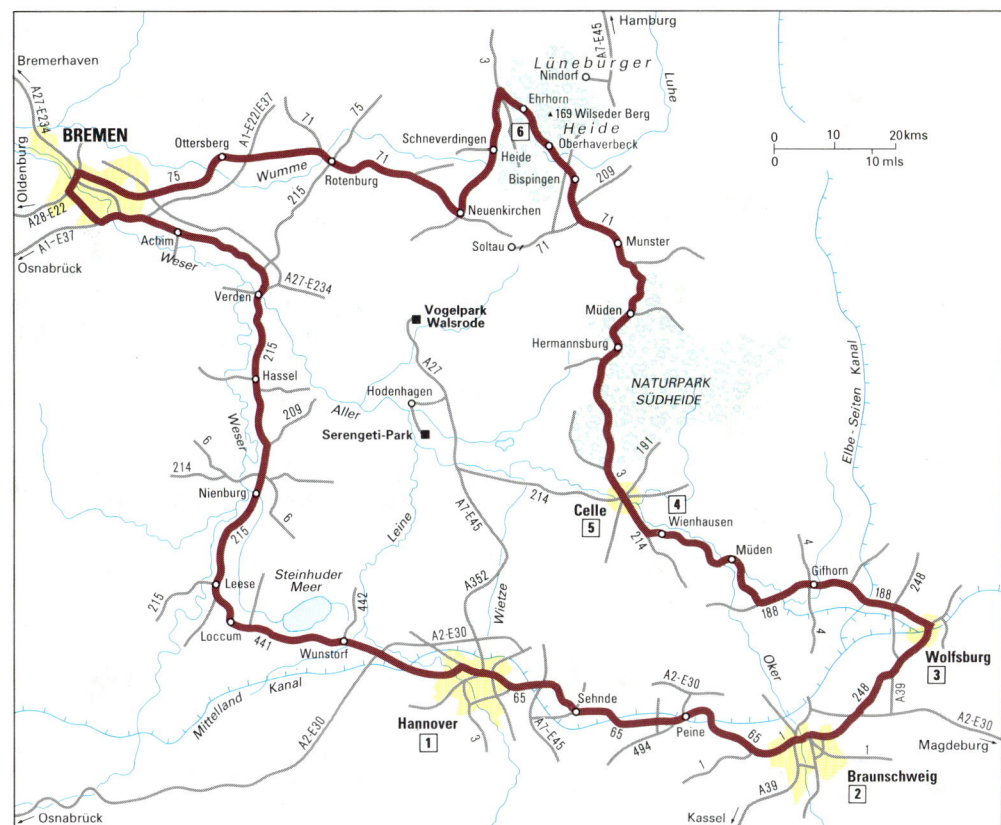

Braunschweig, Niedersachsen

2 Braunschweig is a town very much associated with its mighty prince, Heinrich der Löwe, Duke of Saxony and Bavaria, who made it his residential seat. He himself erected the fine bronze statue of a lion which still stands in the town's central square, the **Burgplatz**. Heinrich also built the **Burg Dankwarderode** (fortress) in 1175, much altered from 1887 on, and greatly restored after World War II. The bomb damage to the town was so extensive that only a few buildings and corners of Old Brunswick remained to be repaired.

Another building which owes its origins to Heinrich's initiative is the Romanesque-Gothic **Dom**, (St Blasius' Cathedral), built between 1173 and 1195. In the central nave lies the tomb of Heinrich and his wife, Mathilda of England.

Built in 1591, the Renaissance-style **Gewandhaus** on the **Altstadtmarkt** (Old Town Marketplace) boasts a superbly ornate east façade and gable. The house belonged to the tailors' and cloth dealers' guild. Apart from trading purposes, it was used as a banqueting hall, and later transformed into a restaurant. The **Altstadt Rathaus** (Old Town Hall) dates back to the 13th century, and overlooks the 1408 **Marienbrunnen** (Mary's Fountain), erected in the middle of the square and cast from molten lead. Consecrated in 1031, the well restored **Magnikirch** (St Magnus' Church) was one of the original buildings to grace *Brunesguik*, which later evolved into Braunschweig. The interior is an interesting mixture, with modern stained glass windows and a 15th-century font. Behind the church a few 16th-century timber-framed buildings remain intact. Last, but not least, the **Herzog Anton Ulrich Museum** is well worth a visit. It houses a collection largely devoted to 17th-century Flemish and Dutch masters with paintings by Rembrandt, Rubens, van Dyck, Vermeer and others.

[i] Hauptbahnhof

*Take the **B248** for 33km (20 miles) to Wolfsburg.*

The rose garden in Hannover's magnificent Herrenhausen Garten

FOR HISTORY BUFFS

2 *Braunschweig, Niedersachsen* South of the old part of Braunschweig lies the **Bürgerpark** (citizens' park) and the adjoining **Schloss Richmond**. This charming castle was built from 1768 to 1769 in late baroque style for the Duchess Augusta.

Decoration runs riot on the Hoppener Haus in Celle

BACK TO NATURE

1 *Hannover, Niedersachsen*
The **Serengeti-Park** at **Hodenhagen** is well worth a visit. Take the **A352/A7** north from Hannover for 30km (19 miles), then left at the Westenholz exit for Hodenhagen. Arranged like a safari park, there are about 600 species of wild animals roaming around, plus reptile and tropical fish displays.

5 *Celle, Niedersachsen* From Celle, take the **B214** west for 28km (17 miles) to join the **A7** north. Bear left (west) at the Walsrode exit and follow the signs. **Vogelpark Walsrode** is an amazing bird sanctuary. Its feathered inhabitants have been gathered from around the globe, but seem quite at home in the attractive gardens, which are a treat in themselves.

FOR CHILDREN

6 *Lüneburger Heide, Niedersachsen* Just west of the **A7**, **Heide Park Soltau** combines the interest of an animal park with the excitement of trips by monorail, narrow gauge train rides, boating excursions on 'rough water' or on rafts and plenty of other attractions – a real fun fair in natural surroundings.

Wolfsburg, Niedersachsen

3 Wolfsburg's great claim to fame is the massive **Volkswagenwerk** (Volkswagen plant), home of the ubiquitous VW Beetle. Austrian engineer, Ferdinand Porsche, was the originator of the company's most famous model which was years ahead of its time. The distinctive outline concealed a revolutionary engine, air-cooled and very simple to maintain. The whole engine block at the rear of the car could be taken out and exchanged in a matter of minutes without any special tools. Volkswagen's factories were built from scratch on empty fields employing state-of-the-art manufacturing and production designs. Subsidised housing was provided for the workers and from a few small villages, Wolfsburg has now grown into a town of 130,000 inhabitants. A visit to the factory is strongly recommended to see the highly automated manufacture and production processes.

Another object of civic pride is mighty **Wolfsburg Castle**. Built during the Renaissance period, it was restored in the 1970s, and serves as a cultural centre and conference venue.

[i] Pavillon Rathausvorplatz

> *Head west from Wolfsburg on the B188. About 10km (6 miles) beyond Gifhorn turn north for Ettenbüttel and continue via Müden and Langlingen to Wienhausen, 59km (37 miles).*

Wienhausen, Niedersachsen

4 A well-kept secret, Wienhausen's medieval treasures attract art experts from far and wide. Its **Kloster** (Convent) and the **Nonnenkirche** (Nuns' Church) contain some of the most valuable works of art in Europe. Originally founded by the Cistercians in the 13th century, and consecrated by the Bishop of Hildesheim, the convent was adopted by a Protestant order after the Reformation. Collections of tapestries, frescos and glass paintings, sculpture and furniture all illustrate tremendous wealth during the 13th to 15th centuries.

The **Nonnenkirche** was built around 1300. Its choir section and Allerheiligen Kapelle (All Saints' Chapel) still retain their original wall paintings, but the medieval tapestries are so valuable that they are only shown once a year for 11 days from the Friday after Whitsuntide to prevent damage. The famous winged altarpiece with its beautifully carved figures is dedicated to the life of the Virgin.

[i] Hauptstrasse 7

> *Continue west to join the B214, then follow the road north to Celle, about 10km (6 miles).*

Celle, Niedersachsen

5 The Dukes of Brunswick and Lüneburg resided here from 1292 to 1866, and the town grew under their patronage. Celle was first documented around 990, by Otto III, who knew the town as *Kellu*, meaning 'a settlement on a river'. Later this was changed to Zelle, and then Latinized to Celle. Heinrich der Löwe was active here, too, granting the settlers privileges for storing goods on the developing long distance trade route via the town.

The **Schloss** was founded in the Gothic period, but rebuilding and alterations changed its shape considerably and only in the last century, after the Prussian takeover, did it emerge in its present form. The reception and banqueting halls are of interest, and the unique baroque-style theatre, which is supposed to be the oldest small theatre in Germany, once had its own company.

The **Altes Rathaus** (Old Town Hall), with its Renaissance gable, stands among a fine collection of richly decorated houses, which exude a comfortably patrician air of days gone by. Take a stroll down attractive Kalandgasse, passing the old **Latin**

Schoolhouse. At the southern end of the narrow lane is the **Stechbahn**, where jousting tournaments were staged. Back on the market place, the **Stadtkirche** (Parish Church) contains the epitaphs and tombstones of the last Duke of Celle, and a burial vault of the Danish Queen, Caroline Mathilde, who died in Celle Castle in 1775.

[i] Markt 6

From Celle drive north to Hermannsburg and continue via Münster and Bispingen to Oberhaverbeck. No cars are allowed from Oberhaverbeck to Wilseder Berg and back, 82km (51 miles).

Lüneburger Heide, Niedersachsen

6 Covering some 7,200sq km (2,800 square miles), Lüneburger Heide (Heath) stretches from Hamburg in the north to Hannover in the south, and from Bremen in the west, east to the Lüneburg/Braunschweig road and beyond. It is the largest expanse of pure heathland in Europe, with its highest point at Wilseder Berg – a small mountain at just 169m (554 feet) above sea level. Residents of the surrounding towns find a welcome respite from the crowds on the heath,

Houses in Lüneburg's old port area. The town's early wealth came from the medieval salt trade

which is best visited in August and September, when the heather is in blossom. At other times, especially in winter, it is a melancholy landscape, scattered with ancient **Hühnengraber** (megalithic tombs) which bear witness to the brief tenure of prehistoric man. Later, the infertile soil prevented any further agricultural encroachments, and now nature reserves maintain the delicate status quo of this unique ecosystem. At the heart of the area, the village of **Wilseder** has a **museum** dedicated to the surrounding heath, and on a clear day there is a spectacular view from the top of the Wilseder Berg. Weather permitting, binoculars can pick out the church spires of Hamburg 40km (25 miles) to the north.

[i] Bispingen, Borsteler Strasse 4–6

*From Oberhaverbeck drive north to Ehrhorn and continue west, crossing the **B3**. Take the next road south to Schneverdingen, continue south, then turn northwest just before Neuenkirchen for the **B71** and the **B75** to Bremen, 94km (58 miles).*

Bremen – Hannover **140 (87)**
Hannover – Braunschweig **66 (41)**
Braunschweig – Wolfsburg **33 (20)**
Wolfsburg – Wienhausen **59 (37)**
Wienhausen – Celle **10 (6)**
Celle – Lüneburger Heide **82 (51)**
Lüneburger Heide – Bremen **94 (58)**

RECOMMENDED WALKS

6 *Lüneburger Heide, Niedersachsen* For a taste of the wide open spaces, nothing beats the trail from Overhaverback to the Wilseder Berg, across the heart of the wild Lüneburger Heide heathland. Spectacular views extend all the way to Hamburg on a clear day, and the heather is alive with honey bees during the late summer. From Bispingen, drive north on the **A7** to the Garlsdorf exit and turn left to **Nindorf Nature Park**. There are idyllic walks through woods here, passing enclosures inhabited by deer, boar, wolves and bears. Paths are well marked, and routes divided into short walks which take about 30 minutes; medium trails of about 45 minutes; and longer walks of around an hour.

1/2 days – 259km (161 miles)

OLD & NEW CAPITAL OF GERMANY

Berlin • Potsdam • Berlin • Lübbenau • Berlin

No city was more in the news during 1989 and 1990 than Berlin, and its emergence from 40 years of division has become one of the historic landmarks of our age. Yet Berlin spent most of its history as a backwater, only achieving prominence in the 19th century as the seat of the Prussian kings.

After World War I, the city suffered heavily from the burden of reparations due to the victors. It was the last bastion of the Third Reich to fall at the end of World War II. Stranded in East Germany after the war, the city was divided into four sectors, each controlled by one of the Allied forces. Soviet attempts to secure the city by blockade were confounded by the Berlin airlift in 1948 to 1949. In 1961, the Soviet-dominated East German regime built a wall between the eastern and western sectors of Berlin, to prevent mass emigration. A death strip was constructed on the eastern side, guarded by barbed wire and watch towers and so it remained until the momentous events of the winter of 1989.

RECOMMENDED WALKS

To get the best of East Berlin in one fell swoop, start at the Brandenburg Gate and follow the length of Unter den Linden, then continue to Alexanderplatz, with its World Time Clock. There is plenty to see and some of the city's best preserved historic buildings are en route.

[i] Berlin West – Europa Centre, Budapester Strasse 45; Berlin Ost – Fernsehturm, Panoramastrasse 1

Kurfürstendamm

1 Berlin itself is made up of a collection of little villages or districts. The Kurfürstendamm is a good starting point. This broad boulevard was the main artery of the prosperous western sector when the city was divided. Known locally as the Ku-Damm, it is lined with prestigious hotels, restaurants, galleries and boutiques. At the top stands the remains of the **Kaiser Wilhelm Gedächtniskirche**, built in memory of Wilhelm I between 1891 and 1895.

Schloss Charlottenburg

2 Northwest of the city centre lies the Charlottenburg district and its castle. Schloss Charlottenburg was founded in 1695 as a summer residence for Queen Sophie Charlotte, the wife of Friedrich I. The original modest building was soon enlarged, and crowned with a dome in 1710. The east wing was added between

Berlin's new unity can go to a souvenir-hunter's head

1740 and 1743. In front of the castle the **Ehrenhof** (Court of Honour) boasts a magnificent equestrian statue of the Great Elector. It was only placed here in 1965, having been brought from the former Royal Palace on the Spree. The castle apartments have been carefully restored to their original appearance and now house a museum of Royal Prussian mementoes. The Prussian rococo-style Goldene Galerie is particularly stunning. Friedrich the Great's notable collection of 18th-century French paintings is exhibited in the east wing, also called the Knobelsdorff Wing, where the king had his living quarters and his own personal library.

The Porcelain Room is largely given over to china from China – delicate plates and figurines cover the walls. An elegantly designed staircase leads up to a large gallery on the first floor, where the insignia of the Prussian Crown are on show.

The **Schlossgarten** (park) was first laid out in the French style in 1697, but later landscaped along English lines at the beginning of the 19th century. There is a mausoleum, in the guise of a small temple, built in 1810. Originally designed to hold the remains of Queen Louise, it now contains the royal tombs of Frederic III, Emperor Wilhelm I and Empress Augusta.

Facing the castle, there are two important museums housed in the guardrooms. The **Antikenmuseum** (Museum of Antiquities) exhibits fine collections of arms, bronzeware and utensils from ancient Greece, Etruria and Crete. However, the real highlights are tucked away in the **Schatzkammer** (treasury), a veritable treasure trove of priceless gold and silver artefacts from the Mediterranean area and Roman objects found in Germany. In the building opposite, the **Ägyptisches Museum** (Egyptian Museum) contains a unique bust of Queen Nefertiti, estimated to have been made around 1350BC. Displays of sarcophagi, jewellery and utensils reveal much about the life and culture of ancient Egypt.

Siegessäule

3 Back at the top of the Ku-Damm, the **Zoologischer Garten** lies due north, and beyond, across the canal, is the **Tiergarten**, which also means 'zoo' in German, but, in this case contains lovely gardens not animals. Several roads through the park converge on the Siegessäule (victory column) towering some 67m (222 feet) above the ground and crowned with a gilt statue of *Victory*. A flight of 285 steps leads up to the observation deck with a bird's eye view of the park and the city.

Brandenburger Tor

4 From the Siegessäule, Strasse des 17 Juni runs due east to the famous Brandenburger Tor (gate) only recently liberated from the eastern side of the Berlin Wall. Erected on the site of an old city gate in 1788, it was made in the style of classical Greek monuments. Above the gate, the

TOUR 3

The war-damaged tower of the Kaiser Wilhelm Memorial Church (Gedächtniskirche)

FOR HISTORY BUFFS

Badly damaged by fire in 1933, and bombing in 1945, the **Reichstag** Parliament Building has been largely restored, and may once again house the German parliament. Meanwhile, it hosts an exhibition of German history from 1800. **Potsdamer Platz**, at the southern end of the Tiergarten, was the site of Hitler's war-time bunker, and where he committed suicide on 30 April 1945.

goddess Victory drives a *quadringa* (ancient chariot) drawn by four horses. The original monument was cast in 1793, and taken to Paris by Napoleon I. It was brought back to Berlin in 1814, but destroyed during World War II. When the original mould was later discovered in West Berlin the statue was re-cast and presented to East Berlin as a gesture of goodwill.

Unter den Linden

5 On the eastern side of the Brandenburg Gate, the poetically named Unter den Linden (Under the Linden Trees) was once a luxury boulevard lined with Old Berlin's most important buildings. An equestrian monument to Friedrich II still stands on the inner promenade. It shows the king in coronation cloak and three-pointed hat, riding on his favourite horse. Further along, **Humboldt University** was originally designed as a palace for Friedrich II's brother between 1748 and 1753. Albert Einstein lectured here. The university faces the **Deutsche Staatsoper** (German State Opera), which was reopened in 1955 after being rebuilt. Behind the Opera House the **Dom** (St Hedwig's Cathedral) is dedicated to the patron saint of the province of Silesia. Near by, the imposing **Kronprinzenpalais** (Palace of the Crown Princes) was built for Prussian royalty in the popular classicist style of the mid-

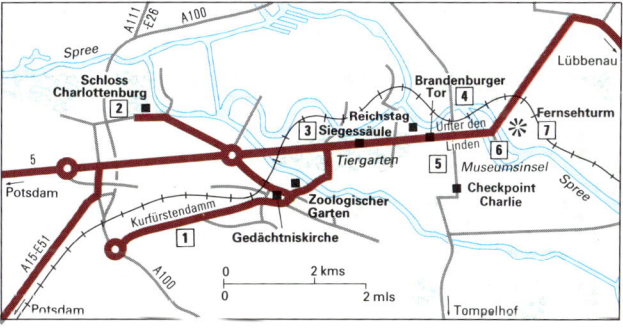

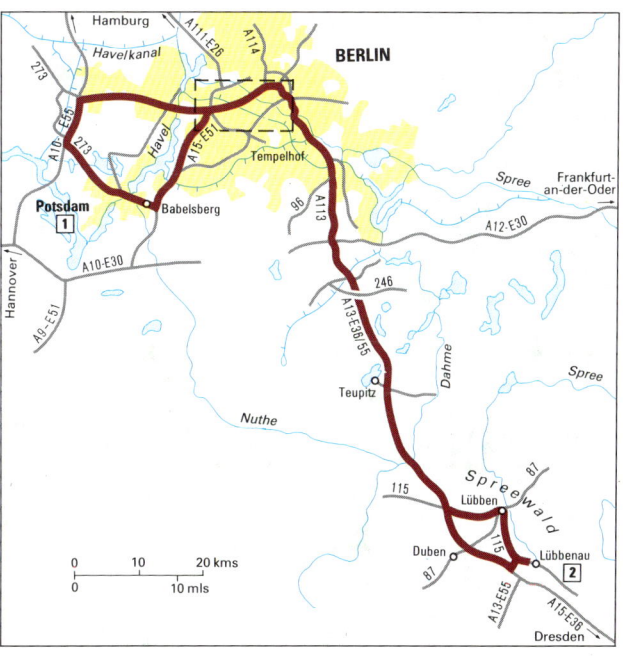

Bridging the culture gap, from Unter den Linden to Museumsinsel

FOR CHILDREN

Although this tour is not specially recommended for children, there is the **Museum für Deutsche Volkskunde** (German Folklore Museum) which has a special toy section with an historical slant exhibiting toy soldiers, dolls and dolls' houses, and old-fashioned games.

The zoos are an obvious attraction for children. The one in the centre of West Berlin is the oldest in Germany, though the animals enjoy well-designed, modern surroundings. (Entrance – Hardenbergplatz.)

The **Tierpark**, in East Berlin, offers special attractions such as a polar bear enclosure, and the **Tropenhalle**, with its collection of exotic fauna and flora. (Entrance via Friedrichsfelde.)

Try **Monbijou Park**, north of the Museumsinsel in East Berlin, a recreation and play centre with a children's bathing facility on the banks of the Spree.

19th century. It was successfully rebuilt after 1945, and used by the former East German government for entertaining. The oldest and perhaps most attractive building on Unter den Linden is the baroque **Zeughaus** (arsenal). Designed by the famous architect and sculptor Andreas Schlüter, it was destined to house the collections of the **Deutsches Historisches Museum** (German History Museum). In the courtyard, Schlüter's *Masken Sterbender Krieger* (Masks of Dying Warriors) is thought one of his finest works.

Museumsinsel

6 Follow the river north to the Museumsinsel (an island created by the Spree Canal and the River Spree) which houses several museums. The **Pergamon Museum** is the best known of these and rates as one of the great museums of Europe, displaying Greco-Roman and Oriental antiquities. The centrepiece is the fabulous *Altar of Zeus and Athene*. Erected at Pergamon, in what is now West Turkey, between 180 and 160BC it is claimed to be one of the wonders of the world. A **Roman market gate** from Milet (Miletus), and sculptures from several early Hellenic cultures further augment the Greek collection. Middle Eastern architecture is represented by the intriguing layout of the Babylonian Processional Way, the Ischtar Gate, and the façade from the throne room of King Nebuchadnezzar II.

Still on the island, the **Bode Museum** is a bit of an all-rounder. Egyptian art and culture, from the prehistoric to the Greek and Roman periods, is revealed in numerous papyri, parchments, wax and wooden tablets from the time of the Pharaohs and examples of early Christian/Byzantine art. Other collections on display here include icons, ceramics and the Apsimosaic from Ravenna in Italy; while yet another section houses sculpture by German, Dutch and French artists from the 12th to the 18th centuries. Coin collectors should not miss the Coin Cabinet which contains around 500,000 items, beginning with early Greek and Roman coins and running through to include modern paper money. North of Bodestrasse, the **National Galerie** exhibits paintings and sculptures from the 18th century to the present day. It faces the **Altes Museum**, which specialises in copper-plate engravings and European prints.

Fernsehturm

7 A modern landmark in former East Berlin, the Fernsehturm (television tower) looms 365m (1,196 feet) above the city. The rotating **Tele-Café**, at a height of 207m (678 feet) affords views which stretch up to 40km (25 miles) into the surrounding countryside. It also reveals the fate of Old Berlin's once attractive and animated central squares and meeting points, which are now vast empty areas, usually surrounded by hideous high-rise blocks built to house the government offices of the former regime. A grim reminder of what life must have been like in this 'worker's paradise', it can only be hoped that these witnesses of the sad past will soon be replaced by more congenial surroundings exuding a true 'Berlinerisch' atmosphere.

EXCURSION 1

*From Berlin Centre drive west on the **A5** to the ring road, **A10/E55**. Head south for exit 'Potsdam Nord' and follow the **B273** southeast to Potsdam, 45km (28 miles).*

Potsdam, Brandenburg

Potsdam, a satellite town for Berlin, is a favourite destination with Berliners wanting a relaxing excursion. Capital of the province of Brandenburg, the town enjoys pleasant woodland surroundings interspersed with lakes formed by the River Havel.

A settlement was mentioned here as early as AD993, but Potsdam's golden hour did not arrive until 1660, when Friedrich Wilhelm, Elector of Brandenburg, chose the town as the residential seat for the ruling Hohenzollern dynasty. He also encouraged the immigration of French Huguenots (Protestant exiles from the reign of Louis XIV), who invested their considerable wealth and craftsmanship into the development of the town. Friedrich der Grosse (the Great) was a great admirer of all things French. He commissioned a mini-Versailles and the result was the delightful **Sanssouci Castle**, the focal point of the town, with grounds that cover a substantial area of Potsdam. This intimate rococo building has only 12 rooms, and was a great success with the king. He paid considerable attention to other parts of the estate, and the architect Knobelsdorff was instructed to build an Orangery, later called the **Neue Kammern** (New Chambers), used to accommodate the king's guests, including the French writer-philosopher Voltaire, and the musician Carl Emanuel Bach. Then followed the **Neptune Grotto**, **Chinese Tea House**, **Drachenhaus** (Dragon's House) and the **Belvedere**. The **Neues Palais**, erected between 1763 and 1769, has a richly appointed interior that boasts the impressive **Marmorsaal** (Marble Hall), and **Schlosstheater**, a private showcase for the ruler's own entertainment.

Other sights include the present **Orangery**, added in the middle of the 19th century and modelled on Italian Renaissance palaces; and the **Raffaelsaal**, which displays 47 copies of paintings by Raphael. Potsdam's **Schloss Cecilienhof** is a copy of an English Tudor-style mansion house. This is where Churchill, Truman and Stalin decided the fate of post-war Germany and signed the Potsdam Treaty on 2 August 1945. The actual conference room and offices of the three leaders can be visited; the rest of the castle functions as a hotel.

[i] Friedrich Ebertstrasse 5

*From Potsdam drive through Babelsberg to join the **A15/E51** and turn northeast back to Berlin Centre, 32km (20 miles).*

Right: Friedrich der Grosse's castle of Sanssouci, of which this is a detail, was built as a mini-Versailles surrounded by splendid gardens

Top right: a gleaming sun motif – another nod towards the Sun King?

EXCURSION 2

*From Berlin Centre take the **A13/E36** southeast to the exit for Lübbenau, and continue west to Lübbenau, 90km (56 miles).*

Lübbenau, Brandenburg

The **Spreewald**, southeast of Berlin, makes an interesting excursion for its special landscape and inhabitants. The people of the Spreewald are mostly of Slavonic descent, refugees from Poland, who have retained their own traditions and language. They are called Sorbs, and have adapted their lifestyle to the special requirements of this wet lowland region, interrupted by sandy islands, which divide the Spree into numerous small rivers and lakes. Houses are built on the islands and transport is mainly by flat bottomed barges or punts. Lübbenau is the starting point for fascinating boat trips into the heart of the Spreewald.

*From Lübbenau take the **B115** north via Lübben to the **A13/E36** and continue north to Berlin, 92km (57 miles).*

Berlin – Potsdam **45 (28)**
Potsdam – Berlin **32 (20)**
Berlin – Lübbenau **90 (56)**
Lübbenau – Berlin **92 (57)**

SPECIAL TO...

At the point where Friedrichstrasse crosses Kochstrasse, the Allied border control post '**Checkpoint Charlie**' is one of the most evocative symbols of the Cold War years. The **Museum** at the checkpoint is a reminder of the human tragedies initiated by the Wall.

1/2 days – 322km (200 miles)

THE UPPER ELBE, ROCKS & CASTLES

Leipzig • Meissen • Dresden • Moritzburg • Königstein
Bad Schandau • Colditz • Leipzig

Leipzig is famous for its literary and musical associations – Friedrich von Schiller, one of Germany's greatest poet-dramatists studied at Leipzig University, and Johann Sebastian Bach lived and worked here, as did Mendelssohn, Schumann and Richard Wagner.

The centrepoint of civic life in Leipzig is the mid-16th-century *Altes Rathaus* (Old Town Hall). Behind the Rathaus lies the *Naschmarkt square*, its northern end adorned with the 17th-century *Alte Handelsbörse* (Old Trading Exchange). In front stands a monument to Goethe, showing the poet as a student at the university. Opposite the Naschmarkt, the *Mädlerpassage* leads into a warren of little passages lined with shops. *Auerbach's Keller* (restaurant) is also there, complete with figures from a scene in Goethe's masterpiece *Faust*. Next to the university stands the cubist-inspired *Neue Gewandhaus*, with several halls and an auditorium designed like an amphitheatre. Close by is the *Kaffeebaum*, Leipzig's famous coffeehouse, which opened in 1694 and later became the meeting point of literary and music circles, frequented by Goethe, Liszt, Wagner and Schumann, among others.

SPECIAL TO...

1 *Meissen, Sachsen* Visitors to the Elbe Valley should keep an eye out for the local wines. **Elbewein** comes from the vineyards along the banks of the Elbe. The **Weinstube Vinzenz Richter** is a famous timber-framed wine cellar dating from the 16th century. Look out for its gory collection of antique weaponry and instruments of torture.

FOR HISTORY BUFFS

2 *Dresden, Sachsen* In Dresden, do not miss the impressive golden equestrian statue of Friedrich August II, Der Starke (The Strong), Elector of Saxony and King of Poland. Erected in 1736, it was designed by French Court sculptor Vinache, cast in copper and gilded by Wiedeman.

[i] Sachsenplatz 1

*From Leipzig take the **B6** for 80km (50 miles) east to Meissen.*

Meissen, Sachsen

1 The 1,000 year-old town of Meissen lies on the River Elbe a short distance northwest of Dresden. Meissen is, of course, known the world over for its beautiful porcelain – identified by the distinctive trademark featuring two crossed swords.

The town's history begins with Heinrich I, who founded **Misni Castle** in 929. Forty years later it became the seat of a bishop, an important step in those days for a growing town. Around AD1000, Meissen was granted *Markrecht*, a decree permitting the settlement to hold its own markets; and in 1150 it was first officially documented as a *Stadt* (town). Further development was hampered by the wars of the Middle Ages, but in 1719 Friedrich August der Starke (The Strong) founded the **Königliche Porzellanmanufaktur** (Royal Porcelain Works) in the Albrechtsburg. It was transferred to the valley of the Triebisch river in the last century.

The best views of the **Albrechtsburg** are from the opposite bank of the Elbe. Founded in 929, the castle is a good example of late Gothic architecture, and was intended to be the seat of Dukes Ernst and Albrecht who ruled over Saxony and Thuringia. The adjoining **Dom** (cathedral) was started in 1260. Its early Gothic origins have almost disappeared under many extensions and annexes, such as two western towers which were partly destroyed by lightning in 1547, and rebuilt between 1903 and 1908. **St Afra's Church** and the former **Fürstenschule** (Duke's School) are interesting.

South of the **Nikolaikirche** (St Nicholas') the head office of the nationalised porcelain manufacturing company is open to visitors, who can inspect a selection of porcelain objects, and there are live demonstrations of the various processes involved in porcelain manufacture.

On a more relaxing note, Meissen is the centre of a wine growing district. There are plenty of traditional old wine cellars in the town where thirsty travellers are welcome to sample the product.

[i] Goldener Löwe, Rathenauplatz 6

Visitors can see porcelain being made at the Meissen factory

*From Meissen continue on the **B6** for a further 24km (15 miles) to Dresden.*

Dresden, Sachsen

2 On a bend of the Elbe, Dresden is now a thriving centre of half a million inhabitants, a far cry from the smoking ruins of a city almost totally destroyed by massive British and American bombing in February 1945. Countless cultural treasures built and acquired over centuries were lost in a single night, and many thousands of lives. Historically, the driving force behind the city's development was the Saxon ruler Friedrich August der Starke (The Strong) and his son, August II. The latter initiated the golden age of Dresden baroque architecture by bringing in Matthäus Daniel Pöppelmann as chief designer, and Balthasar Permoser, the sculptor, to build the **Zwinger Palace**. Originally planned as an Orangery, the building grew and grew between 1709 and 1732. Later it was decided to house a gallery there and Gottfried Semper, another well known architect/builder, was commissioned to design a wing which would close the river end of the garden which had previously remained open. The central view from the gardens to the Wall Pavilion or the Glockenspiel Pavilion (Carillon) on the opposite side, amply demonstrates Semper's genius. The design of the square, with its elegant highly ornate buildings, gives an impression of openness and space. The carillon itself is of Meissen porcelain and was added at the beginning of the century. The Wall Pavilion displays the joint coat of arms of Saxony and Poland, reflecting August the Strong's additional role as King of Poland. Art lovers are in for an enormous treat in the palace Picture Gallery – the emphasis is on old Masters.

The porcelain collection is equally magnificent – the Zwinger Collection is said to be the second largest in the

TOUR 4

Moritzburg Castle stands isolated in the middle of a man-made lake

world, featuring early Chinese ceramics and porcelain together with a unique display of Meissen products. The adjoining Carillon Pavilion houses an unusual Meissen carillon with forty bells, all made of porcelain. Although the Zwinger complex was totally destroyed during the bombing raids of 1945, the structure was carefully rebuilt and completed in 1964, a symbol of Germany's determination to maintain her cultural heritage.

Bordering the Zwinger, **Theaterplatz** (Theatre Square) makes sightseeing easy, as nearly all Dresden's buildings are there. The **Semperoper** (Opera House), built to plans by Gottfried Semper, was one of the most beautiful theatres in Europe, erected between 1871 and 1878. Ruined in 1945, it was rebuilt between 1977 and 1985, keeping as close as possible to the original designs. On 13 February 1985, exactly 40 years after its destruction, it reopened with the Weber opera *Der Freischütz*. Opposite the Opera House stands the **Hofkirche** (cathedral), designed by the Italian architect Chiaveri, and founded in 1738. Chiaveri never finished the baroque-style building, which was subsequently consecrated in 1751 and completed in 1755. The blitz destroyed the interior and sections of the walls, but the tower remained upright and was restored after the war. Notable features of the interior are Permoser's pulpit, carved in 1722, the altar painting, the *Ascension of Christ*, and the magnificent Silbermannorgel (organ). In the catacombs, tombs contain the remains of the kings and princes of Saxony, and August the Strong's heart in its own urn.

Plans exist to rebuild a number of the destroyed buildings in the city, including the **Residenzschloss**. The city gate, the **Georgentor**, has been restored and can be seen on the **Schlossplatz** (Castle Square), next to the Hofkirche.

[i] Pragerstrasse 10/11

From Dresden head northwest for 14km (9 miles) to Moritzburg.

Moritzburg, Sachsen

3 Surrounded by a nature reserve, **Moritzburg Castle** was once a hunting lodge. It escaped war damage, and its well preserved interior houses a good museum. At present the stables are being used to breed race horses. The **Hengstdepot** (stud farm) was founded in 1828 to rear race and cart horses. Now mainly race horses are bred there and during the summer horse shows are staged for buyers and visitors, attracting some 50,000 people to The Parade of Stallions.

*Return to Dresden, then take the **B172** to Königstein, 52km (32 miles).*

Königstein, Sachsen

4 The massive and impregnable, **Königstein Castle** squats on a rocky hill above the Elbe. Although there was mention of a fortress here as early as 1241, the present buildings were erected between 1589 and 1631 by the Elector Christian I. From the 17th century, the castle cellars were used to store huge barrels of wine, the largest holding some 250,000 litres (55,000 gallons). Königstein was also used as a secure prison by various rulers. Christian I locked up his chancellor Krell here; Böttger, the European discoverer of porcelain, spent some time incarcerated at Königstein; then it was the turn of the 1849 revolutionaries. During World War II, several important Allied

FOR CHILDREN

2 *Dresden, Sachsen* A visit to the **Zoologischer Garten** (zoo) in Tiergartenstrasse is always recommended. Its penguin house is particularly appealing. Or try the **Karl May Museum** at **Radebeul**, just northwest of Dresden, which houses fascinating collections of relics from the North American Indians. It is a memorial to author Karl May, who wrote many novels about the white man's early adventures in the Indian territory of North America.

RECOMMENDED WALKS

4 *Königstein, Sachsen* Cross the Elbe, then continue on foot to the Lilienstein mountain on a bend in the river. There are beautiful views from the 414m (1,360-foot) high plateau, and the ruins of a medieval fortress. Or head south to the 427m (1,400-foot) Pfaffenstein, with its interesting rock formations, particularly one called **Barbarine**.

BACK TO NATURE

5 *Bad Schandau, Sachsen* For something a little out of the ordinary, check out the strangely shaped **Schrammstein rocks** south of Bad Schandau. The **Bastei** is another bizarre rock formation to the north of the town. The rock formations in this area are quite unique to Europe and were created by the Elbe river which eroded the sandstone mountains. The most outstanding have been given names and are a favourite spot for rock climbers.

SCENIC ROUTES

The drive from Dresden to Bad Schandau via Königstein runs parallel to the course of the Elbe and offers very attractive scenery.

prisoners pitted their wits against the castle's security, and the French General Giraud succeeded in making a daring escape during 1942.

There are fine views from the castle over the Elbe Valley, which is also called *Sächsiche Schweiz* (Saxon Switzerland).

[i] Goethestrasse 7

*Continue on the **B172** for a further 5km (3 miles) to Bad Schandau.*

Bad Schandau, Sachsen

5 A favourite base for many possible excursions in the area, Bad Schandau also boasts a **sanatorium** offering the popular Kneipp cure. This is based on physiotherapy with the objective of developing resistance to common ailments. Hydrotherapy is also a part of the cure.

The favourite local beauty spot is the **Bastei**, a high stone bridge linking a chain of sandstone peaks above the Elbe. From the bridge, there are fine views over the rocky landscape, which is also ideal terrain for rock climbing schools. Walkers can explore some 1,200km (745 miles) of footpaths around the area. Popular hiking destinations further afield include the Lichtenhainer Waterfall, the Kuhstall and the Obere Schleuse. For more relaxed sightseeing, try a boat trip on one of the pleasure steamers which ply up and down the Elbe.

[i] Ernst Thalmann Strasse 3

*Take the **B172** back to Dresden, then the **A4/E40** to Abzweigung Nossen and turn right for the **A14/E49** to Döbeln. Turn south for the **B175** and right after Hartha on the **B176** to Colditz, 106km (66 miles).*

Main gate to Colditz Castle, most celebrated of World War II prisons

Colditz, Sachsen

6 On the return to Leipzig, a short detour leads to Colditz, a small town in the shadow of its castle. Popularised by a dozen or more films and books, **Colditz Castle** is best known for the daring escapes from it by Allied prisoners of war. A tour of the interior reveals one of the escape tunnels. Most of those sent to Colditz were considered particularly troublesome due to earlier escape attempts, but stories of the castle's impregnability only spurred them on into plotting ever more daring escape plans. Statistics record that of 460 prisoners who tried to escape, 300 were caught at the outset, 130 got out but were captured while still in Germany, while just 30 actually scored the elusive 'home run' and reached their final destination. There are numerous souvenirs of the period displayed in the nearby **Escape Museum**. Since the war, the castle which used to be the seat of the Dukes of Saxony, has been used as a hospital. There are plans to convert it into a hotel and museum.

*From Colditz take the **B107** to Grimma. Head northwest back to Leipzig via Naunhof, 41km (25 miles).*

Leipzig – Meissen **80 (50)**
Meissen – Dresden **24 (15)**
Dresden – Moritzburg **14 (9)**
Moritzburg – Königstein **52 (32)**
Königstein – Bad Schandau **5 (3)**
Bad Schandau – Colditz **106 (66)**
Colditz – Leipzig **41 (25)**

View of the winding Elbe from the towering rock formation known as Die Bastei, near Bad Schandau

Berlin
A9-E51
184
2
87
6
LEIPZIG
Wurzen
Luppa
Oschatz
Riesa
Elbe
Röder
Berlin
0 10 20 kms
0 10 mls
A14-E49
Mulde
87
Nürnberg
Naunhof
95
Grimma
107
176
Colditz
6
176
175
Hartha
Döbeln
A14-E49
169
A14-E49
Nossen
Meissen
1
Wölkisch
182
169
101
3
Moritzburg
Reichenberg
Radebeul
6
A4-E40
173
Dresden
2
170
172
Pirna
5
Bad Schandau
Königstein
4
Pfaffenstein
561
DEUTSCHLAND
TSCHECHOSLOWAKEI
A4-E40
Chemnitz

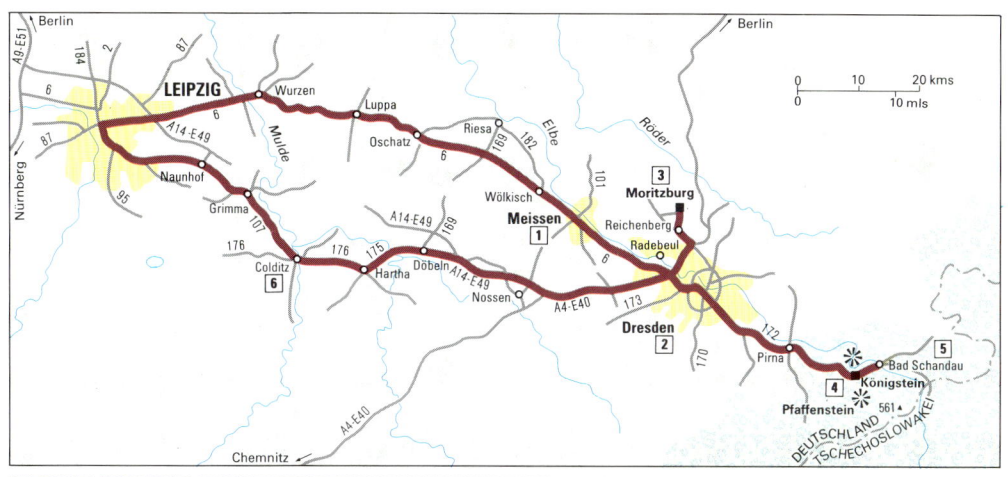

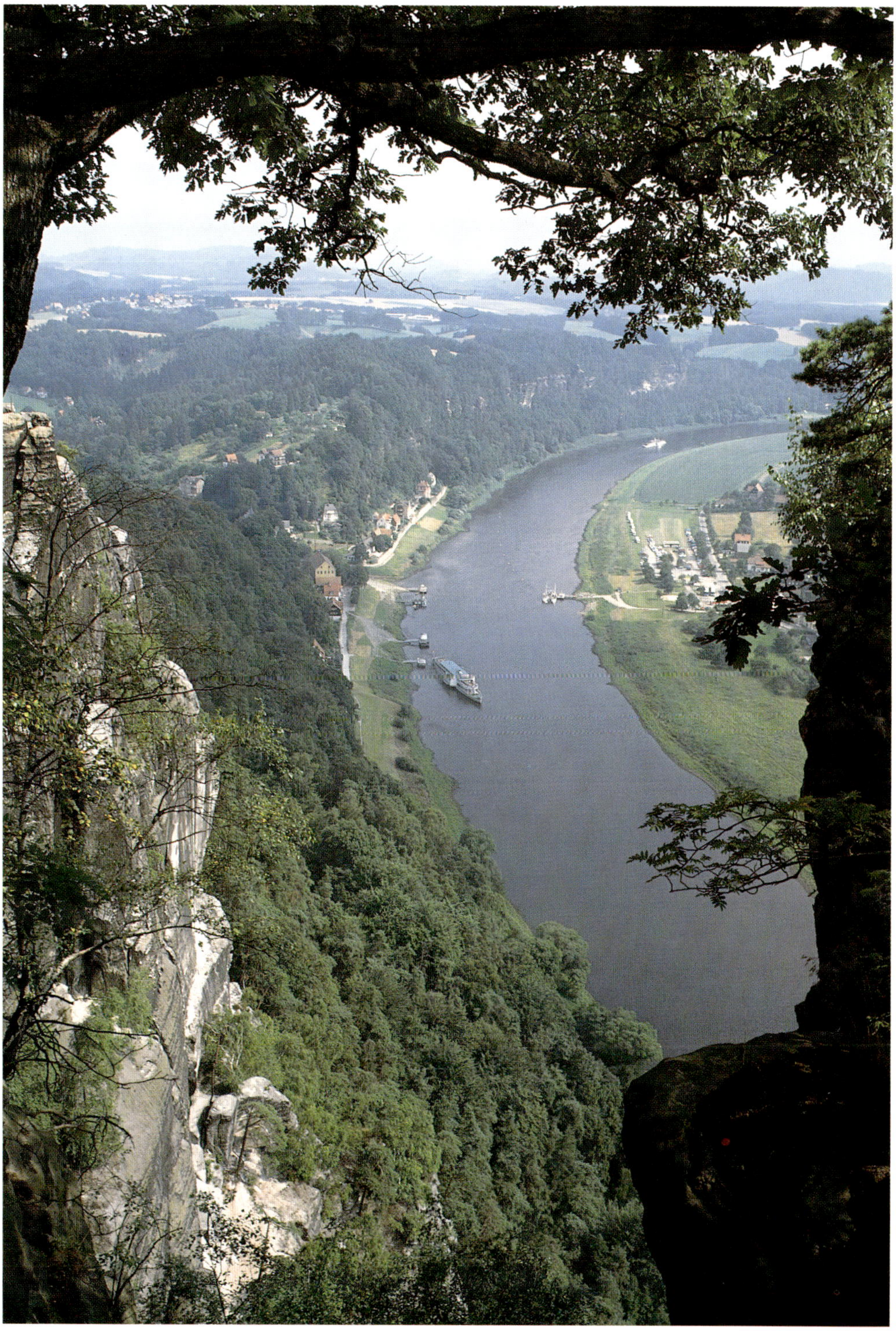

2 days – 246km (215 miles)

TOWNS & FORESTS OF THURINGIA

Weimar ● Jena ● Gera ● Friedrichroda ● Eisenach
Mühlhausen ● Gotha ● Erfurt ● Weimar

Painted shutters in Erfurt's Altstadt, an area full of unconsidered architectural trifles

[i] Markt 15

From Weimar the B7 runs east for 21km (13 miles) to Jena.

Jena, Thüringen

1 Jena used to belong to the Duchy of Saxony and Weimar. In the Middle Ages it flourished as a manufacturer of agricultural products and wine, while later it became famous for more intellectual pursuits. Once accused of being a 'hoarder of knowledge', Jena was the centre of the German philosophy movement, and had its own university. Schiller was invited to lecture here in history and philosophy, and Goethe was one of the university's patrons.

The scientific reputation of Jena rests on the achievement of three men: Carl Zeiss, a mechanic; Ernst Abbe, a physicist; and Otto Schott, a glass manufacturer. Together they laid the foundations for the development and manufacture of optical and other precision instruments using glass. Zeiss installed his mechanical workshop at Jena in 1846. He was joined by Abbe who was experimenting with microscopes; and Schott, the chemical and glass engineer, provided the raw materials.

The **Zeiss Planetarium**, opened in 1926, is one of the oldest of its kind in Germany. It is a listed building, and was renovated between 1983 and 1985 when it was equipped with the latest state-of-the-art advances in technology.

Jena suffered badly during World War II, and the **Marktplatz** (Market Square) is the only reminder of the past. It is flanked by a rare, comparatively small Gothic-style **Rathaus** (Town Hall) with two parallel roofs and a clock tower in between. The statue of the Elector Johann Friedrich der Grossmütige (John Frederick the Generous), stands in the square, an imposing figure with a huge sword in his right hand. He was the founder of Jena's university. To the south of the city centre, the **Optisches Museum** is a fascinating experience. Some 12,000 valuable mechanical and

Weimar emerged from World War II relatively unscathed and remains a charming little town of about 60,000 inhabitants. The entire *Altstadt* (Old Town) is listed as a historic monument. On *Theaterplatz* (Theatre Square) the baroque-style *Deutsches Nationaltheater* (German National Theatre) maintains Weimar's traditional status as an important centre of German literature and music. Franz Liszt and Richard Strauss worked here, among others.

The *Schillerhaus* in the Schillerstrasse was the last home of the poet/dramatist Schiller, until his death in 1805. His living quarters have been carefully preserved in their original state and were recently restored. A separate *Schillermuseum* has been erected next to the Schillerhaus.

The *Goethehaus*, on Am Frauenplan, is an attractive baroque building where Goethe lived for 50 years from 1782 to 1832. From here it is just a short step to the historical tavern *Zum Weissen Schwan* (The White Swan). In the riverside park, Goethe's *Gartenhaus* (country cottage), was where he lived before moving into the town, and many of his nature poems were written here. *Lucas Cranach Haus*, in the market area of Old Weimar, is a pleasant Renaissance building where Cranach the Elder spent his last years.

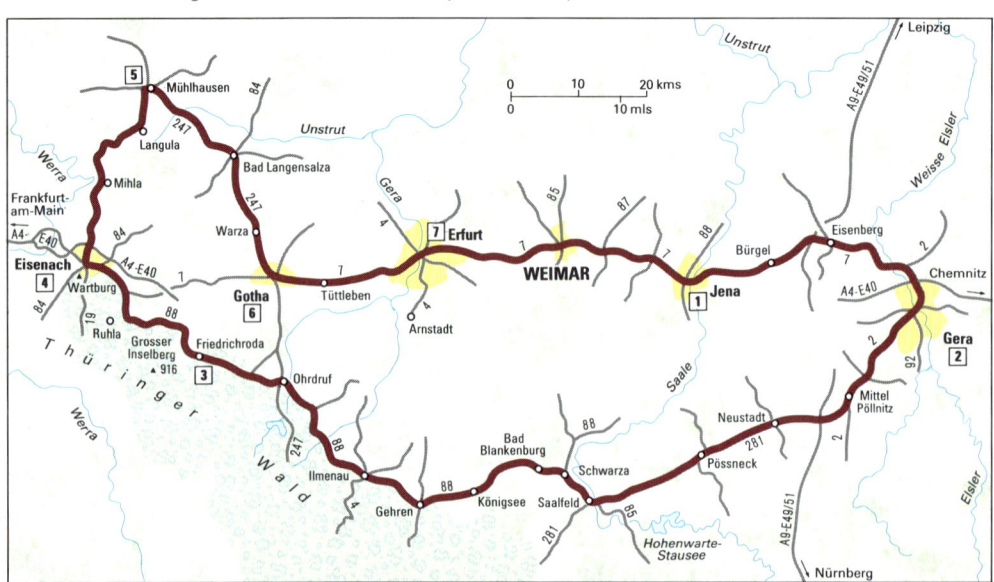

The rolling foothills of the Thüringer Wald. This is splendid terrain for walkers

optical instruments are exhibited here, and there is a model of the type of camera used in space explorations.

[i] Neugasse 7

*Continue east on the **B7**, via Eisenberg, to Gera, 40km (25 miles).*

Gera, Thüringen

2 Gera's name derives from the Old German *Geraha*, meaning a large body of water. Nearly 1,000 years old, the town was chosen as the seat of the von Weida family at the beginning of the 13th century.

The lovely market square is edged by the Renaissance **Rathaus** (Town Hall) and a collection of colourful and well-restored burghers' houses. At the centre of the square is the 17th-century **Simonsbrunnen** (fountain). Also of note is the 17th-century pharmacy, topped with an ornate circular Renaissance oriel.

[i] Dr Rudolf Breitscheid Strasse 1

*Take the **B2** south to Mittel Pöllnitz, turn right on to the **B281** to Saalfeld, then turn north to Schwarza. Turn left for the **B88** for Friedrichroda, via Ilmenau, 134km (83 miles).*

Friedrichroda, Thüringen

3 The road runs through the green hiking countryside of the Thüringer Wald (Forest of Thuringia) and into the resort of Friedrichroda. The town developed around the nearby **Kloster** (abbey) built by Landgrave Ludwig. The abbey was destroyed in the 16th century, and a castle built on its site. The gardens are very attractive with century-old trees and a little Japanese-style garden with artificial cliffs built into the scenery. The monks also created fishponds, which are still used for trout and carp farming.

Friedrichroda prides itself on being one of the oldest tourist resorts and celebrated 150 years of tourism in 1987. The **Thüringer Waldbahn** (Thuringian Forest Railway) provides a handy connection to the **Marienglashöhle**, one of the most attractive and longest crystal caves in Europe, which houses the fabulous **Marienglasgrotte**, a grotto noted for its translucent gypsum crystals of amazing length. Another recommended excursion is a trek up the **Grosser Inselberg**, a 916m (3,000-foot) mini-mountain which can best be reached from the nearby villages of **Ruhla**, **Brotterode** or **Tarbarz**. The final ascent has to be started from the **Kleiner Inselberg** and the **Grenzwiese** near **Rennsteig**, which is the terminal for cars and coaches. There are superb views from the mountain top.

[i] Gartenstrasse 9

*Continue northwest on the **B88** for a further 29km (18 miles) to Eisenach.*

RECOMMENDED WALKS

3 *Friedrichroda, Thüringen*
The town provides a handy *Orientierungstafel* (location/map board) which indicates numerous walking routes around the vicinity.

SCENIC ROUTES

One of the loveliest sections of the route between Gera and Friedrichroda is the stretch between Saalfeld and Bad Blankenburg, before the road actually reaches and runs parallel to the Thüringer Wald. Once you reach the Thüringer Wald, there is a rewarding detour into the forest from Ilmenau.

BACK TO NATURE

The **Rennsteig forest nature trail** runs along the crest of the Thüringer Wald, from Hörschel on the River Werra in the west to Blankenstein and the River Saale in the east. The trail is clearly marked throughout the forest by the letter 'R' painted in white on the tree trunks. Look for middle-spotted and great-spotted woodpeckers, nuthatches, treecreepers and red squirrels. In the autumn, fungi grow in profusion on the forest floor.

Museum pieces in the Wartburg car factory, Eisenach

SPECIAL TO...

6 *Gotha, Thüringen* The town of Gotha prides itself on a long established reputation in the map business. Maps and atlases have been designed and printed here since the 18th century, and the **Museum fur Kartographie** (Cartographic Museum) was opened in 1985 to celebrate 200 years of map craft. Displays illustrate both old-fashioned and modern map-making techniques.

FOR CHILDREN

7 *Erfurt, Thüringen* From Erfurt, travel south on the **A4/B4** for 19km (12 miles) to Arnstadt. Here you will find the delightful **Mon Plaisir Dolls' Museum**, exhibiting 400 dolls in 26 houses with a total of 84 rooms. The entire scenario was created between 1690 and 1750 by ladies-in-waiting to Princess Augusta, together with the help of local craftsmen.

Eisenach, Thüringen

4 Sometimes known as the *Wartburgstadt Eisenach*, the town of Eisenach lies at the northwestern end of the Thüringer Wald (Forest), below the Wartburg Mountain, and its imposing **Wartburg Castle**. One of the most interesting German fortress complexes, the Wartburg is believed to have been founded in the year 1067. As the local lords prospered the castle grew in importance, from a fortress into a seat of government and ducal residence.

The Reformist Martin Luther lived here between 1521 and 1522, under the protection of the Kurfürst (Elector), after he had been outlawed by the reactionary bishops at the Diet of Worms. Within a mere 10 weeks he had translated the *New Testament* from the original Greek into German and, by doing so, laid the cornerstone for the development of the German language. The present fortress was constructed between the 11th and 16th centuries and then renovated in the 19th century. The interior of the Wartburg is enchanting, with timber-framed structures bordering its two courtyards. The castle museum, the **Neue Kemenaten**, displays several exquisite works of art, including paintings by Lucas Cranach the Elder; sculptures by the famous woodcarver, Riemenschneider; a carved trunk designed by Albrecht Dürer; and late-Gothic tapestries.

The market square is the heart of the **Altstadt** (Old Town). At the northern end, the baroque style **Stadtschloss** (Town Castle) houses the **Thüringer Museum**, and its collections of local faïence, porcelain and glass. The **Rathaus** (Town Hall) has a markedly leaning tower. The **Parish Church of St George** boasts a richly decorated interior with tombstones erected for the Counts of Thuringia. Luther preached here and Johann Sebastian Bach was christened in the church. The **Lutherhaus** nearby, and the **Bachhaus** on Frauenplan, can be visited.

[i] Bahnhofstrasse 3/5

Continue north for 35km (22 miles) to Mühlhausen.

Mühlhausen, Thüringen

5 A visit to Mühlhausen is like stepping back into the Middle Ages. This small town of timber-framed houses, narrow streets and numerous churches is still surrounded by its ancient city walls. Historically, it is renowned as the crucible of the German Peasants' Revolt of 1524 to 1525, and is sometimes called *Thomas Müntzer Stadt* after the leader of the revolt. Müntzer's crusade set out to free the peasants from the system of hefty payments demanded by the feudal landlords.

The Parish Church of **Divi Blasii** stands on the square between the Untermarkt and Johann Sebastian

Bachplatz (Bach Square). Near by, the **Annenkapelle** dates back to the 13th century, and a little further on there are several beautiful medieval houses. Parts of the old city walls, interspersed with towers, are still standing, and the largest tower, **Rabenturm**, houses a museum.

[i] Gormastrasse 57

*From Mühlhausen the **B247** runs southeast for 40km (25 miles) to Gotha.*

Gotha, Thüringen

6 Dominating the view of Gotha is **Schloss Friedenstein**, an early baroque building. It stands on the site of the former Grimmenstein fortress, which was conquered in the 16th century and later razed to the ground. The 365-room castle complex includes the **Schlosskirche** (church), which contains the tombs of the rulers of Gotha; and the **Schlossmuseum**, which has a fine art collection. The castle's **Ekhof Theatre** is named after Conrad Ekhof, who established a resident theatre company here. Leave enough time for a visit to the extensive castle gardens, where there is plenty of scope for restful walks.

Overlooking the town centre from the castle, there is a good view of the red-painted **Rathaus**, built between 1567 and 1577. The market square in front of the town hall is lined with burghers' houses. On the right, coming from the castle, stands the house of artist Lucas Cranach (1472–1553).

[i] Hauptmarkt 2

*From Gotha take the **B7** east for 24km (15 miles) to Erfurt.*

Erfurt, Thüringen

7 Erfurt's main claim to fame is its position as a centre for horticultural activities. Its permanent **Internationale Gartenbauaustellung** (International Horticultural Exhibition), attracts many thousands of visitors.

A town with a population of some 200,000 inhabitants, it has undergone an extensive restoration programme and, fortunately, the **Altstadt** (Old Town) remained largely intact after World War II.

The medieval churches on the Domberg, the **Dom** (cathedral) and the **Severikirche** next to it, are impressive ecclesiastical buildings and should not be missed. The cathedral was founded in the 8th century, and then completed in 1154 as a Romanesque basilica. The middle of its three towers contains the **Maria Gloriosa**, one of the largest church bells in the world, and christened the Gloriosa on account of its beautiful sound.

The 600-year-old **Krämerbrücke** (bridge), which spans the River Gera, used to connect the old east–west trading route. Lined with 33 timber-framed and gabled houses, it is one of the town's top sights. Close by, the old **Furt**, a shallow part of the river used as a crossing before the bridge was built, was recently uncovered and can be seen.

A street in old Erfurt. The town had a long history as a place of learning (Luther studied here) and trade up to the 17th century

One of the oldest streets in the town is the **Anger**, a fascinating place for a stroll. Now completely restored, many of its houses hosted a number of important visitors in the past – No 11 **Zum Schwarzen Löwen** (the Black Lion) was visited by Queen Marie-Elenore of Sweden in 1632; and Tsar Alexander of Russia was entertained at No 6 in 1808.

[i] Bahnhofstrasse 37

*Take the **B7** east for 23km (14 miles) back to Weimar.*

Weimar – Jena **21** (13)
Jena – Gera **40** (25)
Gera – Friedrichroda **134** (83)
Friedrichroda – Eisenach **29** (18)
Eisenach – Mühlhausen **35** (22)
Mühlhausen – Gotha **40** (25)
Gotha – Erfurt **24** (15)
Erfurt – Weimar **23** (14)

FOR HISTORY BUFFS

7 *Erfurt, Thüringen* Local legend tells the tale of Count Ernst III who lived in the **Gleiche fortress**. Captured during one of the crusades, he was sold as a slave to the Turks, where he fell in love with a sultan's daughter. They escaped together and although the count was already married, an understanding pope granted him permission to take the baptised Saracen girl as his second wife! Count Ernst's tomb can be seen in Erfurt cathedral where he lies with both his wives.

THE GERMAN MIDLANDS

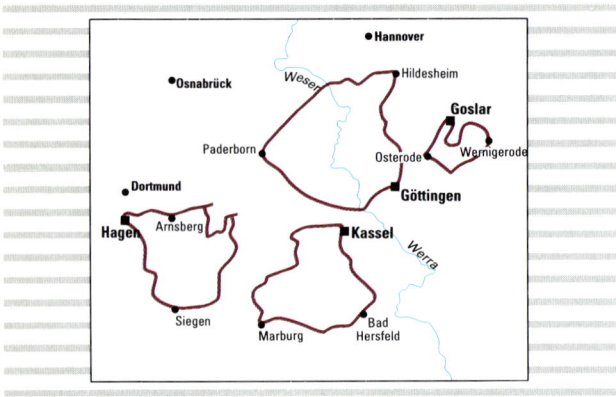

South of the North German plain the map changes and from west to east a hilly and mountainous landscape emerges, cloaked with beautiful forests, lakes and rivers. One scenic route follows another, and as the mountains, with few exceptions, do not reach heights above 1,000m (3,280 feet), there are the advantages of more easy walks. The difficulties encountered crossing from one valley to another in higher mountain ranges do not occur here. Heading into the countryside from the towns and cities of the Ruhr, the visitor is pleasantly surprised by the change in scenery and by the many little villages which present quite a different image of Germany, a Germany for holidays and relaxation. Visitors have been coming to the area since the 19th century, when the dramatic scenery appealed particularly to devotees of the Romantic movement.

The Harz region is called 'The Heart of Germany', and since unification it is definitely more in the middle of the country than before, when it formed the border with the eastern provinces. The Harz mountains were exploited for their valuable ore deposits from as early as the 10th century, with the trees above the mines providing the necessary fuel for the refining operations. Forestry and the creation of hydroelectric power are two major industries to be found here, with tourism adding a more human dimension.

Numerous forests, interrupted by the tributaries of the Weser, make this a very pleasant area to explore. Nature parks compete with medieval towns for attention and it is no wonder that the Deutsche Märchenstrasse (German Fairy Tale Road) runs right along the Weser and its riverside towns. The towns themselves often seem to have been plucked straight from the pages of a fairy tale.

Further down, in the natural northern regions of the province of Hessen, there is no geographical border but visitors arriving from the north are greeted by three large nature parks to the west and east of Kassel, with the Reinhards Wald (forest) bordering the northern approach to Kassel itself. Historic towns full of fine buildings and surrounded by forests provide a balanced landscape between the city and nature. The Sauerland region consists of tree-covered hills, rivers and the mighty dams which supply the industrial might of the Ruhr Valley to the west with water and power. Far from interfering with the natural balance of the surroundings, the dams have actually enhanced the beauty of the scenery and the new lakes have created valuable recreational facilities including a bonus for watersports enthusiasts.

Top: Well restored half-timbered buildings dressed up in flowers make Alsfeld the archetype of a picturesque German town

Tour 6
One of the best areas for recreational pursuits and holiday-making in Germany, the Harz region enjoys a great location – not too far from the capital Berlin, and within quite easy reach of the Ruhr, Bremen and Hannover. No doubt the industrial centre of Saxony will soon provide additional markets for tourism once the economics are sorted out. Although this is a mountainous region, it is not too strenuous for gentle strolls or hikes, and visitors to the area will find the many lakes and rivers provide a wealth of beautiful scenery to just sit and enjoy. There is plenty of history, too, and a great number of superb medieval buildings, many of which are classified as national treasures.

Tour 7
Weserbergland lies between the arms of the River Weser. The river and its main tributaries, the Fulda and the Werra, seem to have inspired many German legends and fairy tales, some of which have achieved international fame. The Deutsche Märchenstrasse (German Fairy Tale Road) links up many of the myths and stories of the past with their original settings. Weserbergland is at the centre of this giant fairy tale, with the Pied Piper's town of Hameln, or Hamelin, its most famous location.

Tour 8
Forests and rivers provide the main backdrop to this scenic tour, and historic towns furnished with beautiful old buildings offer additional interest. It would seem that all the major holiday routes lead here, too. In the town of Alsfeld, the Deutsche Märchenstrasse (Fairy Tale Road) crosses the Deutsche Ferienstrasse (Holiday Road); and Kassel is the starting point of the Deutsche Historische Strasse (Historical Road), while the towns of Frankenberg and Marburg lie on the Romantische Strasse (Romantic Road). It just goes to prove that this is a marvellous area to explore and follow up a wide variety of interests from general sightseeing to boat trips on the Eder Dam near Waldeck and hiking in the plentiful natural parks covering the north of the region.

Tour 9
Bordering the Ruhr Valley, Germany's industrial heartland, the Sauerland is the vital power behind the might of German industry. Its numerous lakes and rivers supply water and hydroelectric power, but on the human side the landscape provides an ideal recreation area. A great variety of watersports can be enjoyed here, and there are some great lakeside walks and camping grounds. In fact, out of 15 artificial lakes, only six do not permit sports and bathing.

Right: Decoration on a doorway in Osterode, birthplace of Gothic sculptor Tilman Riemenschneider

2 days – 176km (109 miles)

THE HARZ MOUNTAINS & FORESTS

Goslar • Bad Harzburg • Wernigerode • Bad Lauterberg
Scharzfeld • Herzberg • Osterode
Clausthal-Zellerfeld • Goslar

Clausthal's Marktkirche was built in the 17th century from two types of wood – spruce for the main church and oak for the tower

Goslar's monumental *Kaiserpfalz* (Emperor's Residence), is an imposing sight and is one of the largest non-ecclesiastical structures of the 11th century. The market square with its 15th-century *Rathaus* (Town Hall) was built by wealthy burghers – the town council still holds its meeting there. The former *Ratsherrnzimmer* (council meeting chamber), open only for viewing, is beautifully renovated and restored, its walls and ceiling decorated with highly colourful images of the Holy Roman Emperors, and scenes from the life of Christ.

Behind the Marktkirche stand the *Bäckergildehaus* (Bakers' Guild House) with its tall gable; facing the church you can see one of the most attractive burghers' houses, the *Brusttuch* (Shawl) named for its steeply pitched roof. Of Goslar's original 47 churches, 23 remain. The largest are the *Frankenbergkirche*, *Jacobkirche* and *Marktkirche* all founded around AD1200 as Romanesque basilicas. The 13th-century *Grosses Heiliges Kreuz* hospice on Hoher Weg was the first charitable foundation in Goslar and is the largest remaining medieval building in town.

BACK TO NATURE

1 *Bad Harzburg, Niedersachsen* The **wild deer park** at Bündheim, near Bad Harzburg, contains moufflon and red deer, among other animals.

2 *Wernigerode, Sachsen-Anhalt* The **Wernigerode Wildlife Park** in the Christinental is a good place to spot all sorts of indigenous animals, from moufflon, red and roe deer, to birds of prey.

[i] Markt 7

From Goslar take a short drive east to Oker, turn south on to the B498, then turn sharp east past Altenau for the B242. Turn north on to the B4 for Bad Harzburg.

Bad Harzburg, Niedersachsen

1 Away from the big towns, skimming the northern end of the Harz Mountain range, Bad Harzburg is a spa town with all the facilities for a relaxing and healthy stay. A natural spring delivers water at a constant 32°C (89°F) to the **Hallenbad** (covered pool), and there is an open-air annexe where the water temperature drops to a mere 29°C (84°F).

The only historical remains here are the ruins of the **Harzburg**, an 11th-century fortress first founded by Heinrich IV, later destroyed by the Saxons then rebuilt under Emperor Friedrich Barbarossa, only to be demolished again in the middle of the 17th century. A cable car ride makes short work of the 500m (1,640-foot) climb up the **Burgberg**. The commanding view from the top explains the positioning of the fortress and there are several gentle strolls around the area which make this a pleasant excursion.

[i] Herzog Wilhelmstrasse 86

Take the B6 east for 21km (13 miles) to Wernigerode.

Wernigerode, Sachsen-Anhalt

2 Located in what was formerly East Germany, Wernigerode is a beautifully preserved town with a medieval centre that is listed as a monument. The focus is the **Marktplatz** (Market Place) with its unique **Rathaus** (Town Hall), which looks as if it has been lifted straight from the pages of a fairy tale. This little jewel of medieval architecture has a raised ground floor entrance which is reached by two staircases, flanked by a pair of oriel spires, and all its façades are painted and decorated. First documented in 1277 as a **Spelhus**, from the word for a play house or theatre (Spielhaus), this was not only a place for entertainment, it also served as a law court administered by the ruling Counts. After a fire in 1543 its function changed to that of a town hall, and weddings still take place there today.

Other interesting buildings include the **Waaghaus**, with its scales which dates back to the 16th century and adjoins the rear of the Rathaus; and there are a number of beautiful timbered houses all around the town centre bearing witness to an era of great and stylish architecture. On Breite Strasse, the **Krummelhaus**, at No 72, was built in 1674 and decorated with carved ornaments which completely conceal the timber-framed façade. The smallest house in town is found on Kochstrasse, just 4.2m (13½ feet) up to the eaves and less than 3m (9 feet) wide. Then there is the **Schiefe Haus** (Leaning House), formerly a mill which started to lean when the water from the stream beneath attacked the foundations.

A few remnants of the old town fortifications can still be seen, including the moat and one of the city gates, the **Westerntor**. A tour of **Schloss Adalbert** gives several insights into the changing demand for creature comforts through the ages.

About 7km (4 miles) from Wernigerode, towards the mountains, is the **Steinerne Renne** with a waterfall and **Ottofelsen** (Otto's Rock). The rock can be climbed with the aid of fixed steel ladders and offers beautiful views from the top.

[i] Breite Strasse 12

Take the B244 south to Elbingerode, and continue on the B27 via Braunlage to Bad Lauterberg, 40km (25 miles).

TOUR 6

Bad Lauterberg, Niedersachsen

3 It is worth considering a stop in Braunlage, before going on to Bad Lauterberg. This resort is one of the most developed in the Harz mountains. It is officially classified as a climatic health resort and offers a great variety of entertainment for all tastes. The sports minded can take their pick of tennis, bowling, swimming, water gymnastics and skiing in winter to name a few. The body conscious can visit the beauty studio or undergo a course of the Scarsdale diet, while the children can enjoy their favourite activities, and competitions are arranged for them in the **Maritim Kinder Club** (Maritime Children's Club). You can take a trip by cable car to the top of the 971m (3,185-foot) **Wurmberg** (Worm Mountain) for fine views and to see the excavations of an

Doorway in Goslar

FOR HISTORY BUFFS

2 *Wernigerode, Sachsen-Anhalt* When walking round Wernigerode, do not miss the house at No 95 Breite Strasse. Built in 1678, it is called **Krell's Schmiede** (smithy), and above the door a horse's head juts out and horseshoes denote the nature of the occupant's trade. There has been a smithy here since the house was built.

SPECIAL TO...

2 *Wernigerode, Sachsen-Anhalt* The **Harzquerbahn** is a real old-timer steam train which runs on narrow gauge tracks from Wernigerode to Nordhausen, a distance of 60km (37 miles). The line was first opened on 27 March 1899, and it was hoped it would eventually run as far as Hamburg in the north and Vienna in the south.

FOR CHILDREN

1 *Bad Harzburg, Niedersachsen* South of Bad Harzburg a stream cascades down on to rocks to the **Radaufall** (waterfall). This forms the background for a **Kinderparadies** (Children's Paradise) which offers all kinds of entertainment and features rides on a miniature railway.

The **Märchenwald**, near the cable car station at Bad Harzburg, exhibits scenes from well-known fairy tales in little wooden chalets. There are some 100 handcarved figures on display arranged on rotating stages.

The Kornmarkt in Osterode is the hub of this medieval gem of a town

ancient place of worship dating back to about 100BC. The **Grosse Wurmbergstrasse** (Great Wurmberg Road) can also be taken from Braunlage and leads along hairpin bends up to the mountain.

Bad Lauterberg is an officially classified health resort. There is no shortage of things to do here as the spa town is at the centre of an extensive network of nature walks, and its other great attraction is the **Oder-Stausee**, an artificial lake which offers a wide range of watersports facilities. Canoeing, rowing and sailing are all available on the 310m (1,016-foot) long stretch of water. On a more relaxed note, a chair-lift operates rides up to the Hausberg, with views over Bad Lauterberg from the Burg-Restaurant.

[i] Haus des Kurgastes

*From Bad Lauterberg take the **B27/B243** west for 5km (3 miles) to Scharzfeld.*

Scharzfeld, Niedersachsen

4 The **Steinkirche** (Stone Church) in Scharzfeld is really a cave once used by prehistoric man as living quarters and then by early Germanic tribes for religious ceremonies. Later transformed into a church, the cave was still used as a place of worship into the 16th century. Its former church bell is now housed in the local village church.

Another interesting cave near by is the 400m (1,310-foot) long **Einhornhöhle** (Unicorn Cave), noted for the skeleton of a prehistoric animal which was found here.

*Continue on the **B27/B243** for 4km (2 miles) to Herzberg.*

Herzberg, Niedersachsen

5 Herzberg's claim to fame is its timber-framed **castle**, formerly a hunting lodge and then seat of the local rulers. Built in 1510, it was the birthplace of Ernst August of Hannover, who later founded what was to become the English-Hanoverian royal dynasty.

[i] Kurverwaltung

*Continue on the **B243** for 11km (7 miles) to Osterode.*

Osterode, Niedersachsen

6 The River Söse flows out of the Harz mountains past the picturesque medieval town of Osterode. The main square, **Kornmarkt** (Grain Market), is edged by a collection of splendid historic buildings, including the Renaissance-style **Englischer Hof** dating from 1610. Near by is the renovated 16th-century **Church of St Agidii**; behind that the old **Rathaus**, built in 1552, stands together with the richly ornamented **Ratswaage** building, which once housed the official weights and measures office erected one year later.

The **Heimatmuseum**, is located in the historical **Ritterhaus** (Knight's Hall), while the baroque **Kornmagazin** (Grain Warehouse) was built between 1719 and 1722. Since 1987 it has been used as the town council chambers. The nearby **Sösetalsperre** (Söse Dam) makes an interesting excursion. Drinking water from the dam is piped as far as Bremen, some 200km (124 miles) away. There is a very pleasant footpath trail that runs around the lake, with traffic restricted to the northern shore.

[i] Eisensteinstrasse 1

*Take the **B241** north for 29km (18 miles) to Clausthal-Zellerfeld.*

RECOMMENDED WALKS

The Harz region has more than 8,000km (5,000 miles) of hiking trails. The distinctly picturesque local term for them is **Wanderwege**, literally 'Wander Ways'. Drive from Wernigerode via Blankenburg to Thale. From Thale climb up to the **Rosstrappe**, which can also be reached by chairlift. It is also possible to walk to the opposite side of the Bode Valley and scale the **Hexentanzplatz** (Dancing Place of the Witches) for another splendid view.

Clausthal-Zellerfeld, Niedersachsen

7 There are two towns rolled into one here, and each boasts its own particular highlight: the **Oberharzer Museum** at Zellerfeld; and the Protestant **Marktkirche zum Heiligen Geist** (Market Church of the Holy Ghost) in Clausthal.

After a serious fire in 1672, Zellerfeld was rebuilt along the lines of a chessboard. The Oberharzer Museum provides an historical overview of mining activities in the Harz region up until the 1930s. Most appropriately, there is a technical university located here with a noted traditional mining faculty.

Clausthal's Marktkirche has several unusual features. The building is totally constructed from timber and inside, daylight is filtered through windows set at an angle, so creating an unusual perspective and a unique atmosphere. The altar dates back to 1641.

Side trips from Clausthal-Zellerfeld include the old **silver mines** which lie 8km (5 miles) to the north and date back to 1551. Also, a trip to nearby **Bad Grund** presents the opportunity to visit the **Iberger Tropfsteinhöhle** (Iberger Caves). Discovered and explored in 1874, the main cave is 150m (490 feet) long, and is made up of a number of smaller caves, with the stalagmites and stalactites mainly found in the upper sections.

[i] Bahnhofstrasse 5a

*Continue north on the **B241** for 18km (11 miles) back to Goslar.*

Goslar – Bad Harzburg **48 (30)**
Bad Harzburg – Wernigerode **21 (13)**
Wernigerode – Bad Lauterberg **40 (25)**
Bad Lauterberg – Scharzfeld **5 (3)**
Scharzfeld – Herzberg **4 (2)**
Herzberg – Osterode **11 (7)**
Osterode – Clausthal-Zellerfeld **29 (18)**
Clausthal-Zellerfeld – Goslar **18 (11)**

A romantic corner in the Harz: the Romerkalle Falls

SCENIC ROUTES

The Harz mountain region offers an abundance of scenic routes. The drive between Braunlage and Bad Lauterberg is particularly lovely. It is always useful to map out a circular drive, and there is a good circuit from Bad Lauterberg to St Andreasberg and back via Herzberg.

From Osterode you can take the scenic **Deutsche Ferienstrasse** (German Holiday Road) to Clausthal-Zellerfeld.

1/2 days – 308km (192 miles)

EAST & WEST OF THE WESER

Göttingen • Northeim • Einbeck • Hildesheim • Hameln
Paderborn • Münden • Göttingen

Situated on the River Leine, Göttingen is mainly celebrated for its university, which produced an impressive clutch of Nobel prize winners. The *university* was founded by George II, King of Great Britain and Ireland, and also Elector of Hannover, in 1737. The *Markt* (market) together with the *Altes Rathaus* (Old Town Hall) forms the centre of the old town. In front of the Rathaus stands the *Gänselieslbrunnen* (Goose Girl Fountain), a delicately ornate fountain erected in 1901 and used as the town's emblem. West of the Rathaus stands the *Johanniskirche*, which dates from the 14th century and is the oldest church in town. Near by, the university's library contains over two million volumes and manuscripts.

The *Marienkirche*, across the river, was founded around 1300 and has an altar dating from 1524. At the southern end of the old town, the *Turmstrasse* reveals a piece of the old city wall dating back to the 13th century, and a former bulwark, called the *Bismarckhäuschen*, is where Otto von Bismarck, who later became Germany's famous chancellor, lived as a student from 1832 to 1833.

Rats are big business in Hameln. These, made of bread, are too hard to be recommended for eating

[i] Markt 9

*From Göttingen take the **B3** north for 21km (13 miles) to Northeim.*

Northeim, Niedersachsen

1 En route from Göttingen to Einbeck, Northeim is a small medieval looking town some 700 years old. The past is still revealed by remnants of the old city wall and a collection of timber-framed houses. Northeim's distinctive emblem is **St Sixti's Church**, a late Gothic edifice built between 1467 and 1498. Notable features of the interior are the winged altarpiece and a bronze font in the Christening Chapel. The church organ and late Gothic paintings in the windows illustrating scenes from *Christ's Passion* will also attract the visitor's eye.

[i] Am Munster 30

*Continue on the **B3** north for 19km (12 miles) to Einbeck.*

Einbeck, Niedersachsen

2 'Einbeck invites you back to the Middle Ages' state the tourist brochures boldly. And it is not far from the truth. The importance of Einbeck stretches back a good few hundred years, and all on account of its beer-brewing activities. The town's famous ale, **Ainpockisch Pier** as it was called, travelled a long way, even as far as Munich, and the Dukes of Bavaria were already purchasing large quantities of Einbeck beer as far back as 1533. It later became the more familiar **Bockbier**. The beer was brewed at home by the citizens of Einbeck, and it is thought that there were as many as 700 of these small breweries in the town at the time.

An aeriel view of the town clearly shows the circular ring of the old town fortifications; there is also a good view from the top of the **Stadtwald**, a wooded hill near by. A few towers, walls and ramparts are still standing, while the remainder make idyllic footpaths and part of the moat has been transformed into little ponds.

A special feature of Einbeck are the wooden houses around the market place. Two of the most outstanding are situated close to a fountain dedicated to the town's famous prankster, Till Eulenspiegel. According to legend, he was a brewery worker, and the composer Richard Strauss set his exploits to music in the symphonic poem, *Till Eulenspiegel*.

The **Brodhaus**, built in 1552, and the **Rats-Apotheke** (Town Pharmacy) opposite, are two beautifully preserved and impressive buildings, with interesting high gables and dormer-like ventilation openings in the roofs. The space under the roof was used by brewers for the storage and drying of raw materials, such as hops, barley and malt. Across the square stands the **Rathaus**, which has become a distinctive emblem with its

The Goose Girl Fountain in Göttingen. Students traditionally kiss the statue after finals

TOUR 7

St Michaelis Kirche, Hildesheim, restored after severe war damage

three asymmetrically set oriel windows. Next door is the **Ratswaage**, the official weights and measures building. Its façade is a picture of Renaissance prosperity, with the doors, window frames and cornices all decorated with mouldings and friezes, and colourfully painted. **Tidexerstrasse** and **Marktstrasse** are graced with a further harmonious collection of old houses, their individuality a potent expression of the style and pride of their architect/builders.

[i] Rathaus

*Continue on the **B3** to Alfeld, then turn northeast via Sibbesse to Hildesheim, 43km (27 miles).*

Hildesheim, Niedersachsen

3 Hildesheim's origins can be traced back by popular legend to 815. Ludwig der Fromme (Louis the Pious), so the story goes, was looking for a good site to found a bishopric in the area. One day, at the height of summer, snow fell unexpectedly where roses normally bloomed. The bishop took this as a sign and built his cathedral here. As long as the roses continue to blossom, it is said that Hildesheim will flourish too. The rose tree was badly burned during World War II, but miraculously it started to

SCENIC ROUTES

You can take the scenic **Wesertalstrasse (B83)** south from Hameln to **Höxter** for 55km (34 miles), then reverse directions by taking the **B239** northwest, through the forests to **Rischenau**, then back through Bad Pyrmont to Hameln. Alternatively you can head north on the **B83** along the Weser. At Veckershagen bear left and drive through the forest of Reinhardswald. From the slopes of the Staufenberg the road carries on to **Sababurg**, the ruin of a 14th-century hunting lodge built for the Landgraves of Hessen.

TOUR 7

The Pied Piper lives again in Hameln every Sunday from May to September in a free street play

SPECIAL TO...

4 Hameln, Niedersachsen A unique feature of Hameln is the **Rattenfängerspiele** (Pied Piper plays) which are performed on the terrace in front of the marriage house during summer. They are scheduled for midday on Sundays from May to September.

BACK TO NATURE

5 Paderborn, Nordrhein-Westfalen From Paderborn, take the **B1** 29km (18 miles) north to **Horn**. West of Horn is a strange rock formation called the **Externsteine**. These bizarre outcrops have been placed under a preservation order. The tallest is 37m (121 feet) high, and one of the rocks is carved with a relief of Christ being taken down from the Cross, the work of an unknown artist around 1130.

FOR CHILDREN

5 Paderborn, Nordrhein-Westfalen Take the **B68** north to Stukenbrock for **Safariland Stukenbrock**. The safari park can be visited either by car or in a miniature train called the **Gläserne Safari Zug**, fitted out with secure protective cages for the passengers. It takes you through a large monkey reservation, then on to see the lions, tigers, elephants, giraffes and antelopes. Other attractions include a **Westernstadt** (western style town), a Hollywood theatre and fun-fair rides.

flower again in the winter of 1945. Believing this to be a good omen for the town's future, the thousand-year-old rose bush which surrounds the walls of the cathedral was adopted as the official emblem of Hildesheim.

Tragedy struck the town in the final stages of World War II when allied bombing destroyed 70 per cent of Hildesheim's early Romanesque architecture and wiped out one of Germany's most important centres of Romanesque art.

Southwest of the **Altstadt** (Old Town) centre the **Dom** (Cathedral) stands on the site of the 9th-century original basilica. The present building is a reconstruction of the 11th-century basilica and was consecrated in 1960. West of the cathedral, the **Roemer Pelizaeus Museum** contains the second most important collection of Egyptian artefacts in Germany, second only to the Bode Museum in Berlin.

St Michaelis Kirche (St Michael's Church) is recognised as the best example of the Gottesburg (God's Castle) Ottonian-Romanesque style; it was, and is again, one of the most magnificent Romanesque basilicas in Germany.

The nearby castle of **Marienburg**, at Nordstemmen, gives the impression of a medieval fortress, but in fact it was only built by King George of Hanover in the 19th century. The castle houses an interesting museum.

[i] Am Ratsbauhof 1c

*Take the **B1** west for 48km (30 miles) to Hameln.*

Hameln, Niedersachsen

4 Hameln, or Hamelin, is the well-known Rattenfängerstadt (rat-catcher's town) of story book fame. The legendary Pied Piper is said to have come to the town in 1284 and promised to rid it of a plague of rats. With the help of his flute he led the rats into the river where they drowned, but when he went to collect his reward, the city burghers refused to pay. In retaliation, he took up his flute again and enticed the town's children to follow him. Neither he nor the children was ever seen again.

As well as the original settlement of *Hamala*, which was founded by peasants and fishermen, monks from Fulda founded an abbey near the River Weser, which was later called St Bonifatius (Boniface).

On the market square stands the early Gothic **Church of St Nicolai**, rebuilt between 1957 and 1958. This was originally the rivermen's church and the top of the tower is decorated with a model of a golden vessel, a reminder of its ancient heritage.

On Osterstrasse, east of the market, stands the Renaissance-style **Hochzeitshaus** (Marriage House), a former reception hall, built between 1610 and 1617. The **Rattenfängerhaus** (Rat-catcher's House) is another imposing Renaissance structure with an ornate front gable and splendid decorations. Around the corner, a plaque commemorates the Pied Piper's tale.

[i] Deisterallee

*Continue southwest on the **B1** for 70km (43 miles) to Paderborn.*

Paderborn, Nordrhein-Westfalen

5 Trading routes between Flanders and Saxony created an early settlement on the site of the present town of Paderborn. Karl der Grosse (Charlemagne) held his first Imperial Diet (Meeting of Rulers) here in AD777, after he had conquered Saxony, and in the same year Paderborn achieved the status of a city.

In the centre of the Altstadt, the mighty **Dom** (Cathedral) stands almost as long as its tower is high, nearly 100m (328 feet). Built over two centuries, from AD100, the church tower is a massive closed construction of Romanesque design. It dominates the view of the cathedral square and the houses around it. Beneath the floor of the cathedral, the foundations of Charlemagne's original basilica were discovered in 1979 to 1980.

Around the cathedral area there are 200 little springs, known as the **Paderquellen**. These form the River Pader, which, at a mere 4km (2½ miles) long, is one of the shortest rivers in Germany. The **Rathaus** is located southwest of the cathedral. A late Renaissance structure with three gables, it houses the natural history museum.

Just 4km (2½ miles) north of town, **Schloss Neuhaus** is a moated castle which has stood here in its present form since the 16th century. It consists of four wings with a massive tower on each corner, and was once the residence of the Prince-Bishops.

TOUR 7

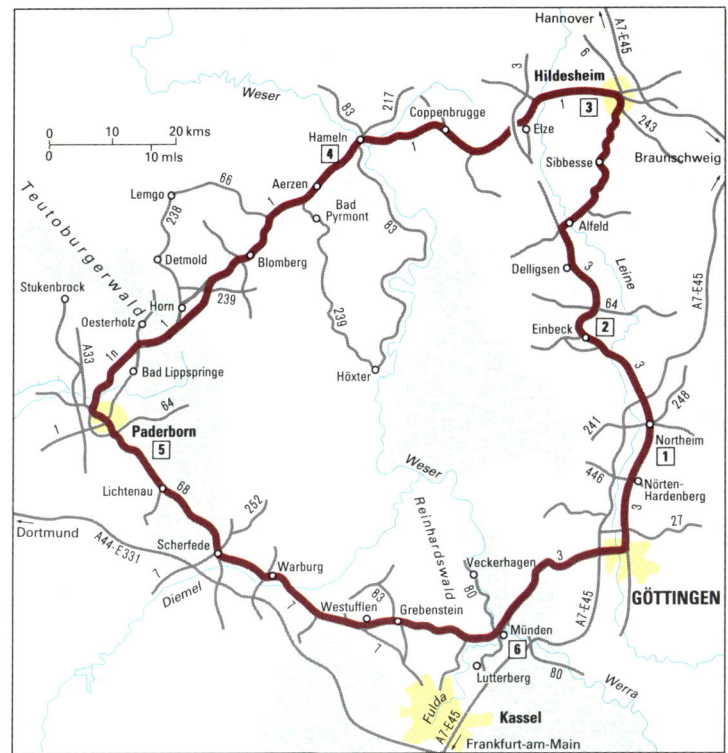

Now the castle houses a school, an exhibition hall for the town's gallery and a concert hall.

[i] Marienplatz 2a

> Drive southeast on the **B68/B7**, via Warburg to Westuffeln, then turn left to Grebenstein and continue east to Münden, 83km (52 miles).

Münden, Niedersachsen

6 The historic town of Münden enjoys a pleasant position in a valley surrounded by woods, close to the confluence of the rivers Werra and Fulda. Excavations have revealed that a large settlement existed here in Charlemagne's time, but the foundation of the town is credited to Heinrich der Löwe (Henry the Lion).

The **Rathaus** stands on Marktplatz (Market Square), surrounded by timber-framed buildings. Its imposing Weser-Renaissance façade was designed by Georg Crossman, and erected between 1603 and 1613, with three ornamented gables, a sumptuous entrance portal and oriel windows. Opposite stands **St Blasius' Church**, which was built between the 13th and 16th centuries. Notable features inside include a bronze font, a sandstone pulpit and the tomb of Wilhelm von Braunschweig (William of Brunswick), who died in 1503.

The former **Welfenschloss** (Castle of the Welfs, an old dynasty) was founded in 1070. It is a picturesque building in Renaissance style and now houses the town's cultural centre and local history museum.

[i] Im Rathaus

> From Münden continue on the **B3** northeast for 24km (15 miles) to Göttingen.

Mummy mask in Hildesheim's Roemer-Pelizaeus Museum, which has a world-famous collection of Egyptian antiquities

Göttingen – Northeim 21 (13)
Northeim – Einbeck 19 (12)
Einbeck – Hildesheim 43 (27)
Hildesheim – Hameln 48 (30)
Hameln – Paderborn 70 (43)
Paderborn – Münden 83 (52)
Münden – Göttingen 24 (15)

RECOMMENDED WALKS

6 *Münden, Niedersachsen* There are about 90 suggested circular walking routes from the car parks in and around Münden. East of Lutterberg, on the **B496** south of Münden, the **Rinderstall** is a popular destination for a stroll. The **Kloster Bursfelde** (abbey), which dates back to the 12th century, can be reached by driving due north along the eastern bank of the Weser, and there are a number of lovely walks around here.

FOR HISTORY BUFFS

5 *Paderborn, Nordrhein-Westfalen* From Paderborn, drive north on the **B1** for approximately 15km (9 miles), then turn left for Oesterholz and Berlebeck and left again at **Hermannsdenkmal**. This enormous monument celebrates 1st-century German nationalist leader Arminius (Hermann) who is seen here brandishing a 7m (23-foot) sword. Hermann's cunning defeated vastly superior Roman forces when he lured them into the forest and beat them in a three-day battle in AD89. The raising of the monument coincided with the birth of the German nationalist movement in the mid-19th century and carries the inscription 'German unity is my strength, and my strength is Germany's power'.

2 days – 311km (193 miles)

NATURE PARKS & FAIRY TALES

Kassel • Wilhelmsthal • Waldeck • Frankenberg
Marburg/Lahn • Alsfeld • Bad Hersfeld • Kassel

On the River Fulda, sheltered by the foothills of the Habichtswald, Kassel has the ideal location for a town. The *Altstadt* (Old Town) no longer exists, wiped out by heavy bombing during World War II. The *Wilhelmshohe Schlosspark* is Kassel's real treasure. Commissioned by Landgrave Karl in 1701, it focuses on the giant statue of Hercules, a copy of the Farnese Hercules in Naples, which stands on a stone pyramid which in turn rests on the Oktogon pavilion. Below the Oktogon, great water cascades flow down the hill and there is a magnificent view of the park, palace and the town below. When all the fountains are switched on it creates an unforgettable scene. The *castle* houses a large museum with collections of Egyptian, Greek and Roman antiquities, but its highlight is the *Gemäldegalerie* (Picture Gallery), with paintings by Lucas Cranach, Dürer and Rembrandt.

The *Brüder Grimm Museum* in the Palais Bellevue presents the life and work of the two brothers, whose collections of fairy tales appear in editions all around the world.

Keep an eye out for quirky details, like this carving, on the old buildings in Alsfeld

[i] Im Hauptbahnhof

*From Kassel take the **B7** northwest for 12km (7 miles) to Wilhelmsthal.*

Wilhelmsthal, Hessen

1 A detour to **Schloss Wilhelmsthal** is suggested en route to Waldeck. The castle in its present rococo form was designed by the French architect Francois Cuvilliès, who built it on the site of an earlier construction dating from the 17th century. The interior is decorated with superb panelling and a whole gallery of beautiful female figures added by the German painter Tischbein the Elder, acting on the instructions of his princely masters.

[i] Calden, Holländische Strasse 35

*Drive about 5km (3 miles) south to the **B251**, turn right and continue on the **B251** to Sachsenhausen. Take the **B485** east for 5km (3 miles), then turn west for Waldeck.*

Waldeck, Hessen

2 Surrounded by woods and an enormous artificial lake, Waldeck is a small town. The **Eder Dam**, which was completed in 1914, is almost 50m (164 feet) high, between 3 and 5m (10 and 16 feet) thick and 400m (1,310 feet) long.

Castle Waldeck, which occupies a commanding position on top of a hill near the town, is said to be a thousand years old, and used to be the seat of the Waldeck princes. Abandoned in the 17th century, it has been restored and is now partly used as a hotel. There is a panoramic view from a terrace overlooking the lake, and the interior decorations carefully preserve the romantic atmosphere of an ancient castle. You can still see the dungeon with three prison cells, one on top of the other, in the **Hexenturm** (Witches' Tower), and there is a museum consisting of two portrait galleries commemorating the glories of the Waldeck dynasty.

A regular boat service plies the lake in summer and there is plenty of opportunity to try out all sorts of watersports. A cabin lift provides an easy connection between the town, the lakes and the castle.

[i] Verkehrsamt, Rathaus

*Continue on the **B485** to Bad Wildungen, then take the **B253** west to Frankenberg, 46km (29 miles).*

Frankenberg, Hessen

3 No fewer than 10 little turrets can be counted on Frankenberg's timber-framed **Rathaus**. A solid tower forms each of the four corners and the space between is filled up by small oriel-turrets, creating a very attractive and unusual outline. The building dates from 1421, but after a fire in 1509 the structure was modified. Its position between the Ober (Upper) and Unter (Lower) market squares links the two. A stroll in the upper half of the town reveals an interesting group of 16th-century wooden houses with the timber often protected by a layer of slate. A little higher up is the **Liebfrauenkirche** (Church of Our Lady), built between the 13th and 14th centuries to a design copied from the Elisabethkirche in Marburg. A notable feature of the interior is the Marienkapelle (St Mary's Chapel) which was erected at the height of the Gothic period.

[i] Rathaus

*From Frankenberg take the **B252** south for 39km (24 miles) to Marburg/Lahn.*

Marburg/Lahn, Hessen

4 On the River Lahn, Marburg was first documented in 1130, as a Thuringian 'marcpurg'. It became part of the province of Hessen in 1248; and in 1527, after the Reformation, it became the seat of the first protestant university.

The **Elisabethkirche** is the main attraction in the **Altstadt** (Old Town), partly for its pre-eminence as the first German Gothic ecclesiastical building, but also because of its connection with Elisabeth of Hungary, daughter of the King of Hungary. The intended bride of the Landgrave Ludwig of Thuringia, she had to leave home in Hungary at the early age of four and was brought up at nearby Wartburg Castle. As a young girl her concern for the sick and poor became well known, then when her husband, the Landgrave, died of the plague in

The Löwenburg near Kassel, an 18th-century sham medieval ruin

BACK TO NATURE

3 *Frankenberg, Hessen* Just outside the town of Frankenberg, the **Stadtforst Finsterbachtal forest** offers a chance to explore a wild deer park inhabited by a wide variety of indigenous wildlife. Look for red squirrels and birds such as middle-spotted woodpeckers and nutcrackers.

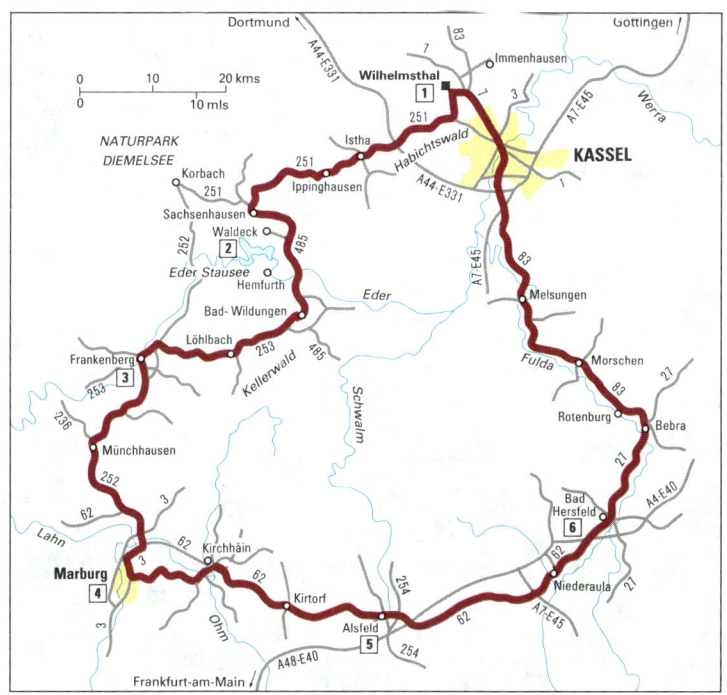

FOR HISTORY BUFFS

3 *Frankenberg, Hessen* Some 15km (9 miles) east of Frankenberg stands a former Cistercian **abbey**, at **Haina**. During the 16th century it was converted into a mental hospital by Landgrave Phillip der Grossmütige (the Magnanimous), when he underwent conversion to Protestantism. The inside of the church consists of a large Gothic hall with columns in a design peculiar to the Cistercian order. The cloister shows a mixture of Romanesque and Gothic.

TOUR 8

RECOMMENDED WALKS

3 *Frankenberg, Hessen* Take the **B252** north from Frankenberg to Korbach, and turn left into the **Naturpark Diemelsee**. Beautiful walking trails explore the forest and the area around the **Diemel Talsperre Dam**.

SCENIC ROUTES

En route from Schloss Wilhelmsthal to Waldeck, a very attractive stretch of road leads through the **Habichtswald nature park**, particularly the section from the village of Ippinghausen to Sachsenhausen. The route from Bad Wildungen to Frankenberg, which passes through the **Kellerwald** forest, is a very scenic part of the tour.

1227, she withdrew to work in a hospital for the incurables below Marburg Castle, where she died from exhaustion at the age of 24. Canonised in 1235, her body was later placed in the church which bears her name.

St Elisabeth's was constructed between 1235 and 1283. Inside, through the main gate, lies the tomb of Field Marshall von Hindenburg, the last German President, upon whom was thrust the unenviable task of leading Germany after its defeat in World War I, and then dealing with the rise of Adolf Hitler and his National Socialist Party. Hindenburg died in 1934.

The most interesting object in the church is the golden shrine of St Elisabeth, which was built by a craftsman from the Rhineland around 1250, and contained the saint's relics until 1539. Reminders of St Elisabeth are to be found in various parts of the church: a 15th-century wooden statue in the nave; a 13th-century painted window and frescos in the chancel; and a statue of her, personifying Charity.

The **Marktplatz** (Market Square) and its upper section, known as the Obermarkt, are still surrounded by some beautiful timber-framed houses, especially numbers 14, 21 and 23. The fountain of St George is a popular meeting place for students; while the Gothic **Rathaus**, erected in 1524, forms one end of the square.

Marburg Castle was built for the former Landgraves of Hesse, and it stands on a hill high above the town with pleasant views from its various terraces. Of special note inside are the large Gothic Rittersaal (Knights' Hall), the Landgrave's study and a small chapel. The **Museum für Kulturgeschichte** (History of Culture) in the Wilhelmsbau wing exhibits precious objects from St Elisabeth's, fragments of stained glass, 15th-century tapestries and a collection of medieval shields.

The **Alte Universität** (Old University) was built in 1870, on a rocky site above the Lahn, using the foundations of a former convent. The **Aula** (Great Hall) is decorated with paintings depicting the history of Marburg; and the **Karzer** (punishment cell for students) is on view complete with graffiti scrawled by former inmates.

[i] Verkehrsamt

*Drive east to Kirchhain and take the **B62** southeast to Alsfeld, 46km (25 miles).*

Alsfeld, Hessen

5 First mentioned in 1069, when it belonged to the Landgrave of Thuringia, Alsfeld became part of Hesse in 1247, and was later made a member of the Council of Rhenish towns. In the 14th century it was the occasional residence of Landgrave Hermann of Hessen, who promoted the local guilds; and during the Reformation Martin Luther stayed here during his appearance before the bishops at the Diet of Worms in 1521.

'European Model Town' in the heritage year of 1975, Alsfeld is very picturesque. The romantic **Altstadt** has retained its medieval charm right up to the present day, and focuses on the **Marktplatz** (market square). In prime position is the **Rathaus**. The two upper storeys are half-timbered and topped by a steeply-pitched gabled roof fronted by two oriel windows. Across a narrow road from the Rathaus stands the **Weinhaus**

The artificial lake and Eder Dam from Castle Waldeck

Bad Hersfeld. The town enjoys a drama festival in July and August

(Wine House). The **Stumpfhaus**, named for former Lord Mayor Jost Stumpf, was built in 1609 and is the most elaborately decorated timber-framed house in the town. Further along there are two fine houses: at No 3, the **Neurath-Haus** is a fine baroque style half-timbered building; and stone-built No 5, the **Minnigerode-Haus**, still boasts its original highly unusual wooden staircase built around a tree trunk.

Behind the Rathaus stands the **Walpurgiskirche**. Built between the 13th and 15th centuries, the church features late Gothic wall paintings and impressive tombs inside. In **Untere Fuldergasse** there are some funny looking crooked half-timbered houses; and further up, one of Alsfeld's few remaining medieval fortifications, a defensive tower called the **Leonhardsturm**.

[i] Rittergasse 5

*From Alsfeld continue on the **B62** for 40km (25 miles) to Bad Hersfeld.*

Bad Hersfeld, Hessen

6 The origins of Bad Hersfeld can be traced to AD769, when Archbishop Lullus founded a Benedictine abbey here. After modifications in the 11th and 12th centuries, it was destroyed by French soldiers in 1761. A free-standing bell tower dating from about 1120, once part of the abbey complex, houses the 900-year-old convent bells, some of the earliest in Germany.

Picturesque old burghers' houses surround Bad Hersfeld's wide market square, and the Gothic **parish church** on the eastern side, with its mighty tower, dates back to the 14th century. Opposite the church, the **Rathaus** was originally built in the 14th century and later enlarged with a Renaissance façade in 1612. The German language expert and lexicographer Konrad Duden (1821–1911) lived here and was responsible for creating the 'bible' of German spelling, since called the 'Duden', the German equivalent of the Oxford English dictionary.

Bad Hersfeld is also one of the country's most popular spa towns, with its mineral-rich spring water which is recommended for the treatment of liver complaints.

[i] Verkehrsbüro

*Take the **B27** north to Bebra and return to Kassel on the **B83**, 73km (45 miles).*

Kassel – Wilhelmsthal **12 (7)**
Wilhelmsthal – Waldeck **55 (34)**
Waldeck – Frankenberg **46 (29)**
Frankenberg – Marburg/Lahn **39 (24)**
Marburg/Lahn – Alsfeld **46 (29)**
Alsfeld – Bad Hersfeld **40 (25)**
Bad Hersfeld – Kassel **73 (45)**

FOR CHILDREN

2 *Waldeck, Hessen* South of Waldeck, near the 400m (1,310-foot) long dam, there is a deer park and power station at **Hemfurth**, with a cable car leading to the water reservoir.

5 *Alsfeld, Hessen* Do not miss the statue of **Little Red Riding Hood** near the **Rathaus** in Alsfeld. The fairy tale favourite is said to have been a former resident of the town.

SPECIAL TO...

1 *Wilhelmsthal, Hessen* From Calden head northeast to nearby Immenhausen, and then a further 6km (4 miles) east is **Glashütte Süssmuth**, one of the few glass factories which still produces hand-blown glass. There are factory tours together with a glass museum.

6 *Bad Hersfeld, Hessen* The ruins of the 1,200-year-old **Stiftskirche** in Bad Hersfeld provide a spectacular background for the annual **Drama Festival** staged here in July and August each year.

DAMS, LAKES & WOODS

2 days – 339km (211 miles)

Hagen • Iserlohn • Arnsberg • Bilsteinhöhle
Meschede • Ramsbeck • Brilon • Siegen
Freudenberg • Hagen

Hagen's boundaries extend to its surrounding villages and suburbs. At the centre of the town stands the *Rathaus* (Town Hall), with a replica of the sun mounted on its tower. The whole solar system is distributed around the town, and bronze plates on the pavements show the orbits of the planets. Hagen has associations with the *Jugendstil* (Art Nouveau) movement which flourished from the 1890s. The best example of this is the *Karl Ernst Osthaus Museum*, which was designed and erected by Henry van der Velde. There are several other Jugendstil buildings around the town.

Hagen is a good centre for excursions into the surrounding area.

BACK TO NATURE

1 *Iserlohn, Nordrhein-Westfalen* Adjoining Iserlohn to the east is **Hemer**, and a further 1km (½ mile) southwest of the town is the **Heinrichshöhle** (cave), which claims to be the wildest and most romantic part of the Sauerland. Close by, the **Felsenmeer** (Sea of Rocks) was formed millions of years ago by corals under the ocean. The boulders were created by the collapse of several adjoining caves, and these towers of rocks were given names like **Teufelskanzel** (Devil's Pulpit) and **Paradies** (Paradise).

2 *Arnsberg, Nordrhein-Westfalen* Visit the **wild deer park** at **Völlinghausen**: take the **B229** north to the Möhnesee, and turn right along the south bank to the park, at the eastern end of the lake. The park is home to indigenous red deer and the Sika-stag.

[i] Friedrich Ebert Platz

*From Hagen take the **B7** east for 17km (11 miles) to Iserlohn.*

Iserlohn, Nordrhein-Westfalen

1 Remnants of the old town fortifications can still be seen at Iserlohn, and another relic of the past is the **Oberste Stadtkirche** (Upper Town Church), a late Gothic building with a Romanesque tower. Inside, there is a valuable carved altar from Flanders dating from around 1400. The **Bauernkirche** (peasants' church) of St Pankratius was originally a Romanesque basilica but was later altered in the Gothic style and became a Protestant church.

The **Dechenhöhle** (Dechen Cave) at **Letmathe**, 4km (2½ miles) west of Iserlohn, was discovered by accident when the railway was being built in 1868. Two men lost their tools in a gap in the rocks and while searching for them discovered the caves. Subsequent excavations at the site have revealed animal bones from the last Ice Age. As the temperature inside never reaches more than 10°C (50°F), even in summer, remember to wrap up warmly. Several easily negotiated paths have been laid out which lead to 15 separate chambers. The **Wolfsschlucht** (Wolves' Ravine) and the **Kaiserhalle** (Emperor's Hall) are the most impressive.

[i] Konrad Adenauer Ring 15

Inside the 300-million-year-old Dechenhöhle near Iserlohn

The Rathaus in Siegen, a town made prosperous by iron-working

*Drive northeast towards Menden, turn right on to the **B515** and continue to Beckum. Turn left and take the **B229** northeast to Arnsberg, 45km (28 miles).*

Arnsberg, Nordrhein-Westfalen

2 Surrounded by **naturparks** (nature reserves), the town of Arnsberg lies just in between the Arnsberger Wald in the north, and the smaller Arnsberg Stadtwald in the south, which extends to the **Naturpark Homert**. The Ruhr flows through the middle with Arnsberg on a hill, caught in a loop of the river.

Its historic importance as former district capital is demonstrated by the picturesque **Altstadt** (Old Town) and its timber-framed houses, fortified towers and the **Hirschberger Tor**, a rococo gate, of 1753. There is a fine **Altes Rathaus** (Old Town Hall), complete with bell tower, and a magnificent view across town and beyond from the ruins of the old Renaissance castle.

An example of early Gothic style architecture, **St Laurentiuskirche** is the only remaining building of an abbey founded by the Prämonstratenser order in 1173, and later disbanded in 1803. The continuous process of building over the centuries has created a mixture of styles, including a surprising early baroque high altar finished in marble and alabaster,

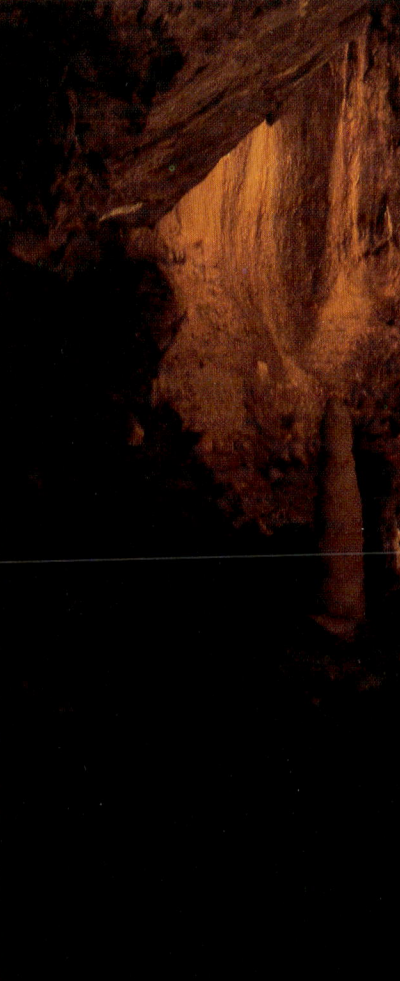

TOUR 9   45

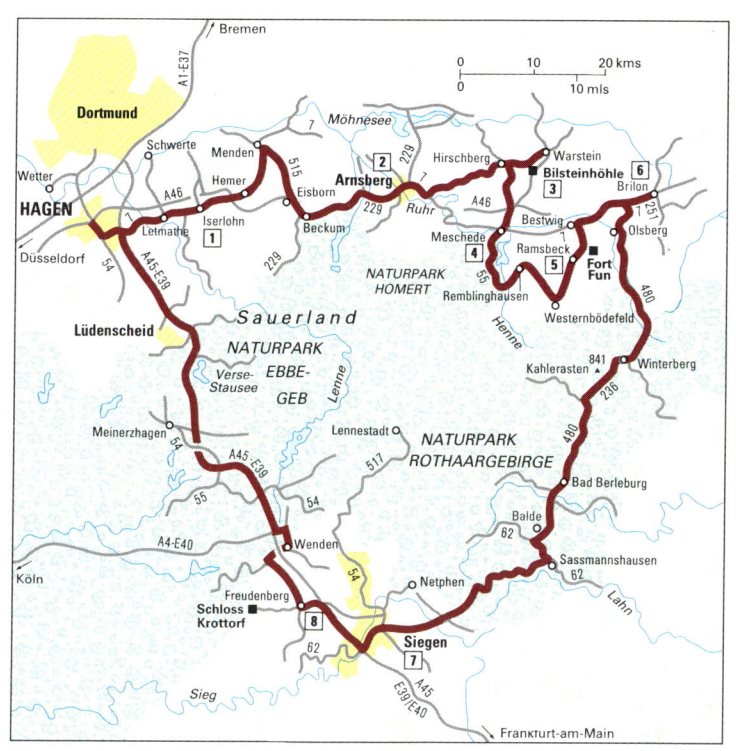

RECOMMENDED WALKS

2 *Arnsberg, Nordrhein-Westfalen* South of the Möhnesee, the **Arnsberger Wald** offers 70 so-called **Wanderparkplätze**, car parks which are also suggested departure points for hikes through the forest.

7 *Siegen, Nordrhein-Westfalen* From Siegen drive north on the **B62**, and follow the road east for Netphen and Brauersdorf. There are pleasant lakeside walks around the **Obernau Stausee** and up the slopes of the **Sanktkopf**.

tombs of local rulers ranging from the 14th to 17th centuries, and a late 18th-century pulpit.

The **Sauerland Museum** exhibits hunting weapons from the 16th to the 19th centuries and finds from the Balver Cave.

Southwest of Arnsberg lies the **Sorpesee** (Sorpe lake), a man-made reservoir with a dam supposed to be the longest in Europe. Built between 1928 and 1935, the dam is 700m (2,295 feet) long and 60m (197 feet) high. It created a lake some 8km

TOUR 9

Inner courtyard of the Oberes Schloss (Upper Castle), one of Siegen's two castles built by the aristocratic Nassau family

SPECIAL TO...

2 **Arnsberg, Nordrhein-Westfalen** A striking architectural contrast to the mighty Möhne dam is provided by the nearby **Druggelter Kapelle** (chapel). Built around 1220, it is said to be the most important Romanesque building in the area. It is a small 12-sided rotunda with sumptuous decorations and sculptures on the capitals.

(5 miles) long, which, apart from supplying electricity, has become a paradise for watersports enthusiasts. Hikers will enjoy walks in the surrounding forests or a stroll round the lake. A motorboat service is also available in summer. Near the southern tip of the lake, in an area called Seidfeld, there is a glider centre. Camping is very popular on the western side of the lake and there is a good choice of sites available.

Due north of Arnsberg, the famous **Möhnesee** is only a short trip through the Arnsberger Wald. Surrounded by a clutch of 15 little villages, the 10sq km (4-square-mile) man-made lake is named for the River Möhne which feeds it. The Möhnesee's fame is derived from the much publicised story and film made of the World War II RAF bomber-raid which destroyed the dam with specially designed bombs and a unique technique which allowed the released bombs to bounce along the water to their target.

There are three crossings over the lake for motor vehicles, opening up a variety of different routes. Only the road along the southwest shore leading to the dam is closed to traffic. There are plenty of opportunities for windsurfing, sailing and rowing as well as boat trips by lake steamer during the summer season.

[i] Neumarkt 6

From Arnsberg drive about 8km (5 miles) to Oeventrop, turn left and head northeast to Hirschberg and west to Bilsteinhöhle (Bilstein Cave), about 4km (2½ miles) southwest of Warstein.

Bilsteinhöhle, Nordrhein-Westfalen

3 A popular tourist attraction, the Bilsteinhöhle (Bilstein Cave) was discovered in 1887. You can visit a 400m (1,310-foot) stretch of the dry upper section of the cave. Close by are the **Kulturhöhlen** (Caves of Culture), which were once occupied by prehistoric people. Finds from the caves are displayed in the local **museum** at **Warstein**, which also contains information on local history.

[i] Warstein, Dieplohstrasse 1

Return to Hirschberg, then continue south to Meschede, 15km (9 miles).

Meschede, Nordrhein-Westfalen

4 Meschede lies at the confluence of the Henne and the Ruhr, near the moated 17th-century **Schloss Laer** which lies about 1.5km (1 mile) west of town. Meschede's **parish church** is an old historic building dating from the mid-17th century while, in complete contrast, **Königsmünster Abbey**, in the north of town, is a modern foundation and the monks run a large Gymnasium, a selective secondary school, similar to the old English grammar school system.

[i] Ruhrstrasse 25

*Take the **B55** south for about 10km (6 miles) to Herhagen, turn northeast to Remblinghausen, southeast to Westernbödefeld and north to Ramsbeck, 33km (20 miles).*

Ramsbeck, Nordrhein-Westfalen

5 The Bergbaumusuem (Mining Museum) in Ramsbeck is well worth a visit for its interesting coverage of centuries of ancient mining techniques in the Sauerland. There is an original mine shaft where the extraction of lead- and zinc-rich ore is demonstrated, and a fun ride on one of the narrow mining railways is part of the enjoyment.

*Continue north, via Bestwig and the **B7** east to Brilon.*

Brilon, Nordrhein-Westfalen

6 In the middle of the high, wide plain, the settlement of Brilon was first documented as early as AD973. Around 1400, it became the capital of the **Herzogtum Westfalen** (Dukedom of Westfalia), and was also a member of the Hanseatic League. The historic central **Marktplatz** (Market Square) is dominated by the Romanesque-style **Propisteikirche**, consecrated in 1276, whose mighty tower overshadows the **Rathaus**, a medieval structure dating from the 13th century with a baroque façade. Another feature of the square is the **Petrusbrunnen** fountain, a fine 16th-century monument.

[i] Verkehrsverein

*Take the **B7** west, then turn south at Altenburen on to the **B480** to Winterberg. Continue southwest on the **B236**, then south on the **B480** again to Balde. Take the **B62** to Sassmannshausen and turn sharp right on the 'Lahn Ferienstrasse' (Lahn Holiday Road) to Siegen, 96km (60 miles).*

Siegen, Nordrhein-Westfalen

7 Siegen lies in a region south of the Sauerland, called the Siegerland. The town's **Oberes Schloss** (Upper Castle) is a successor to the original fortress of the 13th century. It houses an interesting **museum** which, among other things, celebrates 2,000 years of the production and use of iron in industry. Another department deals with a quite different subject, the painter Peter Paul Rubens, who was born here in 1577 after his parents were exiled from Holland. The museum exhibits several original Rubens paintings and also portraits of former rulers. There is a good view over the town and surroundings from the castle's terrace.

The **Unteres Schloss** (Lower Castle) is found in the **Altstadt** (Old Town). Built between 1698 and 1714 in baroque style for Duke Frederick Wilhelm of Nassau, it was the residence of the Protestant branch of the Nassau-Siegen dynasty. The tombs of various counts and dukes are seen below the main building, and the **Dicker Turm** (Fat Tower) is also worth a visit. West of the Unteres Schloss, **Martinskirche** (St Martin's) is a 10th-century Ottonic basilica with a Romanesque font and Gothic features added in the 16th century. East on the market square stands the **Nikolaikirche** (St Nicolas'). It houses the tombs of the Counts of Nassau and has interesting hexagonal foundations.

[i] Rathaus, Markt 2

*From Siegen take the **A45** northwest to the exit for Freudenberg and continue southwest to the town.*

Freudenberg, Nordrhein-Westfalen

8 The timber-framed houses in Freudenberg present an amazing sight as you arrive in the old town centre. Built for miners after a devastating fire in 1666, they are all of roughly the same size and design and give visitors the impression of having just driven into a fairy tale picture book. The **Alter Flecken** (Old Spot), as the town centre is called, has preserved its heritage intact over the centuries and the houses are all listed buildings.

A short 8km (5-mile) detour west of Freudenberg, **Schloss Krottorf** is a moated castle dating back to the 12th century, and offers a deer park in its grounds.

[i] Stadt Verkehrsamt

*Take the **A45** for 80km (50 miles) back to Hagen.*

Hagen – Iserlohn 17 (11)
Iserlohn – Arnsberg 45 (28)
Arnsberg – Bilsteinhöhle 24 (15)
Bilsteinhöhle – Meschede 15 (9)
Meschede – Ramsbeck 33 (20)
Ramsbeck – Brilon 17 (11)
Brilon – Siegen 96 (60)
Siegen – Freudenberg 12 (7)
Freudenberg – Hagen 80 (50)

Jugendstil is well represented in the Hohenhof at Hagen

SCENIC ROUTES

The tour has many scenic stretches of road. Some of the best are from Eisborn, south of Menden, past the **Reckenhöhle** (cave) to Beckum and Arnsberg; between Arnsberg and Warstein; and Sassmannshausen to Siegen, on the Lahn Ferienstrasse.

FOR CHILDREN

5 Ramsbeck, Nordrhein-Westfalen **Fort Fun** is located just east of Ramsbeck and provides entertainment for all the family. There is a true to life model of a **Wild West town**, complete with a western railroad, plus 780m (2,559-foot) long super-slides, a chair-lift and other fun rides.

FOR HISTORY BUFFS

6 Brilon, Nordrhein-Westfalen On the heights of the Istenberg (mountains) near Bruchhausen stands the **Bruchhausen Steine** (stones of Bruchhauser), a monument of great cultural and historical interest. The area shows remnants of a prehistoric fortress and may have been the site of a pre-Christian place of worship. Take the **B7/B251** south from Brilon, then turn right past the Ginsterkopf mountain.

BAVARIA

Picturesque Kaufbeuren has a well preserved medieval quarter

Bavaria forms the southeastern part of Germany, and is one of the largest and most important provinces. In the north is Franken (Franconia), which consists mainly of hilly countryside bordered by the ranges of the Thüringer and Böhmerwald mountain ranges. Further south are the fertile plains of Bavaria and its three main rivers: the Danube, the Isar and the Inn. Towards the Alps, a series of lakes stretches from west to east, before suddenly being confronted by those mighty mountains, with heights of nearly 3,000m (9,840 feet). This district is called Oberbayern, and a turn to the west leads to the Allgäu, well-known for its dairy products. Continuing west towards the Bodensee (Lake Constance), the tour enters Bavarian Swabia, with its distinctive Swabian dialect.

The province is economically strong and now has a vigorous industrial capacity as well as a firm agricultural base. Tourism also plays an important part in the Bavarian economy, principally in the area called Oberbayern. Bavaria was an independent kingdom until the end of World War I; ask a Bavarian about his or her nationality, and the reply will be 'I am a Bavarian' first, with 'and a German' added later.

This is definitely beer country, with the great breweries centred around Munich, although the hops come from the fertile plains of Niederbayern, northeast of the Bavarian capital. Bavarians generally need little prompting to hold a festival. Most are centred round the religious calendar, with Christmas playing the leading role. The traditional fir tree is to be found everywhere and the Christmas celebrations can be very emotional, especially in the Alpine regions. What can be more romantic than Christmas Eve in one of these Alpine villages, with plenty of snow about and the candlelit Christmas trees to be seen in the charming Bavarian houses?

Tour 10

Franken (Franconia) forms the northern part of Bavaria, and the towns have a strong historical background. They include the home of Queen Victoria's consort Albert and a residence of the Holy Roman Emperor. Opera lovers will know it as the home of the Bayreuth festival. There is one big difference to the south of Bavaria: it is wine, not beer, which is the favoured drink, and these wines rate among Germany's best.

Tour 11

This tour covers a wide area, starting with some interesting small towns and then proceeding to the famous forests which form the eastern frontier of Bavaria. At the heart of the tour is Nürnberg, an important historical centre in Bavaria.

Tour 12

Rivers, forests and beautiful scenery are there to be enjoyed on this tour. A famous border town with a unique location – Passau – is the starting point, and from there it is straight into the forests. A much treasured jewel of a town set on a famous river, Regensburg, is a highlight.

Tour 13

The tour starts along a large Bavarian lake with two famous islands dominated by the fairytale splendour of one of the best-known Bavarian castles. The route then turns south to the real mountains of the Alps, where breathtaking scenery can be enjoyed, not only from the mountain-tops, but also from the valleys below.

Tour 14

This tour concentrates on a series of the Bavarian Alpine lakes which lie at the foot of the mountains. Remarkable scenery can be admired on the drive between the lakes, as the road leads up and down some magnificent mountain passes.

Tour 15

You will start this tour gently by a lake at Starnberg, the favourite weekend destination of visitors from the nearby capital of Bavaria. This is followed by resorts famous for their sports and their religious affiliations. A charming mountain retreat fit for a king provides an unforgettable experience.

Tour 16
The River Danube appears several times during the course of this tour, but it has quite a different appearance here to the river it becomes after it leaves Bavaria. The tour enters Bavarian Swabia, where smaller towns will attract the interest.

Garmisch-Partenkirchen, at the foot of the Zugspitze, is Germany's top wintersports centre

Würzburg: the Marienberg fortress

Tour 17
This tour begins and ends on an island in the Bodensee (Lake Constance), but driving on and off it presents no problems. The scenery becomes gradually more dramatic as the tour proceeds. Later on, fantasy becomes reality, with a magic castle unmatched by frequent reproductions.

2 days – 341km (212 miles)

FRANCONIA & ITS HISTORIC TOWNS

Würzburg • Coburg • Kronach • Bayreuth • Bamberg
Ebrach • Würzburg

Fountain in Bayreuth. The town is one of Germany's cultural highspots, thanks to Wagner

Würzburg's prosperity dates from AD741, when St Burchard became the first bishop. In the 17th and 18th centuries the Prince-Bishops used their wealth to commission outstanding works of art. World War II bombing raids destroyed most of the old town, but much has since been rebuilt.

The *Würzburg Residenz* is a major example of south German baroque architecture. The fires of 1945 left some main parts intact, such as the staircase by Balthasar Neumann, and the ceiling frescos by the Venetian Tiepolo. The Kaisersaal is often used as an ideal setting for Mozart concerts.

The first *cathedral* was consecrated in AD788; the present building was finished in 1700. Near the cathedral stands the *Rathaus* (town hall), which has functioned since 1316. Work by Franconian artists is displayed in the *Städtische Gallerie*. The *Martin von Wagner Museum*, located in a wing of the Residenz building, exhibits Greek and Roman antiquities. On the other side of the river is the fortress *Marienberg*, which features the 1482 Scherenberg gate.

RECOMMENDED WALKS

1 *Coburg, Bayern* A pleasant stroll leads from the gardens of Schloss Ehrenburg in Coburg up to the medieval castle of Veste.

2 *Kronach, Bayern* In Kronach walk westwards from the centre of the town to the part called Gehölz and look out for 'Trimm Dich Pfad' ('the path to get you into trim')!

FOR HISTORY BUFFS

3 *Bayreuth, Bayern* The **Eremitage**, 4km (2½ miles) east of Bayreuth, was established between 1715 and 1750 as a pleasure park for the Landgrave, with castles and fountains cleverly arranged.

[i] Palais am Congress Centrum

*From Würzburg take the **B22** west to Schwarzach, then north to Volkach, turn left and drive along the west bank of the Main river to Schweinfurt, then on the **B303** to Coburg, 129km (80 miles).*

Coburg, Bayern

1 Coburg lies on the River Itz, and its fortress is a major local landmark. The town is more than 900 years old, and from the 16th century the ruling dynasty of Saxe-Coburg had connections with many royal families of Europe. Queen Victoria's beloved Albert was a prince of Saxe-Coburg. His childhood home, the Ehrenburg, is open to the public.

The Festungstrasse leads up to the fortress, which is known as the 'Fränkische Krone' (crown of Franconia) because of its layout, well protected by a double ring of walls and numerous watch towers. The original structure dates back to the 12th century, although the present castle is mostly 16th-century. The castle is famous as the place where the Protestant reformer Martin Luther sought refuge. His room, the **Lutherstube**, can still be seen. In the central wing, a museum displays an art collection acquired over 900 years. It also has the largest weapons collection in Germany, with a special chamber devoted to armaments used in the Thirty Years' War (1618–48).

The **Herzoginbau** (Duchess's building) has a carriage museum, art exhibitions and a fabulous display of armour.

The **Ehrenburg**, Prince Albert's childhood home, has a wonderful collection of French tapestries. Stroll through an arcade up to the Hofgarten, the palace gardens which lead up to the **Veste** (from the German word *festung*, for fortress).

The **Marktplatz** (market square) is typically Bavarian – a feast of Renaissance and baroque buildings, immaculately kept in characteristic German order. Also of interest is a **nature museum**, which has a collection of over 2,000 birds and exhibits of the natural world. The **Rathaus** (town hall), started in 1500, has a figure called the Bratwurstmännle. He carries a staff supposed to indicate the correct length of the Bratwurst, the celebrated local sausage. The many gables and spires of the town hall give it a most attractive appearance.

[i] Herrngasse 4

*From Coburg take the **B303** for 29km (18 miles) to Kronach.*

Kronach, Bayern

2 In the old town stands the **Festung Rosenberg** (Rosenberg fortress), one of the largest and best preserved fortresses of the Middle Ages. Although building began in 1128, the last touches were not put to the structure until the 18th century. The numerous wars of the 15th, 16th and 17th centuries meant that the castle was turned into a formidably defended bulwark. Since 1867 it has been used for peaceful purposes and houses both the municipal **Frankenwald museum** and the **Franconian Gallery**.

Kronach's most famous son was the 16th-century master Lucas Cranach the Elder; three of his paintings are on display here. His house, a timber-framed building, can be seen in the old part of the town.

[i] Fremdenverkehrsamt, Marktplatz 5

*From Kronach take the **B85** south for 42km (26 miles) to Bayreuth.*

Bayreuth, Bayern

3 Bayreuth received its town charter in 1231 and was later destroyed by the Hussites, the followers of Jan Hus, during their revolt against the clerical privileges in neighbouring

Bohemia and Moravia. Hus was excommunicated in 1410 and asked to explain his views at the Council of Constance (1414–18). It suited both the clergy and the Emperor to eliminate him, and he was subsequently burned at the stake.

Bayreuth recovered fairly quickly and became the seat of the Margraves of Brandenburg-Kulmbach in 1604. The town blossomed under the rule of Margrave Friedrich and his wife Wilhelmine, the favourite sister of Frederic the Great, King of Prussia. They ruled from 1753 to 1763 and created a building boom, but the fine baroque buildings later decayed,

The huge Veste Coburg sits above the town that shares its name

SPECIAL TO...

1 *Coburg, Bayern* Look out for a statue of the British Queen Victoria at Coburg, as a reminder that her consort – and therefore the great-great grandfather of the present Queen – was Prince Albert of Saxe-Coburg.

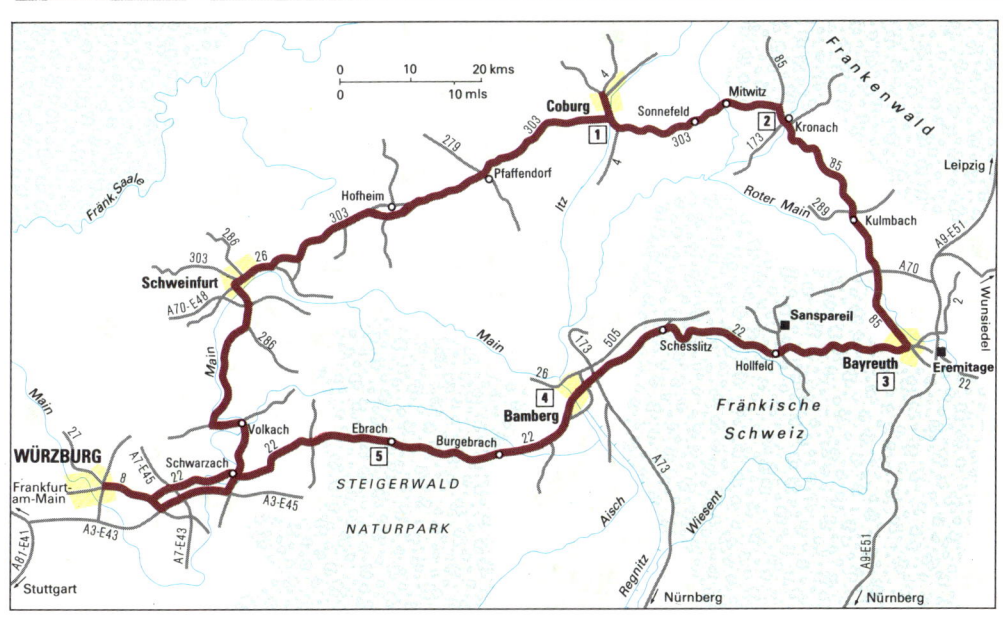

BACK TO NATURE

3 *Bayreuth, Bayern* Leave Bayreuth, heading north on the **A9**, turn right and follow through the Steinach valley and the Fichtelgebirge (Fichtel mountains) to Wunsiedel. Watch the skies for birds of prey soaring overhead. These may include black kites, red kites, honey buzzards and sparrowhawks. The **Felsenlabyrinth Luisenburg** is a fascinating agglomeration of rocks of granite. Marked paths guide the visitor through caves, grottoes and ravines.

presumably through lack of funds. The town became part of Bavaria in 1810.

In 1847 Richard Wagner had his **Villa Wahnfried** built by the architect J Wolfel. The villa is an uninspiring cube-shaped building in neoclassical style. Wagner and his wife Cosima, daughter of the composer Franz Liszt, are buried in the grounds of the villa.

The **Richard Wagner Festspielhaus** (festival theatre) was built between 1872 and 1876 on the hill northeast of the town, now called **Festspielhügel** (Festival Hill). King Ludwig II, the 'Mad King' of Bavaria and an ardent admirer of Wagner, supported his work and the Festspielhaus was opened with four operas of the performances of the *Ring Cycle*. Composers Tchaikovsky and Grieg were among the audience, but even a full house could not meet the costs of mounting these extraordinarily lavish operas. Today, the composer's family still carries on the tradition and the annual festivals continue to be a highlight of the international music calendar. The Festival Theatre and the ornate Opera House are open to visitors when no performances or rehearsals are in progress.

The **Altes Schloss** (old castle) in the Maximilianstrasse is easily recognisable, with its octagonal tower, which has a spiral ramp inside, for horses to be ridden up to the top. The castle was burnt out in 1945 but has since been rebuilt. In the Ludwigstrasse stands the **Neues Schloss** (new castle), commissioned by Wilhelmine in 1753. The interiors were decorated to her taste with motifs of nature. Birds, insects, palms and Chinese dragons can be seen: the latter were fashionable features of 18th-century interior decoration. The Neues Schloss also contains the municipal museum and a Bavarian state paintings collection.

[i] Luitpoldplatz 9

*From Bayreuth take the **B22/B505** west for 60km (37 miles) to Bamberg.*

The beautiful townscape of Würzburg surrounded by vineyards

Courtyard of the Alte Hofhaltung, Bamberg, the homely face of a former imperial palace

Bamberg, Bayern

4 The path of the River Regnitz created an island here, which became the centre of this historical town dating from the 10th century. Most of the buildings were erected under the rule of Holy Roman Emperor Heinrich II, the Saint (1002–1024), who upgraded the town to an imperial residence.

The **Altes Rathaus** enjoys a commanding position on an artificial island on the left arm of the river, and is connected to the other parts of the city by bridges on either side. The building itself is an attractive Gothic structure which dates from 1467, and the long façades facing the river are decorated with fine frescos. The present Dom, or **Kaiserdom** (cathedral) dates from the 13th century and contains many typically beautiful German sculptures, including the enigmatic **Bamberger Reiter** (Bamberg horseman). The tomb of Heinrich II is the work of the great Renaissance sculptor Tilman Riemenschneider, a native Bavarian. Not only an eminent sculptor, Riemenschneider became Mayor of Würzburg, but fell into disgrace when he took the side of the oppressed peasants during a rebellion. Imprisoned and tortured, he died in 1531.

Next to the cathedral stands the **Alte Hofhaltung** (old residence), a half-timbered Renaissance structure, once the residence of the former imperial and episcopal rulers. Also of note is the **Reiches Tor**, the richly decorated entrance portal to the old residence, which offers a fine view into the old courtyard. The **Alte Residenz** now houses the museum of history, which exhibits documents and maps relating to Bamberg's history.

Look out for the **Neue Residenz**, built between 1693 and 1703 to express the opulent wealth and power of the Prince-Electors. The **church of St Michael** dates from the 11th century, although the site is even older, and the lovely baroque façade was added in the late 17th century.

Bamberg is well-known for its *Rauchbier*, a beer made from smoked malt using an old recipe.

[i] Hauptwachstrasse 16

From Bamberg take the B22 west for 34km (21 miles) to Ebrach.

Ebrach, Bayern

5 Ebrach's former **Abbey of the Cistercians**, once considered to be one of the finest examples of the order's building style, is now part of the **Steigerwald Naturpark**, which lies east of Würzburg and has one of the largest concentrations of beech trees in central Europe. The massive church building is decorated with rich stuccos, and its organ pipes are arranged around the large round window, the diameter of which is over 23 feet (7m) and composed of 259 pieces of glass. The **Kaisersaal** (Emperor's Hall) boasts beautiful frescos.

[i] Verkehrsamt, Rathausplatz 4

From Ebrach continue west on the B22/A3 for 47km (30 miles) to Würzburg.

Würzburg – Coburg **129 (80)**
Coburg – Kronach **29 (18)**
Kronach – Bayreuth **42 (26)**
Bayreuth – Bamberg **60 (37)**
Bamberg – Ebrach **34 (21)**
Ebrach – Würzburg **47 (30)**

SCENIC ROUTES

A very attractive stretch is along the Wiesenttal en route from Bayreuth to Bamberg. The route is actually through a nature park and the area is called Fränkische Schweiz (Franconian Switzerland), which emphasizes its scenic and Alpine beauty. A small detour of 6km (3½ miles) from Hollfeld takes you to the **Sanspareil park**, a romantic rock garden with natural caves and grottoes.

FOR CHILDREN

5 *Ebrach, Bayern* Take the children about 14km (8½ miles) south of Ebrach to the **Märchenpark Ebrach**. This fairytale park exhibits 30 ponies and about 1,000 exotic birds. Children can enjoy rides on motorised swans!

2/3 days – 489km (307 miles)

AROUND NÜRNBERG & REGENSBURG

Nürnberg • Altdorf • Amberg • Weiden • Vohenstrauss
Kallmünz • Kipfenberg • Eichstätt • Weissenburg
Ellingen • Abenberg • Roth • Nürnberg

Nürnberg (Nuremberg), on the banks of the River Pegnitz, had its most prosperous times in the 15th and 16th centuries, when its position at the crossroads of commercial traffic attracted merchants, craftsmen and artists. Between the 11th and 16th centuries, 32 emperors and kings were based at the castle of Nürnberg, called the *Kaiserburg*. The city suffered from heavy wartime bombing raids, but restored buildings blend well with new ones, and the layout of the town has been preserved. The well-known 'Nuremberg Trials' were held here after World War II.

The *Frauenkirche* (Church of Our Lady), on the east side of the square in the old town, is a magnificent Gothic building with a clock which comes to life at noon. In the *Germanisches Nationalmuseum* you can see works by famous German artists and the Behaim globe – the oldest in the world – made in the late 15th century, minus the still-to-be-discovered continent of America.

FOR HISTORY BUFFS

1 **Altdorf, Bayern** From Altdorf, a short trip southeast via Gnadenberg and Oberölsbach leads to Berg and the ruin of the oldest **Birgittenkloster** (abbey of St Bridget) in southern Germany. It was donated in 1426 by Pfalzgraf (Count Palatinate) Johann I and erected to house both monks and nuns. Its church was finished in 1483 but a fire in 1635 destroyed both the church and the convent. Today's parish church was erected out of the remnants of the former convent. Easily recognisable among the ruins are the remnants of the three walls, which were a special feature to which all Birgittenklöster had to adhere.

FOR CHILDREN

3 *Weiden, Bayern* The **Model Railway Club** of Weiden has opened a museum at the station building. The trains are in operation on certain days, usually Sundays and public holidays. Check first with a tourist information centre.

[i] Im Hauptbahnhof and Frauentorgraben 3

> Leave Nürnberg by the **B4** southeast, turning off right to Feucht and turn east to Altdorf, 28km (17 miles).

Altdorf, Bayern

1 Altdorf is an historic town with 15th-century gates, city walls and burghers' houses. The old university buildings date back to the 16th century and many famous scientists and inventors have passed through the gates. The university was dissolved in 1809. The Protestant **church of St Lorenz** used to be the university church, and more than 1,100 students of theology received their degrees before the altar.

If you have time, take the **A3** south-east from Altdorf for about 32km (20 miles) to Velburg. From there a short and very enjoyable walk past a special rock formation called the **Schwammerl** (mushroom) leads to the **König-Otto Tropfsteinhöhle** (King Otto Cave). The cave, with its stalagmites and stalactites, was discovered in 1895 and is 280m (918 feet) long. It consists of seven grottoes and can be visited daily from April to October.

[i] Stadtverwaltung, Oberer Markt 2

> From Altdorf take the **A3** southeast, turn left at exit Neumarkt and take the **B299** northeast to Amberg.

Steins on display in Nürnberg

Amberg, Bayern

2 'Fortunate Amberg' has almost totally preserved its medieval appearance. It has an imposing circle of city walls with four gates, numerous towers and other fortifications. One part of the former line of defence crosses the River Vils in the form of two arches above the water, whose reflection in the water led to the nickname 'Stadtbrille' (the city's spectacles). Two Gothic parish churches, **St Martin** and **St Georg**, dominate the city centre. Of special note inside the former is the painting by C Crayer, of the *Coronation of Holy Mary*, an imitation of the style of Rubens. This work, completed in 1658, was removed from its original place over the altar and is now above the sacristy. The tomb of Ruprecht Pipan, the Pfalzgraf (Count Palatinate), who died in 1397, stands behind the High Altar. The religious denomination of the church was changed from Protestant to Catholic when the Jesuits acquired the building during the Counter-Reformation. The adjoining library hall of the former Jesuit college is well worth seeing. The **Rathaus** (town hall), on the market square, is a very attractive building, also in Gothic style, with a Renaissance annexe. It features a tall, narrow gable and has various council chambers inside. The small hall has outstanding wood panelling.

Other buildings worth seeing in Amberg are the former residence of the Pfalzgrafen (Counts Palatinate), now used by the local government; the former **Kurfürstliche Zeughaus** (Electors' arsenal), dating back to the 15th century; and the **Ratstrinkstube** (councillors' drinking chamber).

[i] Zeughausstrasse 1a

> From Amberg take the **B229** north to Gebenbach, continue on the **B14** east to Wernberg and from there north on the **B15** to Weiden, 51km (32 miles).

Weiden, Bayern

3 Weiden lies on a major crossroads, between Regensburg and Leipzig, and between Nürnberg and Prague. The town is associated with the composer Max Reger, who came here as a child and received his musical education here.

The original Gothic **parish church of St Michael**, with its onion-shaped spire, was reconstructed in baroque style in the 18th century. Of note inside are the High Altar (1791) and the chancel, built in 1787. The **Rathaus** (town hall) was built between 1539 and 1545 in Renaissance style.

Weiden is an excellent centre for exploring the nearby forests, especially the **Böhmerwald**, where some areas are still almost completely unspoiled.

[i] Altes Rathaus

> From Weiden take the **B22** southeast to Bernrieth/Wittschau, where it crosses the **B14**. Continue on the **B14** northeast and turn left after about 8km (5 miles) for Vohenstrauss, 20km (13 miles).

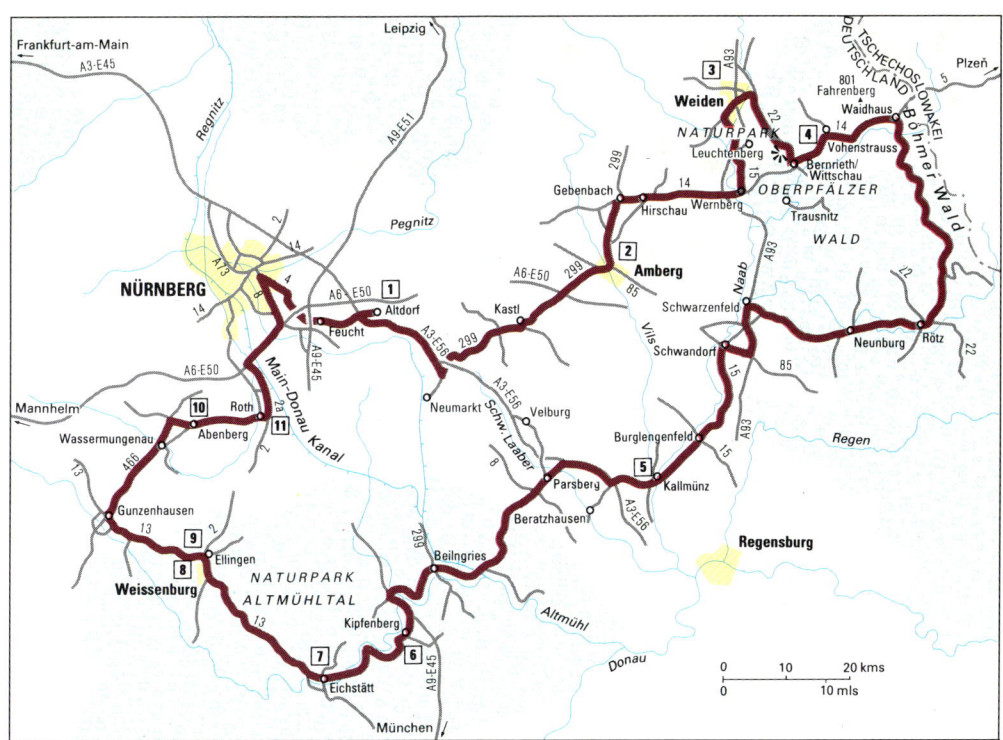

Vohenstrauss, Bayern

4 Situated on the former military road between Nürnberg and Prague, this town's main attraction is the castle **Friedrichsburg**. Six massive round towers encircle the building, with a very high gabled roof and a wall

Street scene in Weiden, a good centre for seeing eastern Bavaria

RECOMMENDED WALKS

4 *Vohenstrauss, Bayern* There are very pleasant walks by the Kainzmühl and Reisach Stausees, artificial lakes near Trausnitz, a short drive south from Vohenstrauss. A marvellous view can be obtained from the top of the mountain near Tannesberg.

BACK TO NATURE

4 *Vohenstrauss, Bayern* The route from Vohenstrauss to Kallmünz passes through **Neunburg vorm Wald**, which is 12km (8 miles) past Rötz. A seam of the mineral quartz protrudes in certain places in this area and one spot where this occurs is **Pfahl**, near Neunburg – a great attraction for geologists.

surrounding the castle yard. The building is quite unique in its design: a Renaissance structure erected between 1586 and 1593.

Short detours to the ruin of the fortress **Leuchtenberg**, 7km (4 miles) southwest, and to the **Fahrenberg** mountain, 8km (5 miles) northeast, offer fine views to the Fichtel mountain range and the Bohemian forest.

i Verkehrsamt, Marktplatz 9

From Vohenstrauss turn south to the B14 and continue northeast to Waidhaus. Turn sharp right south to Rötz, and from there west to Schwarzenfeld. Continue south to Schwandorf and Burglengenfeld via the A93 and B15. From there drive southwest to Kallmünz.

Kallmünz, Bayern

5 At the meeting of the Vils and Naab rivers lies Kallmünz, a picturesque medieval town. A good view can be had from the River Naab to the rococo-style **parish church of St Michael**, with the ruins of the former fortress of Kallmünz in the background, delightful for painters or photographers.

The excellent strategic position of the fortress suggest earlier settlements here and some archaeological findings confirm this. A 10m (33-foot) wall around the fortress was probably erected in the 10th century to protect the inhabitants against attacks from the north. The walls from the fortress went right down to the river, presumably to provide additional protection for the village below.

The bridge over the River Naab is noteworthy for its massive pillars and arches, dating back to 1550.

i Marktgemeindeverwaltung

From Kallmünz drive 9km (5½ miles) west to the A3 entry to Beratzhausen, continue northwest and leave the A3 at exit Parsberg in a southwest direction for Beilngries. Continue along the Altmühl river to Kinding and turn south to Kipfenberg, 77km (49 miles).

Kipfenberg, Bayern

6 Kipfenberg is a romantic little town surrounded by woods, with its proud **Burg** standing on a hill. The present fortress was built in the 13th and 14th centuries, but fell into decay and was restored between 1914 and 1925. Remains of the **Limes**, the wall protecting the Roman Empire against invaders from the north, are near by.

i Marktplatz 2

From Kipfenberg continue along the Altmühl valley southwest for 22km (14 miles) to Eichstätt.

Eichstätt, Bayern

7 Eichstätt is dominated by the imposing **Willibaldsburg** (St Willibald's castle), which dates from the 14th century and was fortified and extended in later centuries into a fine castle.

The town centre is basically baroque in style and the former

Amberg's best known spectacle – the arches forming the Stadtbrille

Dürer's house in Nürnberg's Altstadt. The great artist lived and worked here from 1509 until his death in 1528

bishop's palace has an impressive interior with a double staircase. Some remains are left of the 8th-century cathedral. The 'new' one was built over four centuries and is therefore an intriguing mixture of Romanesque, Gothic and baroque styles. The gardens of the summer residence of the Prince-Bishops are arranged in the English manner. There are three pavilions at the southern end – one features a fountain and ornate stuccos: a true rococo work of art.

[i] Domplatz 18

From Eichstätt take the B13 northwest for 27km (17 miles) to Weissenburg.

Weissenburg, Bayern

8 The old city walls have survived and the **Ellinger Tor** and the **Spitaltor** (gates) remain as formidable entrances to the town. The thermal springs were enjoyed by the Romans, and the layout of their baths was rediscovered in 1977.

The Protestant **parish church of St Andreas** stands behind the Ellinger Tor and was built in several stages, work finally being completed in 1520. The well-appointed interior includes a remarkable High Altar, the Sebaldusaltar and the Mariaaltar. The **Rathaus** (town hall) in the market square was built between 1470 and 1476 and is easily recognisable by its richly decorated gable.

[i] Städtisches Fremdenverkehrsamt, Martin-Luther-Platz 3

From Weissenburg continue for a short drive north on the B13 to Ellingen.

Ellingen, Bayern

9 The **castle** at Ellingen is a huge baroque creation, built for the Teutonic Order of Knights. Work began in 1708, and it is one of the most important castles among many created for this order. Napoleon banned the order in 1809, and the building now serves as a museum. The baroque **Schlosskirche** (castle church) is ornately adorned with stucco and frescos.

[i] Verwaltungsgemeinschaft

From Ellingen continue on the B13 northwest to Gunzenhausen, turn right for the B466 and turn right again 3km (2 miles) after Wassermungenau for Abenberg, 40km (25 miles).

Abenberg, Bayern

10 Abenberg is a beautiful old town with a walled fortress. The **fortress** is first mentioned in 1071, but the present building dates from 1250. The 30m (96 foot) square tower offers fine views of the area. Of interest too are the gate, in early Gothic style, the circular wall and the moat.

The Countess Stilla, who was canonised in 1927, founded a small church in 1132, later turned into a convent. After a fire in 1675, the church was rebuilt in a mixture of Renaissance and baroque styles. There are 68 nuns buried here, the graves being arranged in a design adopted from the catacombs in Rome. The gravestone of Countess Stilla shows the lady in a long pleated robe, with a small replica of the church on her arm.

Abenberg is also a traditional centre for the manufacture of lace tassels.

[i] Stadtverwaltung

From Abenberg head northwest for 12km (7½ miles) to Roth.

Roth, Bayern

11 Roth is pleasantly situated on the River Regnitz, among green parkland. George the Pious had the **Schloss Ratibor** (castle) built from 1535 to 1537, although the towers were only completed 50 years later. A visit to the **Prunksaal**, a lavishly appointed banqueting hall which is part of the **Heimatmuseum** (local museum) is recommended. The main edifice has six gables and surrounds an idyllic court. The **Riffelmacherhaus** on the market square, with its carved façade, belongs to one of the finest timber-framed houses in the area.

A more unusual museum shows the processes of manufacturing leonic wire and its uses in woven metal products and in the textile industry.

[i] Stadtverwaltung, Kirchplatz 2

From Roth take the B2a north to the A6, then northeast to the B8 to Nürnberg.

Nürnberg – Altdorf **28 (17)**
Altdorf – Amberg **54 (34)**
Amberg – Weiden **20 (13)**
Weiden – Vohenstrauss **20 (13)**
Vohenstrauss – Kallmünz **129 (80)**
Kallmünz – Kipfenberg **77 (49)**
Kipfenberg – Eichstätt **22 (14)**
Eichstätt – Weissenburg **27 (17)**
Weissenburg – Ellingen **2 (1¼)**
Ellingen – Abenberg **40 (25)**
Abenberg – Roth **12 (7½)**
Roth – Nürnberg **27 (17)**

SPECIAL TO...

2 *Amberg, Bayern* Amberg celebrates the **Bergfest** at the beginning of July. The origins of the festival go back to the days when pilgrims came to the Mariahilf church and were fed by the townspeople.

6 *Kipfenberg, Bayern* Kipfenberg celebrates the **Limesfest** in the middle of July. The festival's name refers to monuments of Roman times, but in fact it is a real Bavarian feast, which lasts for four days.

SCENIC ROUTES

The stretch between Weiden and Leuchtenberg en route to Vohenstrauss leads through the nature park called **Oberpfälzer Wald**. Take a look at the **Burgruine Leuchtenberg** (castle ruins) from which there are fine views over the forests.

One of the most enjoyable routes will be the drive between Waidhaus and Rötz. Lakes and small rivers with a few ruins here and there, and an abundance of forests, will make this drive quite memorable.

THE DANUBE & THE BAVARIAN FOREST

2/3 days – 456km (283 miles)

Passau • Regen • Cham • Regensburg • Donaustauf
Kelheim • Essing • Riedenburg • Ingolstadt • Landshut
Passau

The border town of Passau lies in a unique position. Three rivers – the Donau (Danube), the Inn and the smaller Ilz – join together here to form just one: the mighty Danube.

In 1219, Bishop Ulrich II erected a fortress on the rock which stands at the confluence of the Ilz and Danube rivers, and the *Veste Oberhaus* was used by the bishops as a refuge from citizens seeking independence. The town had been ruled by a bishop since AD739, but in the 13th century it became a Free Imperial City, and its bishop a Prince of the Empire. Fires in 1662 and 1680 destroyed the city, but it was rebuilt and now boasts beautiful baroque buildings.

The *Dom* (cathedral) *of St Stephen* could date back to Roman times, but it was largely destroyed by the 1662 fire and three Italian architects, Lurago, Carlone and Tecalle, were commissioned to replace it. The interior is wonderfully ornate, and the organ is claimed to be the world's largest.

SCENIC ROUTES

Soon after leaving Passau the road passes through some charming small villages, lined with forests on the **Bayerische Ostmarkstrasse**.

A detour from Bodenmais en route from Regen to Cham is strongly recommended. It leads to the Risloch waterfalls and the remote Arbersee (lake) and into the beauty of the unspoiled Böhmer Wald (Bohemian Forest).

FOR HISTORY BUFFS

3 *Regensburg, Bayern*
Regensburg can lay claim to two of the oldest constructions in Germany: the **Porta Praetoria** from AD179 is the oldest city gate, and the old stone bridge across the Danube is the earliest bridge of its kind in Germany.

[i] Rathausplatz 3

*From Passau take the **B85** north for 60km (37 miles) to Regen.*

Regen, Bayern

1 Although *Regen* means rain – and the visitor may feel this is an ominous sign – the name of the town actually comes from the Regen river, flowing through the town. The ruins of the fortress **Weissenstein**, 3km (2 miles) south, date back to the 11th century, and the keep affords wide views over the Bayerischer Wald (Bavarian Forest). Regen is a good centre to stop and plan side trips into the Bavarian Forest, especially to Arbersee, near the Czech border.

[i] Verkehrsamt, Stadtplatz 2

From Regen drive north via Bodenmais and Kötzting for 59km (37 miles) to Cham.

Cham, Bayern

2 Having left Regen, a stop is suggested en route at Bodenmais in the **Bavarian Nature Park**. In the **Silberberg** (silver mountain) there is an old mine, dating back to the 12th century, which is open in summer.

In Cham the market square is dominated by the 13th-century **parish church of St Jakob**. Many alterations and extensions over the centuries have meant that the church is now an attractive mixture of Gothic, baroque and rococo styles. The **Rathaus** (town hall), with its many gables and oriels, was originally built in the 15th century but has been added to many times since.

[i] Propsteistrasse 46

*From Cham take the **B85/B16** southwest for 53km (33 miles) to Regensburg.*

Regensburg, Bayern

3 Regensburg, set on the Danube, must be one of Germany's loveliest cities. The great German poet and philosopher, Goethe, said that so beautiful a location was bound to attract a city, and Regensburg lives up to its setting. The Roman fort was built here in AD179 by the Emperor Marcus Aurelius. Later, the Bavarian Dukes made Regensburg their capital, and in the Middle Ages it became a European centre for politics, science and economics. Many Imperial Diets (assemblies) met here, dealing with issues which involved the entire Holy Roman Empire. Napoleon was wounded here in 1809, an event recalled by a plaque; but otherwise Regensburg remained unscathed by

Stone carvings on the portal of Regensburg's splendid cathedral

centuries of war.

Entering the old town from the north, drivers cross the Danube over the **Steinerne Brücke** (stone bridge). If traffic allows, stop for a memorable first glimpse of the town before crossing the bridge, which is said to be the oldest in Germany. It dates from 1135 and is a masterpiece of medieval engineering. The old town is entered through the southern bridge gate, which was erected in the 14th century. Not far away on the left is the former North Gate of the Castra Regina, the Roman fort. On the site of a former Romanesque basilica stands the **cathedral**. Building began in the 13th century, but its 105m (344-foot) spires were finished only 600 years later. The beautiful stained glass windows date back to the 14th century. Other features of note are the 14th- to 16th-century cloisters, the Romanesque All Saints' Chapel and the Annunciation group of 1280. The cathedral also boasts one of the finest boys' choirs in the land – the Regensburger Domspatzen.

The **Altes Rathaus** (old town hall) dates from the 13th century, although parts of the building were added much later, up to and including the 18th century. In the large **Reichssaal** (Imperial Hall) many Diets were held. Later this became a permanent institution and could be called a forerunner to the first German parliament. Also on view are the dungeons where prisoners were 'interviewed'.

The **Thurn and Taxis Castle** belongs to the old dynastic family of Thurn and Taxis, who became powerful by holding the first German mail delivery monopoly until 1867. The **Johannes Kepler Museum** is housed in a building which dates from 1500, in which the famous mathematician and astronomer lived. Interesting displays describe his life and work.

Regensburg has numerous churches, and among those of special interest are the **Karmeliterkirche** and the rococo **Alte Kapelle** next door. The Protestant **Neupfarrkirche** is noted for its fine Renaissance interior, while the **Niedermünster** parish church has interesting excavations underneath, revealing remains from Roman, Merovingian, Carolingian and Ottonic times. The Scottish **church of St Jacob** has a Romanesque portal. The confessor of Mary, Queen of Scots, is buried here.

[i] Im Alten Rathaus

From Regensburg drive east for 12km (7 miles) to Donaustauf.

Landscape in the Bavarian Forest, tamed here but largely wilderness

RECOMMENDED WALKS

1 *Regen, Bayern* Parts of the Bohemian Forest are still left to their natural devices and are largely untouched by human hand. Fallen trees form intriguing natural 'sculptures' and some areas are totally covered in moss. The areas around the Arber and Falkenstein mountains are designated as maintained 'wild' forests. To get there, drive from Regen towards Bayerisch Eisenstein on the **B11** or branch off from Bodenmais en route to Cham. Beautiful walks into remote unspoiled nature can be enjoyed there.

5 *Kelheim, Bayern* A walk from the Kloster Weltenberg to see the Danube gorge along the cliffs is very rewarding. The gorge cannot be seen by car, but a boat trip provides another opportunity to see this phenomenon. Take the river boats from Kelheim or Schloss Weltenberg.

TOUR 12

The busy market square in the modest little town of Cham

*From Donaustauf turn back to Regensburg and take the **B16** south for 20km (13 miles) to Kelheim.*

Kelheim, Bayern

5 The Befreiungshalle (Liberation Hall), which stands above the town, was built in 1842 and commemorates the liberation of Germany from Napoleon. The rewarding views from the gallery of the circular temple make the trip worthwhile. Inside the temple are memorials to Napoleon's defeaters.

The **Kloster Weltenburg** church, near by, stands on an ancient site, though the present structure dates back to the first half of the 18th century. The two architects have left their own images inside – one looks down from a railing, and one is painted in a fresco. Clever use of light through a window draws attention to the statue of St Georg in front of the large High Altar painting.

[i] Ludwigsplatz 14

From Kelheim take a short drive of 8km (5 miles) west to Essing.

Essing, Bayern

6 The ancient past is evident here, as Essing lies below rocky cliffs with many prehistoric caves. In the cave known as the **Grosse Schulerloch Höhle**, excavations have revealed remains of a former hunting station from the Stone and early Bronze Ages. In the nearby smaller cave, **Kleine Schulerloch Höhle**, drawings were found which date back to about the 15th century BC. One interesting sight is the old wooden bridge over the Altmühl river, its exit guarded by the **Altmühltor** (gate). The ruin of the fortress **Randeck** stands right above the town and there is an excellent view from the keep.

[i] Marktplatz 1

From Essing continue northwest for 8km (5 miles) along the Altmühl valley to Riedenburg.

BACK TO NATURE

Almost any part of the Bavarian Forest can be good for wildlife. Explore forest tracks on foot looking for orchids such as lady's slipper and dark red helleborine growing in clearings. Mezereon – with red berries in autumn – and butcher's broom are also frequently found here.

Donaustauf, Bayern

4 The **Walhalla**, near Donaustauf, should definitely be seen if time allows, although it may not be to everybody's taste. Surrounded by trees, it is a copy of the Parthenon in Athens, dedicated to men and women whose achievements benefited the German state. King Ludwig I of Bavaria had the temple built between 1830 and 1842, and laid an obligation upon his successors to add to it. The Bavarian government has added nine more marble busts since 1945, and the total of dignitaries exhibited is now 122. Although the Walhalla is set in a charming site, visitors expecting an exact replica of the Athenian original will be disappointed.

[i] Gutenbergstrasse 5

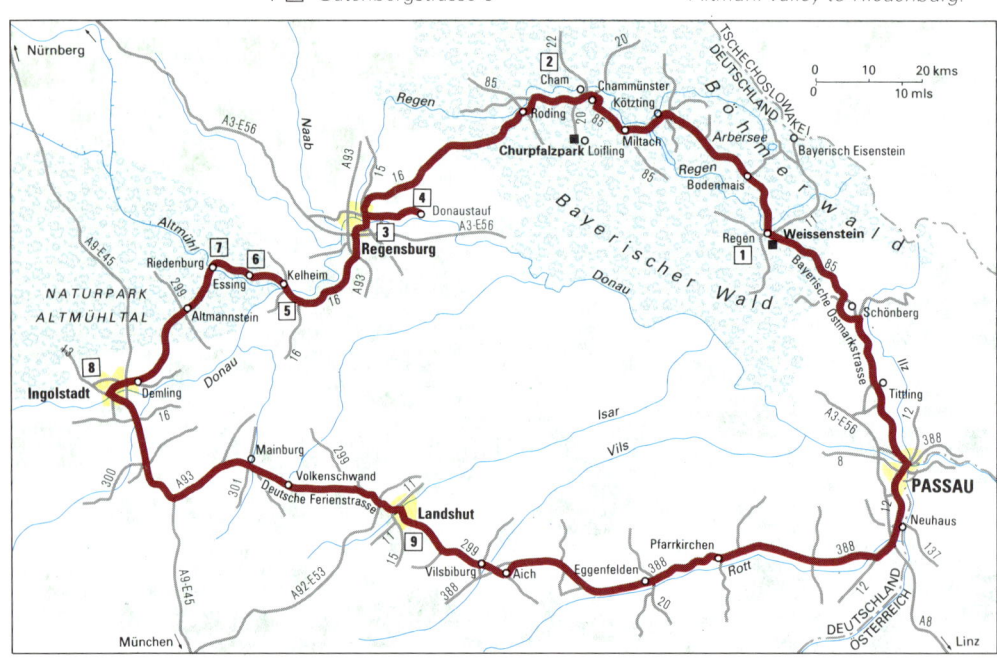

Riedenburg, Bayern

7 This is an area rich in castles, and one worth stopping for is the **Rosenburg**, dating from the 12th century. The 16th-century part, which is well preserved, houses the local museum and the Bavarian centre for falconry. Displays of flying eagles, vultures and falcons are presented in medieval surroundings.

Perched on the top of a rock above the river is the nearby castle of **Prunn**, one of the best kept knights' castles in Bavaria. The entry to this mighty building is over a bridge, and there is a museum.

Schloss Eggersberg, situated a bit further away in a more remote setting, used to be a hunting lodge before its conversion into a hotel.

[i] Fremdenverkehrsamt, St-Anna-Platz 2

From Riedenburg turn south and drive for 36km (22 miles) via Altmannstein and Demling to Ingolstadt.

Ingolstadt, Bayern

8 Ingolstadt is now an important industrial town, but reminders of its past make it attractive to visit. The **Kreuztor** (Cross Gate), with its seven small towers, is one of the most interesting remaining parts of the old city fortifications, and dates back to the 14th century. Other, later landmarks are the churches designed and built by the famous Asam brothers. The **church of Maria de Victoria** is a jewel of Bavarian rococo style, finished in 1736. Inside there is an enormous fresco on the ceiling and a richly ornate High Altar.

The **Liebfrauenmünster** (Minster of Our Lady) is one of the larger Bavarian churches in the late Gothic period, dating from 1425. The High Altar reaches a height of 9m (29 feet) and is decorated with 91 paintings. The centrepiece is the *Madonna of the Cloak*, significant because the Virgin Mary is the patron saint of Bavaria.

The **Bavarian Army Museum** is housed in a former Duke's Palace built by Ludwig the Bearded.

[i] Hallstrasse 5

*From Ingolstadt take the **A9** south to the junction with the **A93**. Continue on the **A93** northeast to exit Mainburg, drive 9km (6 miles) east towards Mainburg and take the Deutsche Ferienstrasse via Volkenschwand to Landshut, a total distance of 74km (46 miles).*

Landshut, Bayern

9 Landshut provides perhaps the best picture of an elegant medieval city in Bavaria. The old town has hardly changed, and the houses in the main street, with their high gables and painted façades, are still dominated by **St Martin's Church**, with its 133m (436-foot) spire, which starts off square but becomes octagonal as it rises! The church was designed by Hans von Burghausen, and took 110 years to complete. One of the treasures inside is the larger than life woodcarving of the Virgin Mary. Called the Landshuter Madonna, this statue is renowned as an important example of late Gothic woodcarving. Stone was used as material for the High Altar and the pulpit, both of which were built between 1424 and 1429.

Trausnitz Castle was the residence of the Dukes of Wittelsbach, and is one of the largest and most impressive castles in Germany. One of the Dukes, called Ludwig the Rich, arranged a magnificent wedding for his son

Regen, pleasantly situated on the river of the same name

Georg, so impressive that it has become part of local legend.

The **Stadtresidenz** (town palace) consists of two wings: the 16th-century Italian Renaissance and the 18th-century German wing, which faces the **Altstadt** (old town).

[i] Altstadt 315

*From Landshut take the **B299** southeast to Aich, turn left and continue for 126km (77 miles) on the **B388** east to Passau.*

Passau – Regen **60 (37)**
Regen – Cham **59 (37)**
Cham – Regensburg **53 (33)**
Regensburg – Donaustauf **12 (7)**
Donaustauf – Kelheim **20 (13)**
Kelheim – Essing **8 (5)**
Essing – Riedenburg **8 (5)**
Riedenburg – Ingolstadt **36 (22)**
Ingolstadt – Landshut **74 (46)**
Landshut – Passau **126 (78)**

SPECIAL TO...

1 *Regen, Bayern* In Regen is the **Pichelsteinerfest**, which takes place around the last Saturday in July and lasts for five days. A special dish of meat, potatoes and vegetables is served, cooked in one pot. The festivities continue in the evenings with a romantic atmosphere provided by gondolas on the River Regen with candlelit lanterns.

9 *Landshut, Bayern* Every four years the wedding of Georg, the son of Ludwig the Rich, is recreated in Landshut. The original wedding took place in 1475 and was such a splendid occasion that it has passed into local history. For those interested, the next celebration is in 1993.

FOR CHILDREN

2 *Cham, Bayern* The **Churpfalzpark** at Loifling has a special section for children with a fairytale garden and playing fields.

8 *Ingolstadt, Bayern* In the Gerolfinger Strasse at Ingolstadt is a small zoo called **Wasserstern**. Snakes, crocodiles, bears, monkeys and birds of prey are on show here.

2 days – 248km (155 miles)

AROUND LAKE CHIEM & BERCHTESGADEN

Rosenheim • Prien • Herrenchiemsee • Seebruck
Traunstein • Bad Reichenhall • Berchtesgaden
Ruhpolding • Reit im Winkl • Rosenheim

Taking refreshment in Rosenheim

Rosenheim is situated at the meeting point of the rivers Inn and Mangfall, and its position makes it an ideal base for touring the mountains and the lakes in the area.

The focal point in town is the *Max-Josefs-Platz*, surrounded by the houses of noteworthy residents of former times, with beautifully painted fronts and stucco ornaments. The romantic *Laubengänge* (arcades) recreate the feel of a medieval town. Two churches – the *Heilig Geist* and *Heilig Blutkirche* – are well worth a visit. The former was built in the 15th century and has remarkable wall paintings and the latter was erected in the 17th century.

A local gallery houses various exhibitions by artists of the past and present, including Defregger, Busch, Leibl, Kokoschka, Hundertwasser and others. The *Heimatmuseum* (local museum) is located in the Mittertor, the 14th-century town gate.

SCENIC ROUTES

The road from Berchtesgaden to Ruhpolding is an experience in itself, through valleys and between mountains. But drive carefully! The river is often perilously close to the road.

The stretch between Ruhpolding and Reit im Winkl leads through more magnificent scenery, with small lakes on either side of the road.

[i] Stadthalle

*From Rosenheim go south and join the **A8** east towards Salzburg. Leave at exit Frasdorf northeast for Prien, 27km (17 miles).*

Prien, Bayern

1 The **parish church** was built in 1653 and enlarged in 1736. The ceiling was painted by the locally famous J B Zimmermann. The **Heimatmuseum** is located in a house built in 1681, and the displays show what peasant life around the lake was like during times past.

[i] Alte Rathausstrasse 11

From Prien drive 2km (1 mile) to the lake shore at Prien Stock. This trip can also be done from the railway station by the historical Chiemsee Railway, built in 1887 with the original engine and coaches. Then take a boat to Herrenchiemsee, 3km (2 miles).

Herrenchiemsee, Bayern

2 Herrenchiemsee Castle was the idea of Ludwig II, the Mad King, who, after a visit to Versailles, decided to build a similar castle for himself here on the island. Work began in 1878, but in 1885 the project ran out of money, after an enormous amount had already been spent. It was eventually finished much later, and today houses a museum with rare antique furniture and many valuable artefacts. Guided tours are available through the highly ornate rooms. The gallery of mirrors is about 77m (253 feet) long and the State Room is often used for candlelit concerts during the summer months.

The **Altes Schloss** or old castle, built in 1700, was once part of a monastery, which explains the name Herren ('men'). The library hall is beautifully decorated by the master of rococo, Dominikus Zimmermann; many churches and buildings in this area display his work.

The **Fraueninsel** ('ladies' island') is much smaller but more romantic and intimate. The **Benediktinerinnen Kloster**, a convent founded in AD782 by the Duke Tassilo, is still used by nuns as a religious retreat, and is also a boarding school for girls. It is therefore closed to the public, although the little 13th-century **church** offers visitors the chance to write down their thoughts in a book which is located

behind the altar.

Brighten up your visit with a taste of the local spirit, *Klostergeist*. Each Kloster (cloister) has its own traditional recipe.

[i] Verkehrsamt Frauenchiemsee

After returning by boat to Prien drive along the lake in a northerly direction via Gstadt to Seebruck, 19km (12 miles).

Seebruck, Bayern

3 Seebruck is worth a stop to see the Roman remains in the **Heimathaus** and enjoy a swim in the lake in the large open-air enclosure called the **Freibad**, weather permitting.

A short northwesterly detour is recommended to visit the **Kloster Seeon**, situated on an island in the Klostersee. Of special interest are the combinations of architectural styles in the church, which dates from the 10th

TOUR 13

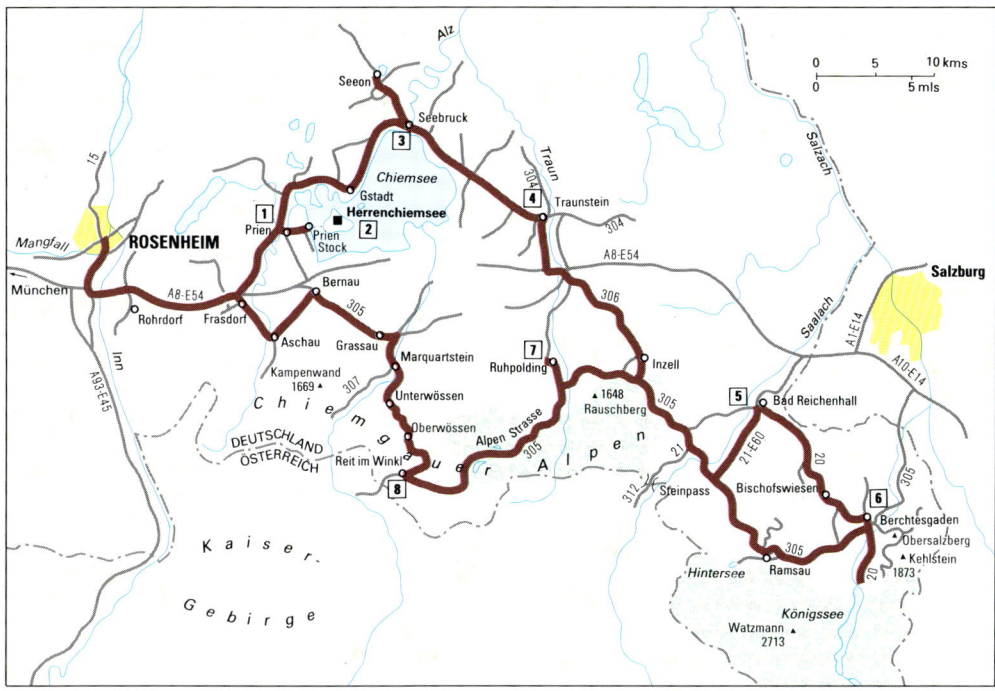

century. The wall paintings were rediscovered in 1911, having been lost for generations.

An attractive journey northwest from here, on the **Deutsche Ferienstrasse** (German Holiday Road), leads to **Wasserburg** on the Inn river, about 25km (15½ miles) away. The **Burg** (castle) which gave the town its name was first built in the early Middle Ages, but Herzog (Duke) Wilhelm IV ordered that it be dismantled, and in 1531 work began on the new castle. Step gables are a distinctive feature of the high roof and, inside, vaulted passages provide the link to the staircases and an attractive hall on the first floor. The chapel between the castle and the adjacent corn store was built in 1465, and stucco decorations were added in 1710.

The **parish church of St Jacob** was the work of architect and builder Hans Stethaimer and the main building was

Fraueninsel in the Chiemsee, Bavaria's largest lake. The island, with its ancient convent, is a pleasant holiday resort

built between 1410 and 1445, with the tower added in 1478. The baroque pulpit was beautifully carved by the brothers Zürn in the 17th century. The **Frauenkirche** (Church of Our Lady) was built in the 14th century, but the light interior and ornaments show all the characteristics of baroque, and date from the late 18th century.

The **Rathaus**, with its tall gable, was built in the 15th century, when the town was earning its riches from a strategic position on the main salt trading route between Augsburg and Salzburg.

Drive back to Seebruck and continue in a southeasterly direction to Traunstein.

FOR HISTORY BUFFS

1 *Prien, Bayern* The steam railway line from Prien to Stock on the lake shore dates back to the end of the 19th century. The old train could well be a museum piece, but luckily for visitors, is still in operation.

SPECIAL TO...

3 *Seebruck, Bayern* At Amerang, a few kilometres west of Obing between Seebruck and Wasserburg, is the **Bauernhausmuseum** (museum of farmhouses). Old farmhouses from the area between the Inn and Salzach rivers have been reconstructed to demonstrate the farming life of the past. The museum is open daily from the middle of March until November, except on Mondays.

RECOMMENDED WALKS

1 *Prien, Bayern* The island of Fraueninsel near Prien is ideal for gentle strolls and pleasant views, and is a favourite spot for artists.

6 *Berchtesgaden, Bayern* Take a left turn at Ramsau en route from Berchtesgaden and proceed to the Hintersee. Away from the busy tourist routes, you can enjoy a relaxing walk along the lake shore – or, if you prefer, take a boat to admire the scenery.

Traunstein, Bayern

4 Traunstein calls itself the 'Green Town on the German Holiday Road', as it hosts a research centre for forestry, which has an international reputation.

On Easter Monday the **Georgritt** takes place here. Riders in historic armour and local costumes proceed on beautifully decorated horses to the little church at **Ettendorf** to receive a blessing for their horses.

[i] Verkehrsamt in Stadtpark

*From Traunstein take the **B306** south to the junction with the **B21** and turn sharp left northeast to Bad Reichenhall, 25km (16 miles).*

Bad Reichenhall, Bayern

5 This is one of the main spas in the area, well-known for the salt deposits in its mountains. The healing effects of salt are used here to treat many ailments, including asthma, rheumatism and even pneumonia.

The **Münster** (Minster) **of St Zeno** was destroyed by fire and rebuilt in 1512. Ironically, St Zeno is the patron saint who protects against the danger of water and flooding! This is the largest Romanesque church in Upper Bavaria, and the jewel of the town. The gate and the Gothic font are noteworthy and there is a woodcarving of the coronation of the Holy Mary, which dates back to the early 16th century. As with many other Bavarian churches, there is a great deal of superb woodcarving.

King Ludwig I had the **Alte Saline** (old saltmine) built in 1834 and a visit today gives a good idea of what working in the saltmines was really like. Visitors are provided with protective clothing. Salt was an important trading item during the Middle Ages and in the past brought enormous wealth to the owners of the mines.

[i] Wittelsbacher Strasse 15

*From Bad Reichenhall take the **B20** for about 21km (13 miles) to Berchtesgaden.*

Berchtesgaden, Bayern

6 Geographically an enclave in Austria, Berchtesgaden is surrounded by beautiful mountains. Its environs make it a good centre for day trips in the area. The town itself has a castle dating from 1410, which became the home of the ruling Wittelsbach dynasty in the 19th century. Crown Prince Rupert, son of the last king of Bavaria, lived here until his death in 1955. The castle is now a museum showing the many treasures which the Crown Prince collected during his lifetime. The **Salzbergwerk** (saltmine) is also open to visitors. As the salt deposits in this area are exploited by both Austria and Bavaria, the mine tunnels often run between both countries.

From the town one of the most

The spa rooms at Bad Reichenhall. The salt springs near the town have been exploited since Celtic times and salt is still important

TOUR 13

View over Berchtesgaden in its spectacular mountain setting

rewarding trips is up to the **Kehlsteinhaus**, or Eagle's Nest, named because of its precipitous position on the mountain. Cars are only allowed as far as Obersalzberg, and the journey is then completed by bus, foot and lift. The lift rises 124m (407 feet) up into the mountain. The views defy description. Allow plenty of time for the excursion: walkers may want extra time to enjoy some of the summit paths on the Kehlstein. On the way down from the parking area you may wish to stop at the **Hotel Türken** to see something of the remains of the Third Reich, with which this area is so closely associated. The Berghof, Hitler's Alpine retreat, once stood here. The air-raid shelter network under the houses belonging to Nazi leaders still remains, although there is not much left to see. The brochures available here provide a good insight into the way things were then. After the war, the Bavarian government decided to destroy all traces of the buildings associated with the Third Reich; the groundwork had already been done by an RAF bombing raid on 25 April 1945, when most of the buildings were left in ruins.

The area around the Obersalzberg is also served by the **Rossfeld Ringstrasse**, a circuit often used for motor rallies. It is not unusual to see immaculately maintained vintage cars coping gracefully with the bends and steep gradients of this road. Another rewarding excursion leads from Berchtesgaden to the **Königssee**, a ride which takes only about five minutes, depending on traffic. The Königssee is surrounded by steep mountain slopes descending to the lake, with no road around the shores. Motorboats are available, however, to make the journey around the lake. The picturesque **chapel of St Bartholomä**, perched on the eastern face of the Watzmann mountain, dominates the whole area with its formidable height and contours.

[i] Königseerstrasse 2

*Take the **B305** west for 45km (28 miles) to Ruhpolding.*

Ruhpolding, Bayern

7 In Ruhpolding stands one of the most beautiful churches of the Alpine area – the **parish church of St Georg**, right in the middle of the town. Elaborately decorated, its main attraction is the Ruhpoldinger *Madonna*, dating back to the 13th century.

[i] Hauptstrasse 60

*From Ruhpolding go south and rejoin the **B305** southwest to Reit im Winkl, 23km (14 miles).*

Reit im Winkl, Bayern

8 Reit im Winkl is a favoured destination for excursions from many surrounding areas. It is a perfect example of a typically delightful Alpine village. A short stroll up the hill called Grünbühel is worth it for the superb views of the nearby Kaiser Gebirge (Kaiser Mountains).

From Reit im Winkl, a short detour northwest to **Aschau** is suggested; take the B305 via Bernau. The main attraction here is the castle **Hohenaschau**, which was built around 1100. The original complex was enlarged to include a brewery and iron-foundry. The first beer was brewed in 1549 and it has kept its reputation ever since. A cable-car can take visitors to the top of the Kampenwand mountain, which reaches an altitude of 1,669m (5,575 feet). The views are breathtaking.

[i] Rathausplatz 1

From Aschau go northwest to Frasdorf and back to Rosenheim, 54km (34 miles).

Rosenheim – Prien 27 (17)
Prien – Herrenchiemsee 3 (2)
Herrenchiemsee – Seebruck 19 (12)
Seebruck – Traunstein 31 (19)
Traunstein – Bad Reichenhall 25 (16)
Bad Reichenhall – Berchtesgaden 21 (13)
Berchtesgaden – Ruhpolding 45 (28)
Ruhpolding – Reit im Winkl 23 (14)
Reit im Winkl – Rosenheim 54 (34)

FOR CHILDREN

7 *Ruhpolding, Bayern* Two parks should keep children amused at Ruhpolding. The **Märchenpark** has a mini railway, a playground and decorative models from fairy tales. The **Minatur Städte Park** has models of famous German buildings, made to a scale of 1:25.

BACK TO NATURE

Woodland birds are diverse in the Bavarian Forest. Seven species of woodpecker occur, most easily seen in the spring, when males drum loudly on trees. Roe and red deer are common but shy – look for their tracks on muddy forest paths.

2 days – 213km (132 miles)

THE BAVARIAN LAKES

München • Schliersee • Rottach-Egern • Tegernsee
Gmund • Bad Wiessee • Walchensee • Kochel
Benediktbeuern • Bad Tölz • München

München (Munich) owes its origins to the 12th-century Duke, Henry the Lion, who diverted the lucrative trade in salt via a new bridge over the Isar so that he could levy taxes. München suffered terribly from World War II bombing; it has since been sensitively restored. This is a cultural city, alive with theatres, galleries and museums. The *Frauenkirche* (Church of Our Lady), with its two domed towers, is its chosen emblem. The stained glass windows miraculously survived both wars. The heart of München is the *Marienplatz* (square), with the neo-Gothic *Neues Rathaus* (new Town Hall). Its Glockenspiel can be heard twice daily when the tower becomes alive with figures. The tower has a fine view, but there are 300 steps to climb first! Near the opera house and the theatre, both restored, is the *Königsbau* (King's Building) and the entrance to the palace of the Wittelsbach dynasty, which ruled Bavaria for 700 years.

Above left: buskers in München, Bavaria's lively capital

BACK TO NATURE

2 *Rottach-Egern, Bayern* Take the cable-car from Rottach-Egern up to the Wallberg. For those who wish to venture into more remote areas, a walk of about 45 minutes leads to the mountain-top, 1,722m (5,650 feet) high. From there the scenery is superb. Look out for Apollo butterflies and colourful alpine flowers. Rock buntings and citril finches can also be seen, along with alpine accentors – birds which are characteristic of higher altitudes.

SCENIC ROUTES

The toll road south of Josefsthal passes through magnificent alpine scenery, with gradients of up to 1 in 7. Remote alpine roads can sometimes face sudden closure for long periods. It is always advisable to check the road conditions at the local information office.
Another scenic mountainous drive starts along a pleasant stretch on Lake Tegernsee. Continue in a southerly direction and face a 1 in 6 gradient up to the Achenpass, followed by a leisurely drive alongside Lake Sylvenstein. Your destination is reached at the Walchensee.

[i] Sendlingerstrasse 1

*Leave München on the **A8** southeast. Leave at exit Irschenberg and proceed southwest on the **B472** to Miesbach and south on the **B307** to Schliersee, 52km (32 miles).*

Schliersee, Bayern

1 Situated on the northern end of a lake, Schliersee is the centre of activities in this area. The town is in the foothills of the surrounding mountains, with a steep slope from the upper part of the town to the lake.
The 18th-century **parish church** in baroque style is worth visiting, as is the **town hall**. There is a cable-car connection to the peak of the Schlierberg, 1,256m (4,120 feet) high, which has a leisure park. Another excursion takes you from the upper part of the town, called Spitzingsee, to the mountain lake of the same name. From there a cable-car rides up the 1,640m (5,380-foot) Taubenstein, with extensive views over the lake and its surroundings. A bit further south along the lake from Schliersee town lies the ruin of the fortress **Hohenwaldeck**, which is over 1,000 years old.

[i] Kurverwaltung, Bahnhofstrasse 11a

From Schliersee head south to Josefsthal and take the toll road to Valepp. Turn northwest to Rottach-Egern, 25km (16 miles).

Rottach-Egern, Bayern

2 The mountains between the lakes prevent a more direct connection, but this small detour is worth it for the beautiful scenery.
The twin towns of Rottach and Egern have combined to form a health resort and winter sports centre on the southern end of Lake Tegernsee. The 15th-century **parish church** was formerly a centre for pilgrims who came to venerate a picture of the Madonna, called the *Egerner Gnadenbild*.
In the past Lake Tegern was popular with German writers and composers, a few of whom are buried here. A small detour south via a toll road, called the Wallbergstrasse, leads to the **Moosalm**, but the most magnificent views can only be enjoyed by continuing on foot to the Wallberghaus.

[i] Kuramt, Nördliche Hauptstrasse 9

*From Rottach-Egern drive north on the **B307** for 2km (1½ miles) to Tegernsee town.*

Above: The beautiful Tegernsee, haunt of the rich and famous

Tegernsee, Bayern

3 Tegernsee town was founded by Benedictine monks, who came from St Gallen in Switzerland in the 8th century. The **monastery** was converted into a castle in 1803 and became a country home for royalty. Parts of the castle are open to visitors, especially the main hall (Kapitelsaal), which is also part of the local museum. Another attraction is the **Braustüberl** in the northern part of the castle, formerly a brewery, now serving beer. The castle was also on the visiting list of one Walther von der Vogelweide, the famous Minnesinger of the Middle Ages, who went from castle to castle cheering up the knights and their ladies in their forbidding surroundings with his medieval version of pop music! The castle also houses displays on the lives and works of various local celebrities such as the satirist Ludwig Thoma. Steamer trips on the lake and the many cable cars provide enjoyable excursions.

[i] Kuramt Hauptstrasse 2

From Tegernsee go north on the B307 for 3km (2 miles) to Gmund.

Gmund, Bayern

4 Set on the northern end of the lake, Gmund is a small resort noted for its **parish church of St Aegidius**, the architects of which introduced the Italian baroque style seen in many church buildings in Upper Bavaria during the late 17th and early 18th centuries. The church obtained its High Altar from the Kloster at Tegernsee, after the rest of the building had been destroyed by fire.

[i] Verkehrsamt Kirchenweg 6

From Gmund go south on the west side of the lake for 4km (2½ miles) to Bad Wiessee.

Bad Wiessee, Bayern

5 This spa offers a thermal spring containing iodine and sulphur, with a water temperature of 27°C (77°F). The water is supposed to have healing effects on heart and circulatory diseases, as well as rheumatism and disorders of the skin. The resort is now one of the most elegant in Germany.

[i] Kuramt, Adrian-Stoop-Strasse 20

From Bad Wiessee go south to the B307 to Wallgau, then take the B11 north to Walchensee, 48km (30 miles).

FOR CHILDREN

3 *Tegernsee, Bayern* Children and adults alike will enjoy a boat trip around Lake Tegernsee.

9 *Bad Tölz, Bayern* The **Alpamare leisure park** at Bad Tölz makes a good day out. A swim in artificial waves is great fun and there is a multitude of other attractions.

RECOMMENDED WALKS

1 *Schliersee, Bayern* It is possible to walk right around the Schliersee and when you feel you have had enough, there is a pleasant lake steamer to take the weight off your feet.

5 *Bad Wiessee, Bayern* A short walk from Bad Wiessee in a southerly direction leads to Abwinkl, from where the route branches off into the mountains to **Bauer in der Au**, a popular resting place. Along the way, the walk passes through delightful mountain scenery and serene grazing cattle.

TOUR 14

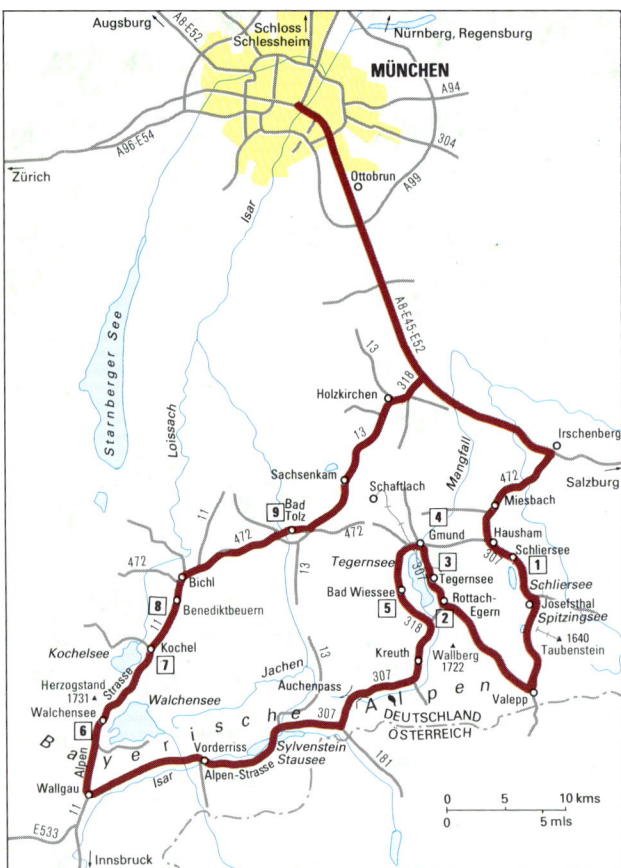

to the 16th century. The route then changes direction to go north to the **Walchensee**, Germany's biggest mountain lake, which reaches a depth of 200m (656 feet). It is also the highest alpine lake in the country, 800m (2,625 feet) above sea level. An excursion by chair-lift to **Herzogstand** offers panoramic views of the surrounding area.

[i] see Kochel

> From Walchensee continue north on the **B11** for 13km (8 miles) to Kochel.

Kochel, Bayern

7 As with other mountain lakes, motorboats are not allowed here on Kochelsee, but there is ample opportunity for hiring rowing and sailing boats as well as paddlers. Swimming is also possible, of course, but will only appeal to the hearty, as the water in the mountain lakes tends to be chilly. Kochel also has a modern leisure centre called 'Trimin' to keep you in trim.

[i] Kalmbachstrasse 11

> From Kochel drive 5km (3 miles) north to Benediktbeuern.

Benediktbeuern, Bayern

8 The former **Benedictine abbey** was founded as early as AD740, with the assistance of St Bonifatius, but was partly destroyed by the marauding Huns from Hungary in the 10th century. It has survived and been rebuilt twice, and the existing structure, completed in 1686, has frescos by Asam. Apart from their religious duties, the monks also enjoyed painting and literary activities.

The abbey contains the **Fraunhofer Glashütte** (glassworks), which are situated in the former laundry.

FOR HISTORY BUFFS

7 *Kochel, Bayern* The monument to Balthasar Mayr in Kochel was erected in commemoration of his attempt to liberate his Bavarian homeland from the Austrian Habsburgs in 1705. He was killed as a result and became a symbol of Bavarian patriotism.

Walchensee, Bayern

6 After Wildbad Kreuth the road climbs steeply up to the Achenpass. The Alpenstrasse (Alpine Road) then leads to **Lake Sylvenstein**, an artificial lake which creates hydroelectric power, but also prevents flooding when the winter snow melts. The route crosses the lake by bridge and then continues on a toll road to **Wallgau**, a picturesque mountain village where some of the farmhouses have decorative frescos dating back

The Walchensee, in whose depths, it is said, lie treasures dumped there by the defeated Nazis

Fraunhofer was a scientific researcher, whose work rooms have been kept in their original state. The Fraunhofer firm continues a long tradition of glass-making, specialising in the preservation of medieval stained glass windows in the churches of Europe.

[i] Prälatenstrasse 5

*From Benediktbeuern continue on the **B11** to Bichl and then on the **B472** via Bad Heilbrunn to Bad Tölz, 15km (9 miles).*

Bad Tölz, Bayern

9 Bad Tölz, originally a fishing village, produces the highest output of iodine-containing water in Germany, thus offering a variety of cures based on this chemical. The spa also has other amenities connected with the health springs, such as a Trinkhalle, where you can 'take the waters', and a moorbath. These establishments have become focal points in the recent past for social gatherings of the healthy and unhealthy alike.

The **parish church of Mariahilf** is a centre for pilgrimages, and is adorned with a fresco by Mathias Günther, depicting the Tölz plague procession of 1634. A **Kreuzweg** (Way of the Cross) to the top of the **Kalvarienberg** (Calvary) leads past seven stations with seven chapels.

[i] Ludwigstrasse 11

*From Bad Tölz take the **B13** northeast via Holzkirchen to the **A8** and return north to München, 46km (28 miles).*

München – Schliersee **52 (32)**
Schliersee – Rottach-Egern **25 (16)**
Rottach-Egern – Tegernsee **2 (1¼)**
Tegernsee – Gmund **3 (2)**
Gmund – Bad Wiessee **4 (2½)**
Bad Wiessee – Walchensee **48 (30)**
Walchensee – Kochel **13 (8)**
Kochel – Benediktbeuern **5 (3)**
Benediktbeuern – Bad Tölz **15 (9)**
Bad Tölz – München **46 (28)**

SPECIAL TO . . .

3 *Tegernsee, Bayern*
Tegernsee town has a special private railway, which runs to Schaftlach to connect with the main line to München. On most Sundays and public holidays an old steam engine is used, to the delight of old and young alike.

9 *Bad Tölz, Bayern* The **St Leonhardtsritt** (ride of St Leonard) takes place each year on 6 November in Bad Tölz. A procession of horse carts and wagons drives through the town and up past the Stations of the Cross to the 'Hill of Calvary', where a service is held at the chapel.

The Marienplatz, München's hub, with the neo-Gothic Rathaus

2 days – 288km (178 miles)

THE ALPS SOUTH OF MÜNCHEN

München • Starnberg • Berg • Seeshaupt
Garmisch-Partenkirchen • Schloss Elmau • Mittenwald
Ettal • Schloss Linderhof • Oberammergau • München

The München (Munich) museums appeal to all tastes and many happy days can be spent exploring their treasures. The *Glyptothek* exhibits Greek and Roman sculpture, including the famous figures from the Aegina temple. One of the great picture galleries of the world is the *Alte Pinakothek*, a large building in Venetian Renaissance style, built in 1836 to house the paintings acquired by the Wittelsbach dynasty from the early 16th century. Almost every great name – and every nationality – in painting is represented here, from Peter Bruegel the Elder to da Vinci, from Van Dyck to Tiepolo and El Greco. The *Neue Pinakothek*, opposite, houses German and French work. The *Deutsches Museum* is one of the most comprehensive science museums in the world. A visit to *Schloss Nymphenburg* is recommended: this lavishly decorated palace was once the summer residence of the Bavarian rulers.

FOR HISTORY BUFFS

1 *Starnberg, Bayern* The former Austrian Empress Elisabeth, being Bavarian born, chose **Feldafing** on the western side of Lake Starnberg as her favourite summer retreat. Her former villa is now a luxury hotel bearing her name, and a commemorative statue stands in the hotel park.

2 *Berg, Bayern* Every year on 13 June a service is held at the **Votivkapelle** in Berg in memory of the tragic death on that day of King Ludwig II in the lake near by.

[i] Sendlingerstrasse 1

From München take the A95 south, then take the exit for the A952 to Starnberg, 20km (12 miles).

Starnberg, Bayern

1 This is a very popular holiday resort, partly due to the excellent connections to and from München, and offers many leisure activities such as sailing, windsurfing, boating and diving. The adjoining villas, with their beautiful gardens, enhance the general holiday atmosphere around the lake.

The **parish church of St Josef** was built between 1764 and 1766 in the rococo style. The High Altar built by Ignaz Günther is flanked by statues in white marble and altogether the interior seems filled with light, no doubt enhanced by its position on top of a hill.

During the 16th and 17th century 'playgrounds of the rich' developed in Europe and Starnberg Lake claims to be one of the first. In 1663, the Elector Ferdinand invited 500 guests to a gondola party on the lake, with 100 oarsmen in charge of the boats. Now there is a yacht harbour, and more modest sailing regattas during the summer. A **Heimatmuseum** (local museum) advises on local activities during the past and present and a notable picture gallery features works by painters of the Romantic period.

Monument to Mathias Klotz, Mittenwald's most honoured son

[i] Kirchplatz 3

Continue along the east side of the lake for 4km (2 miles) to the village of Berg.

Berg, Bayern

2 Berg is famous as the place where King Ludwig II met his tragic death. Having been certified insane and deprived of his throne, Ludwig was ordered to be taken to Schloss Berg and kept under medical supervision. An outing in a small rowing boat proved fatal for him and his doctor: both bodies were found by a search party, next to their boat, in shallow water. The exact circumstances leading to their deaths remain a mystery. Ludwig drained Bavaria's coffers to build the extravagant castles which are a monument to him. A cross in the Starnberg lake denotes the spot where the bodies were found, and a **Memorial Chapel** was built on the shores near by.

[i] Ratsgasse 1

Continue south along the lake for 21km (13 miles) to Seeshaupt.

Seeshaupt, Bayern

3 Seeshaupt, on the southern end of the lake, is less crowded than the northern shores and is a good centre to explore the nearby **Ostersee**, a group of numerous tiny lakes from the Ice Age. It is of special interest to ornithologists because of the ideal nesting conditions in the tall reeds for all kinds of birds. Geologists will find the soil and rock formations of interest.

[i] Weilheimerstrasse 1

Turning southward for 8km (5 miles), rejoin the A95 at Penzberg/Iffeldorf and proceed to Garmisch-Partenkirchen, a total of 48km (30 miles).

Garmisch-Partenkirchen, Bayern

4 Two adjoining towns, united in a double name, are best known as the major German wintersports resort and host to the Winter Olympics of 1936. One of Germany's busiest resorts, it offers magnificent views of the surrounding mountain ranges, especially the massive **Zugspitze**, Germany's highest mountain – 2,963m (9,718 feet). King Ludwig's lodge is now a museum of local history. The German composer Richard Strauss lived here and met American troops when they occupied Garmisch-Partenkirchen at the end of World War II.

An excursion to the top of the Zugspitze should not be missed – first by cogwheel train to Eibsee, then by cable car – or by a more leisurely route, continuing by train to **Schneefernerhaus**, followed by a short ride by cable car to the top. The latter route avoids the very sudden change in altitude of about 2,000m (6,600 feet) in 10 minutes.

Glacier skiing is practised on the top all year round, and if you wish to venture into Austria, there is a tunnel link between the two countries, with windows cut into the rocks so that passengers may enjoy the views over the mountains.

[i] Bahnhofstrasse 34

*From Garmisch turn east on the **B2** to Klais, 12km (7 miles) and then southwest on a toll road to Schloss Elmau.*

Schloss Elmau, Bayern

5 Still owned by the family who built it during World War I, this stately home offers a sort of English house party atmosphere with a mixture of cultural and intellectual pursuits on a residential basis for paying guests. Meals are taken communally, many of the staff are highly educated and guests can enjoy painting, music and dancing classes, concerts and music weeks, sometimes attended by famous musicians. A visit to the Schloss is worthwhile, even for day visitors who do not wish to stay.

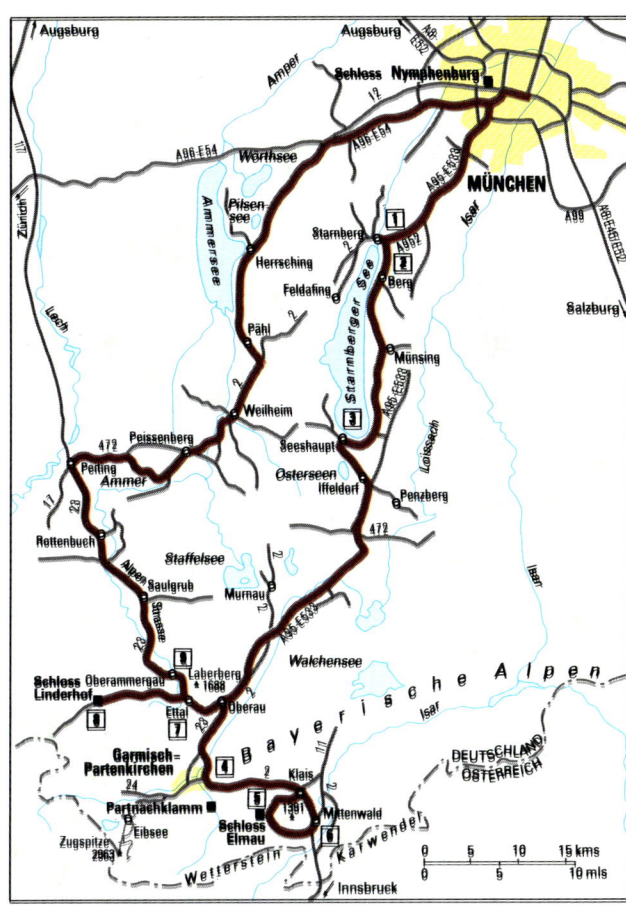

Mittenwald is a centre for summer walking and winter skiing

BACK TO NATURE

3 *Seeshaupt, Bayern* The Osterseen (lakes) south of Seeshaupt are in a designated nature reserve and their formation dates back to the Ice Age. In all, 21 small lakes have been counted in the group and birdwatchers will find it interesting – there are numerous species to be seen, including great crested grebes, spotted crakes and pochards.

4 *Garmisch-Partenkirchen, Bayern* Between Garmisch-Partenkirchen and the Austrian border, there are several forest tracks that can be explored on foot. Hazel hens and capercaillies – gamebirds – live on the wooded slopes and unusual orchids grow beside the paths.

RECOMMENDED WALKS

3 *Seeshaupt, Bayern* A stroll along the Starnberg lake from Seeshaupt to Seeseiten or to the Ostersee can be very pleasant. The southern side of the lake is less crowded and more relaxing.

4 *Garmisch-Partenkirchen, Bayern* A fascinating walk is from Garmisch-Partenkirchen in a southerly direction to the **Partnachklamm** (ravine). A well laid-out path leads on one side of the ravine through many tunnels. The walk is highly recommended.

SCENIC ROUTES

The toll road from Klais near Mittenwald is very scenic. Not only that, but drivers benefit from the scarcity of traffic, which makes it doubly enjoyable.

From Ettal to Linderhof castle the drive is through a valley which is a nature reserve. It is easy to appreciate the uniqueness of the grand alpine scenery. If there is time, continue from Linderhof towards the Austrian border for a while, when it becomes even more scenic and blissfully deserted.

The feeling of space in the big halls and corridors, and the elegance of days gone by, are combined with modern comforts.

[i] Schlosshotel

From Elmau drive about 7km (4 miles) southeast along the Lautersee to Mittenwald (toll road).

Mittenwald, Bayern

6 This name, which means 'in the middle of the woods', describes the beautiful surroundings of this health and wintersports resort, situated in a valley between two massive mountain ranges, the Karwendel and Wetterstein.

The town flourished in the Middle Ages, when it was a staging point for trade between Venice and northern Europe, and reminders of this boomtime can still be found in the marketplace. In 1684, Mathias Klotz founded the town's unique industry, which continues to this day: violins, violas, cellos, zithers and guitars are all made here, often using local wood. The descendants of Mathias Klotz continue the family business. The **Geigenbau museum** and the **Heimatmuseum** offer more insights into local history and crafts. At the Geigenbau, it may even be a descendant of Mathias Klotz who demonstrates the art of violin-making. All the work is done by hand. Numerous excursions can be taken from Mittenwald. The western peak of the Karwendel mountains can now be reached by cable car and offers a magnificent panorama of the Bavarian and Austrian Alps and beyond. Chair- and cabin-lifts take you to other peaks in the region.

[i] Kurdirektion, Dammkarstrasse 3

*From Mittenwald drive northwest to Klais, take the **B2** west to Garmisch, 12km (7 miles) and north to Oberau 8km (5 miles), then turn left on the **B23** to Ettal.*

Schloss Linderhof. This baroque fantasy of King Ludwig II, with its elegant park, sits snugly among forested hills

TOUR 15

FOR CHILDREN

1 *Starnberg, Bayern* A round trip by lake steamer on the Starnberger See makes a pleasant outing for the whole family.

4 *Garmisch-Partenkirchen, Bayern* Skaters will have the opportunity to enjoy an all-year ice-rink at Garmisch-Partenkirchen. The **Alpspitz Wellenbad** in Garmisch provides plenty of entertainment for children and adults. The leisure complex offers self-drive boats, sauna, solarium and swimming in a pool with artificial waves.

9 *Oberammergau, Bayern* The **Wellen Berg Pool** at Oberammergau is a large, circular pool with artificial waves and a special safe area for children.

Ettal, Bayern

7 Visitors are attracted to the Benedictine Abbey, a monastery founded in 1330 by the Holy Roman Emperor for his knights and monks. To add to the confusion, it is also called 'Kloster', which means convent, although only monks live here. The Gothic building took 50 years to complete, and contains an enormous fresco, 25m (82 feet) wide. Today, the abbey houses a school and the monks distil a special liqueur, called **Klosterlikör**, which is made from health-giving herbs in accordance with a centuries-old recipe, which is, of course, secret.

[i] Ammergauerstrasse 8

From Ettal continue west 12km (7 miles) to Schloss Linderhof.

Schloss Linderhof, Bayern

8 A charming, comparatively small castle built for Ludwig II, this is idyllically set, surrounded by woods, mountains and a small lake. The lavish interiors reflect the King's desire to emulate the grandeur of Louis XIV of France. The Hall of Mirrors is said to represent Ludwig's dreamworld. There is a collection of paintings portraying French celebrities during the reigns of Louis XIV and Louis XV. The extensive gardens are in harmony with the landscape, with waterfalls tumbling down rocks, fed by water from mountain streams. There is also a grotto dedicated to the goddess Venus and many fountains, dominated by the Neptune Fountain. This spouts out great jets of water into the air, rising higher than the top of the castle itself. A Moorish pavilion was brought here straight from the Paris exhibition of 1867.

From Schloss Linderhof return east for about 7km (4 miles), then take a left turn to Oberammergau.

Oberammergau, Bayern

9 Oberammergau is famous the world over for its **Passion Plays**, which have been performed since 1634, and

*Above: an heraldic lion decorates a house in Garmisch-Partenkirchen
Right: religious frescos in Oberammergau – appropriate to a town famous for its Passion Play*

in 10-year cycles since 1680. The houses in the main streets are decorated with colourful frescos, showing that woodcarving is the local industry here. The **Passion Play Theatre** should be visited, even when no plays are taking place. The auditorium seats around 5,000 and the stage is open-air, with remarkable acoustics.

Woodcarvers are at work at all times and the variety of their products, mainly religious objects, can be seen in shop windows all over the town. The **parish church** was built by the famous Josef Schmuzer and the frescos are by Mathäus Günther. Oberammergau also offers a variety of recreational facilities, including tennis, swimming, keep-fit, hang-gliding, canoeing and, of course, walks through the countryside. Or take the chair-lift to the Kolbensattel or the cable-lift to the Laberberg: both offer panoramic views over the countryside.

*Take the **B23** northwest to Peiting, and turn due east on the **B472** to Peissenberg. After Peissenberg, take the left fork to Weilheim. Continue north on the **B2** for about 8km (5 miles), then turn left for Pähl and the Ammersee. Drive along the eastern shore to Herrsching, then northeast along the Pilsensee for the **A96** to München, a total of 112km (70 miles).*

München – Starnberg **20 (12)**
Starnberg – Berg **4 (2)**
Berg – Seeshaupt **21 (13)**
Seeshaupt – Garmisch-Partenkirchen **48 (30)**
Garmisch-Partenkirchen – Schloss Elmau **18 (11)**
Schloss Elmau – Mittenwald **7 (4)**
Mittenwald – Ettal **34 (21)**
Ettal – Schloss Linderhof **12 (7½)**
Schloss Linderhof – Oberammergau **12 (7½)**
Oberammergau – München **112 (70)**

SPECIAL TO...

9 *Oberammergau, Bayern* The Oberammergau **Passion Play** is known the world over. It started during a plague epidemic, when the village councillors vowed that if God would halt the spread of the disease they would stage a play every 10 years. The plague stopped suddenly, and the survivors put on the first performance in 1634. The next one is scheduled for the summer of 2000.

The annual beer festival has to be mentioned, although it is very well advertised all around the world. The official title is Oktoberfest, but it takes place in the second half of September and ends at the beginning of October. Basically it is a popular carnival devoted to the consumption of large quantities of beer. Obviously, it is necessary to be in the right mood to enjoy this festival, and participants also need a good stomach!

2 days – 311km (193 miles)

BAVARIAN SWABIA

Augsburg • Donauwörth • Dillingen • Günzburg • Ulm
Memmingen • Ottobeuren • Kempten • Kaufbeuren
Landsberg • Augsburg

Founded 2,000 years ago by one of the family of the Roman Emperor Augustus, Augsburg prospered in the 15th and 16th centuries, mainly due to two wealthy merchant families: the Fuggers and the Welsers. The Fuggers founded a housing estate in 1519 where rents were low, on condition the tenants were married, Catholic, poor and of unblemished character! The *Fuggerei* still stands; its gate is closed at 22.00 hours.

The *Stadtpalast*, one of Augsburg's outstanding buildings, was completed in 1515. It was destroyed in World War II but completely rebuilt by the present Fugger family. The *Dom* (cathedral) was started early in the 9th century, and now houses many unique art treasures, including the oldest known stained glass paintings in central Europe. The altar paintings are by Hans Holbein, a citizen of Augsburg. The *Rathaus* (town hall), built between 1615 and 1620, has seven floors. Adjacent is a 78m (256 foot) watch-tower, the *Perlachturm*.

[i] Bahnhofstrasse 7

*Leave Augsburg north on the **B2**, the 'Romantic Road', for Donauwörth, 40km (25 miles).*

SPECIAL TO...

1 *Donauwörth, Bayern* At Schloss Leiheim, 9km (6 miles) east of Donauwörth, candlelight concerts are held from May to September.

4 *Ulm, Baden-Württemberg* The **Ulmer Schachtel** (box of Ulm) was a specially designed boat for use on the Danube. A replica can be seen at the Edwin Scharff House museum in Neu-Ulm.

Donauwörth, Bayern

1 Donauwörth lies at the point where the Wörnitz river enters the Danube. The Fuggers of Augsburg left their mark here, too, and the **Fuggerhaus**, built in 1539, has had many famous visitors, such as the Swedish King Gustavus Adolphus and Emperor Charles VI.

The **Reichstrasse**, with its **parish church**, dominates the centre of the town. The church was built in the 15th century and contrasts in style with the **Heiligkreuzkirche**, which is in lavish baroque and was built much later, in about 1717. The builder was Josef Schmuzer, who is known for many Bavarian churches of this period. Of special note inside is the High Altar, which is richly decorated.

[i] Rathaus

*From Donauwörth take the **B16** southwest for 26km (16 miles) to Dillingen.*

Ulm cathedral: carved choir stalls

Dillingen, Bayern

2 Dillingen was a university town for over 200 years from the 16th century onwards. The university was founded by Cardinal Bishop Otto Truchsen von Waldburg, who had to request permission from the Emperor and the Pope. The **Aula**, or Goldener Saal, as it is called here, is a masterpiece of late rococo. The hall is about 30m (98 feet) long, 12m (39 feet) wide and only 6m (19 feet) high, but the combination of design and ornament is truly magnificent.

The **Schloss** (castle), where the Bishop of Augsburg used to live, now has a more secular use: law courts, tax and forestry offices. The **church of St Peter** was founded in 1619, and the **Königstrasse** provides a good example of how the streets and their surrounding buildings looked between the 16th and 18th centuries.

[i] Königstrasse 37

*Continue on the **B16** for 24km (15 miles) to Günzburg.*

Günzburg, Bayern

3 Günzburg warrants a short stop to see the **Frauenkirche**, built between 1736 and 1741 by Zimmermann – a masterpiece of south German rococo.

Another building worth visiting here is the **castle** of a former Austrian Margrave, which was started in 1579 and completed in 1609. Only the chapel, which was erected in 1754 by Zimmermann's pupil, J Dossenberger, has survived in its original style. The rest of the castle was converted into government offices.

[i] Rathaus

*Take the **B10** for 25km (16 miles) to Ulm.*

Ulm, Baden-Württemberg

4 Ulm is really a border town: the new town of Neu-Ulm across the river is still in Bavaria, while Ulm is in Swabia. The **Münster** (minster) is known for its high spire, 161m (528 feet) high, and is Germany's second largest Gothic church. The foundation stone was laid in 1377, but work extended over many centuries.

Many families of builders dedicated their working lives to the minster. The robust may decide to climb the 768 steps up the main spire, but the view is a reward – as far as the Alps on a clear day. The **Rathaus** (town hall) building was started in 1370 with a simple design but, like the minster, it became the work of many artists and took a long time to complete. The paintings on the walls and the figures date back to 1540. The interior was totally redesigned after the bomb damage of 1944.

The **Schwörhaus** (house of swearing-in) is a reminder of the still practised annual tradition, in which the Mayor and the Guilds swear their loyalty anew to the constitution of the town. Crossing the Danube into Neu-Ulm, there are some fine old gabled houses. The leaning tower of Ulm, the **Metzgerturm** (butcher's tower), is about 2m (6 feet) off balance. Part of the old city walls can also be seen from here.

The idiosyncratic façade of the Rathaus in Memmingen

Ulm also prides itself on its fountains – the **Brunnen** – which were created in the 15th century in connection with the building of two waterworks. They all have names, and the **Delphinbrunnen** has 53 water jets. Lovers of the rococo style will want to visit the library at the **Benediktinerkloster**, while the **Klosterkirche St Martin** is a baroque masterpiece.

The **German Bread Museum** gives information on the manufacture of bread and on the ancient bakers' guilds, as well as the present world food situation.

[i] Münsterplatz 51

From Ulm drive via Neu-Ulm and the B28 and B19, along the Bavarian/Württemberg border to Memmingen, 55km (34 miles).

Memmingen, Bayern

5 The **Rathaus** (town hall), built in 1589, with a façade of 1765, is the major attraction in the Old Town, which is well preserved in its original state. An architectural curiosity is the **Siebendächerhaus** (house with seven roofs), three either side and one on top. This former tanners' house was unfortunately totally destroyed by bombing during World War II, but rebuilt according to the original design.

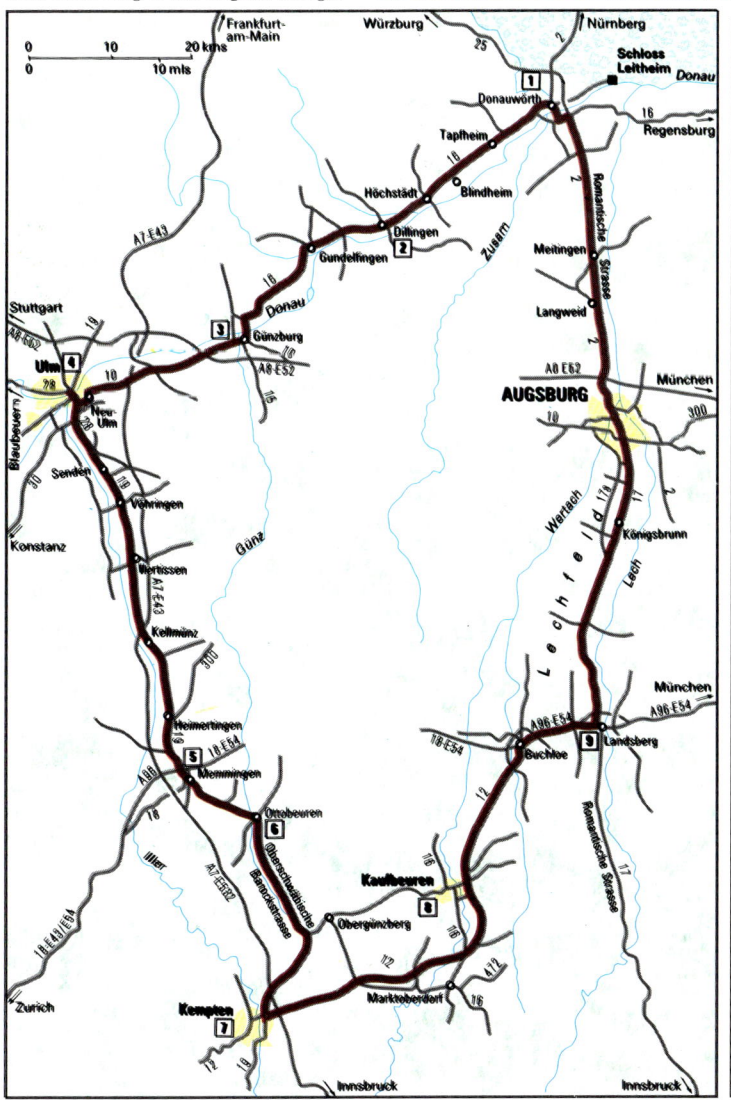

RECOMMENDED WALKS

4 *Ulm, Baden-Württemberg*
Take a stroll in the **Glacis-Stadtpark** at Neu-Ulm to the fortress, which was built in the mid-19th century. In the summer, open-air concerts are held within the enormous walls of the fortress. Another pleasant walk can be taken on the other side of the Danube, at Ulm. East of the town centre, the **Friedrichsau park** offers relaxing strolls, with an Aquarium and Tropical House as special attractions.

BACK TO NATURE

4 *Ulm, Baden-Württemberg*
Blaubeuern lies 17km (10 miles) west of Ulm and at the northern end of the town is the **Blautopf** (blue pot), the source of the River Blau. The crystal-clear water emerges from a depth of 22m (72 feet) and flows along rocks and ravines, which provide a perfect natural setting. The River Blau joins the mighty Danube a little later. You may see dippers here – little black and white birds which bob up and down, and flit from rock to rock.

TOUR 16

FOR CHILDREN

8 *Kaufbeuren, Bayern* The **Tänzelfest** takes place on the third Sunday in July, when the history of Kaufbeuren is presented by about 1,600 children in historical costume. The procession is led through the town and the evening is crowned by a torchlit tattoo and fireworks display.

SCENIC ROUTES

Before and after leaving Dillingen, the route is particularly scenic as it follows the course of the Donau (Danube). From Obergünzburg onwards, the route takes you through memorable country landscapes until it reaches Kaufbeuren.

Look out also for the **Steuerhaus** on the market square, which dates back to 1495; pretty arcades lead through to the market. The Gothic style of architecture dominates in the town, but parts of this building, as well as the town **museum**, show baroque influence.

The old city gates are still standing, as are parts of the city wall, and the Gothic **Martinskirche**, with its 66m (216-foot) spire, is the symbol of the town. The choir is a masterpiece of local woodcarving. The Fugger dynasty also erected a building here in 1589: the **Fuggerbau**.

i Ulmer Strasse 9

From Memmingen drive southeast for 11km (7 miles) to Ottobeuren.

Ottobeuren, Bayern

6 The church in Ottobeuren represents one of the most important buildings in baroque style in Germany, although there has been a church on this site since AD 764. This structure was begun in 1737, and while many craftsmen created different parts of the church, the end result shows a remarkable artistic harmony, which makes the church unique. The

Below: the abbey church at Ottobeuren is regarded as the peak of German baroque architecture

Above: bird's-eye view over the towers and roofs of the former imperial city of Kaufbeuren

foundations for other parts of the **Kloster** were laid in 1711, and the **Kaiser Bibliothek** (library) and **Theatersaal** should also be seen.

i Marktplatz 12

Continue on the Oberschwäbische Barockstrasse south for 27km (17 miles) to Kempten.

Kempten, Bayern

7 Kempten lies on the River Iller, and has a Celtic and Roman past, but like so many towns and cities in this area is now a living reminder of the exuberant architectural glories of the 17th and 18th centuries. The Residenzplatz is dominated by the **palace** of the former Prince Abbots. The lavishness of the interior reflects the worldly part of the Prince Abbot's role, rather than the spiritual. Purists may disagree about whether the style is really late baroque or early rococo, but to most visitors it will simply seem opulent.

The **Basilika** of St Lorenz adjoins the west wing of the Residenz and was erected at about the same time, in the mid-17th century. The basilica was built over a period of four years,

the Residenz took 13 years to complete. Architecture apart, Kempten is also an important centre for dairy farming.

[i] Rathausplatz 29

*From Kempten take the **B12** east for 34km (21 miles) to Kaufbeuren.*

Kaufbeuren, Bayern

8 A free imperial city until 1803, Kaufbeuren's old quarter dates back to the Middle Ages. Since 1945 it has been the home of the Gablonzer glass industry, the craftsmen and their families having been expelled from their former homes in Gablonz, now in Czechoslovakia. They brought their craft here and Neugablonz is the area in which they work. The **St Blasien-Wehrkirche** was built in 1436 on the city wall, thus adding to the defences of the town. Five towers of the wall still stand. The church altar is distinguished by wonderful 16th-century woodcarvings.

More woodcarvings can be found at the **St Martinskirche** in town. The local **Volksmuseum** is worth a visit, and an exhibition celebrates the work of the famous local writer, Ludwig Ganghofer, who died in 1920.

[i] Kaiser Max Strasse 1

*Continue on the **B12**, then the **A96** north to Landsberg.*

Landsberg, Bayern

9 Enter the city through a beautifully decorated gate, the **Bayertor**, erected in the 15th century. From the top of the tower, which formed part of the city's defences, there is a wide view over the town. The marketplace, with its **Maria Brunnen** fountain, is also the main square. On one side stands another tower, the **Rathaus**, built between 1699 and 1702. The famous architect Dominikus Zimmermann worked here and erected the exterior stucco façade of the Rathaus. He was also Lord Mayor of the town for five years from 1759. The interior of the **parish church** is decorated in rich baroque style and was built between the years 1458 and 1488. It contains several treasures, including a rosary altar by Zimmermann and the sculpted Landsberger *Madonna* by a sculptor from Ulm.

[i] Altes Rathaus

*Take the **B17** north for 36km (22 miles) back to Augsburg.*

Augsburg – Donauwörth **40 (25)**
Donauwörth – Dillingen **26 (16)**
Dillingen – Günzburg **24 (15)**
Günzburg – Ulm **25 (16)**
Ulm – Memmingen **55 (34)**
Memmingen – Ottobeuren **11 (7)**
Ottobeuren – Kempten **27 (17)**
Kempten – Kaufbeuren **34 (21)**
Kaufbeuren – Landsberg **33 (20)**
Landsberg – Augsburg **36 (22)**

FOR HISTORY BUFFS

2 *Dillingen, Bayern* At Höchstädt, 6km (4 miles) before Dillingen, stands a memorial commemorating the battle which took place on 13 August 1704 between the 'allies', Austria, Holland and England, against Bavaria and France. The battle was fought to decide the succession to the Spanish throne and was won by the allies. The English army was led by the Duke of Marlborough, who named his palace in England 'Blenheim' after the village of Blindheim, near the battlefield.

9 *Landsberg, Bayern* West of the road from Landsberg to Augsburg lies the **Lechfeld**, where an important battle was fought in AD955. The invading Huns from Hungary, who had looted and destroyed throughout southern Germany and Austria, were finally defeated by Otto the Great, who became Emperor Otto I in 962.

2 days – 286km (177 miles)

THE ALPS EAST OF LINDAU

Lindau • Oberstaufen • Immenstadt • Sonthofen
Oberstdorf • Klein Walsertal • Füssen • Isny • Wangen
Lindau

Lindau is set on an island in the Bodensee (Lake Constance), connected to the mainland by a causeway. Cars are discouraged in the centre; there is free parking near the station. It is in any case a place to wander around on foot – an enchanting maze of medieval streets, with the magic of the lake never too far away. The town's recorded history goes back to AD882, with the mention of a convent called Our Lady under the Linden Trees. In 1220 it became a Freie Reichsstadt, meaning direct rule under the Emperor. Lindau changed ownership many times between the Austrians and the French, but finally became part of Bavaria in 1805. The climate here is surprisingly mild: wine-producing grapes are grown on the lake shores. The port, which is guarded by the *Old Lighthouse*, is now only used for pleasure craft. *St Peter's Church* is noteworthy for the only remaining frescos by Hans Holbein the Elder.

SPECIAL TO...

2 *Immenstadt, Bayern* In September in Immenstadt is the **Berglerfest**, when cowherds drive their cattle down from the mountains back to their stables. Traditionally, beards grown during the summer stay on the alpine pastures are measured, with prizes given for the longest specimens!

3 *Sonthofen, Bayern* On the second Sunday in December, the **St Nikolaus balloon race** takes place at Sonthofen, which provides a very rewarding way of viewing the mountains.

[i] Bahnhofplatz

From Lindau drive a short stretch on the B12 before turning off for the B308 via Scheidegg to Oberstaufen, 40km (25 miles).

Oberstaufen, Bayern

1 In the 19th century a Silesian peasant made a useful discovery: a cure for the effects of over-eating and drinking! The cure involves fasting – although mulled wine is part of it – and Oberstaufen is always busy with customers for the 'Schrothkur'. An alternative cure might be a drive to Steibis near by, and a cable car ride and walk to the summit of **Hochgrat** with its breathtaking views. This clears the head just as well!

[i] Schlosstrasse 8

One of Wangen's atmospheric narrow streets. Many buildings here date from the 16th century

From Oberstaufen take the B308 east for 15km (9 miles) to Immenstadt.

Immenstadt, Bayern

2 Immenstadt has the ideal alpine setting – a lake encircled by mountains. It offers sailing, surfing and rowing on the lake and plenty of walks through the attractive countryside. The **parish church of St Nikolaus** was built in late baroque style in 1707, and the **Rathaus** (town hall) slightly earlier in the 17th century. Two 17th-century ruins, the **Laubenbergstein castle**, north of the town, and the **Schloss Königsegg** in town, are worth visiting.

[i] Marienplatz 3

From Immenstadt take the B308 southeast for 7km (4 miles) to Sonthofen.

Sonthofen, Bayern

3 This well-known resort should be mentioned for the great variety of facilities it offers to sport enthusiasts, including swimming, bowling, canoeing, tennis, squash and cycling. In winter there is an equal variety, with sports such as skiing, curling and skating. A camp site is also open all year round.

[i] Verkehrsamt, Rathausplatz 3

From Sonthofen proceed south on the B19 for 13km (8 miles) to Oberstdorf.

Oberstdorf, Bayern

4 The old village of Oberstdorf has grown into an excellent resort. It is very much associated with winter sports and well-known for its long ski-jump. Exciting summer sports are also available, such as hang-gliding and parasailing: enthusiasts can take advantage of the many cable cars which travel to the mountain-tops.

The **Nebelhornbahn** cable car goes from Oberstdorf – 828m (2,717 feet) above sea level – up to 1,933m (6,342 feet), a good starting point for hikes and mountain walks. To reach the summit of the Nebelhorn, just continue from the last station by chair-lift. The **Fellhornbahn** is a grander affair, the largest cable car in Germany, the cabin taking 100 people at a time. A second stage goes to a point just beneath the summit. In winter, five ski-lifts provide the usual 'Skicircus' atmosphere. Lastly, the **Sollereckbahn** rises 1,400m (4,593 feet) in 11 minutes to a superb area for walking and hiking.

Down in the valley, the sight to see is the **Breitachklamm** – a ravine sometimes only 2m (6 feet) wide, so that in certain places the sky can hardly be seen. The curious rock formations along the way add to the impression of being in a cave.

[i] Marktplatz 7

From Oberstdorf drive on the B19 southwest into the Kleinwalsertal. The road becomes the B201 when in Austria, 15km (9 miles).

TOUR 17

Klein Walsertal, Vorarlberg (Österreich)

5 Politically, this valley is in Austria, but as there are no rail or road links with that country, it is economically allied with Germany. Visitors who buy postcards will need Austrian stamps, but will pay for them with German marks. Apart from these man-made peculiarities, nature has created a little paradise here, and walkers and hikers will really feel at home. An abundance of alpine flowers, most of them protected, adorn the meadows.

There are four main villages in the valley: **Riezlern, Hirschegg, Mittelberg** and **Baad**. As there are no plans for any changes in the present status of the valley, it can be hoped that this special place will stay unspoilt for some time.

Hohenschwangau, a Bavarian castle not built by Ludwig II

[i] Klein Walsertal, Verkehrsamt Hirschegg

*Drive back on the **B201/B19** to Sonthofen, then due east on the **B308** via Hindelang along the Jochstrasse. Turn left before the Austrian border to Oberjoch on the **B310** and along the Grüntensee. Turn southeast to Füssen, 89km (55 miles).*

Füssen, Bayern

6 The parish church of St Mang was erected between 1701 and 1717 in baroque style by the builder and painter Jakob Herkomer, who studied in Venice. As a consequence, his work shows a strong Italian influence.

The former Benedictine abbey now serves as the **Rathaus** (town hall); the **Fürstensaal** (hall of the princes) and the **Papstzimmer** (room of the Pope) are also well worth visiting. The **Hohes**

RECOMMENDED WALKS

4 *Oberstdorf, Bayern* A spectacular walk leads from south of Oberstdorf through the **Breitachklamm**, a ravine which constantly creates waterfalls. The walk is about 1.6km (1 mile) long, and waterproof clothing is necessary.

5 *Klein Walsertal, Vorarlberg (Österreich)* A climb up the Widderstein mountain from Baad in the Klein Walsertal is a worthwhile experience for the energetic. An early rise followed by a $4\frac{1}{2}$-hour climb are the necessary prerequisites for the beautiful scenery to be seen up at the top.

6 *Füssen, Bayern* Many lakes around the Füssen area provide good opportunities for gentle walks.

TOUR 17

FOR HISTORY BUFFS

6 *Füssen, Bayern* From Füssen drive the 22km (13½ miles) along the **B17** to Steingaden, turn right after 3km (2 miles) and right again to Wies; here, the **Wieskirke** is a pilgrimage church designed and built by Dominikus Zimmermann. Work started in 1746 and was finished eight years later, and both the exterior and interior decorations are fine examples of baroque and rococo. On the return journey, stop in **Steingaden** to visit the former **monastery church of St Johannes der Täufer**, which dates from the mid-12th century, although the interior was extensively decorated in the 18th century.

BACK TO NATURE

6 *Füssen, Bayern* The River Lech has to pass through a narrow ravine just south of Füssen, near the Austrian border. The nearby **Lech waterfall** completes this natural spectacle, which can be admired from a small bridge across the ravine. For the birdwatcher, the ravine by the castle at Neuschwanstein is a renowned haunt of the wallcreeper.

FOR CHILDREN

8 *Wangen, Baden-Württemberg* **Miniland** at Wangen on the **B12** is a treat for model train enthusiasts. Trains run through a beautifully presented miniature landscape called 'from the sea to the Alps'. The whole set is mounted on an enormous table, and is open to visitors from mid-March to the end of October and during the Christmas holidays.

Schloss, built on a hill, has origins from around 1330, although the present building dates from the 15th century.

Near Füssen are two important castles: Hohenschwangau and Neuschwanstein. **Hohenschwangau** stands above the village of Schwangau; a steep walk leads up to the castle from the car park. The architect was chosen by Crown Prince Maximilian of Bavaria for his theatrical connections, and he favoured the English Tudor style. The drawing rooms and salons feature designs inspired by old German sagas, including parts of the legends used by Richard Wagner for his operas. Wagner was a frequent visitor and his piano is still kept tuned. The castle was used as a summer residence and its terraces offer tranquil views over the countryside and lakes – and to the castle of Neuschwanstein, a spectacular sight.

Neuschwanstein must be seen to be believed, but photographers beware – it is very difficult to get a good shot of it, and the best ones are usually done from the air.

The castle was the brain-child of Ludwig II, and work began on it in 1869. The plans were drawn up by a stage designer, instructed to make real the King's dream-world. The mythical world of Wagner's operas – heroic and magical – influences the interiors. It truly is a fairy tale in stone and paint, and fascinating to visit. The castle took 17 years to build, but the tragic King only lived here for 102 days. Since his mysterious death (see page 70), millions of visitors have been enthralled by his living fantasy.

[i] Augsburger-Tor-Platz 1, Füssen

*From Füssen take the **B310** northwest until it becomes the **B309** to the Kempten ring road, then turn left and take the **B12** to Isny, 71km (45 miles).*

Surrounding alpine meadows form one of the charms of Obertsdorf

Isny, Baden-Württemberg

7 Isny is a border town between Bavaria and Württemberg, and actually lies in the latter. The **Rathaus** prides itself on having a mighty stove, which reaches from floor to ceiling, and is decorated with coloured tiles of clay. On the ground floor is a copy of a Roman milestone from AD202.

The Romanesque **St Nikolaus Church** has a library housed in its spire. The Gothic choir and font are also interesting. The **church of St Georg** was built in baroque style in 1661. However, the rococo

The old lighthouse and the Lion of Bavaria guard the entrance to the port of Lindau on the Bodensee

decorations are mostly 18th-century.

The climate around Isny, which is an officially designated health resort, is known to be beneficial for many respiratory illnesses, as well as heart and circulation problems.

[i] Untere Grabenstrasse 18

Continue on the **B12** westwards, but turn right before Staudach for Wangen, 18km (11 miles).

Wangen, Baden-Württemberg

[8] Wangen's interesting past still shows through its buildings and streets. Most of the houses were built after the great fire of 1539 and the fronts painted with motifs in traditional colours. The end of the Herrenstrasse (gentlemen's road) runs most appropriately to the **Frauentor** (ladies' gate), again beautifully decorated, and was built in 1608.

[i] Rathaus

Return on the **B18**, then the **B12** to Lindau, 18km (11 miles).

Lindau – Oberstaufen 40 (25)
Oberstaufen – Immenstadt 15 (9)
Immenstadt – Sonthofen 7 (4)
Sonthofen – Oberstdorf 13 (8)
Oberstdorf – Klein Walsertal 15 (9)
Klein Walsertal – Füssen 89 (55)
Füssen – Isny 71 (45)
Isny – Wangen 18 (11)
Wangen – Lindau 18 (11)

SCENIC ROUTES

One of the most picturesque drives is south of Oberstdorf into the Klein Walsertal. The road passes through beautiful countryside and the charming villages of Riezlern, Hirschegg and Mittelberg to Baad.

The stretch from Sonthofen onwards is a scenic and dramatic drive through the Alps. Many hairpin bends have to be negotiated on the Jochstrasse up to Oberjoch. However, only the passengers should enjoy the scenery: the driver will need to concentrate hard on the road. Later, from Nesselwang to Füssen the scenery is enhanced by Lake Weissensee near Füssen.

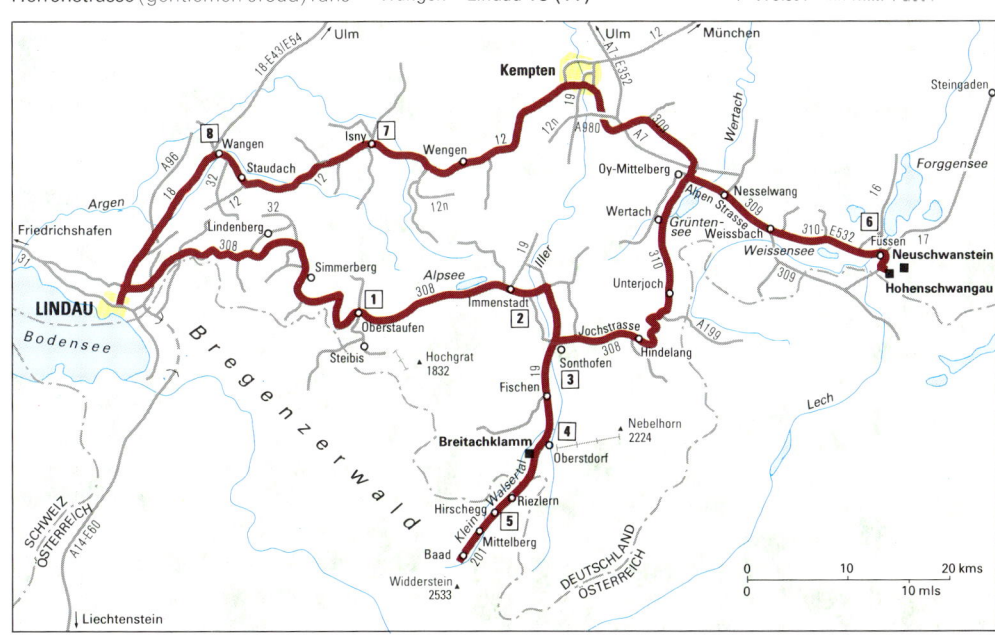

BADEN-WÜRTTEMBERG

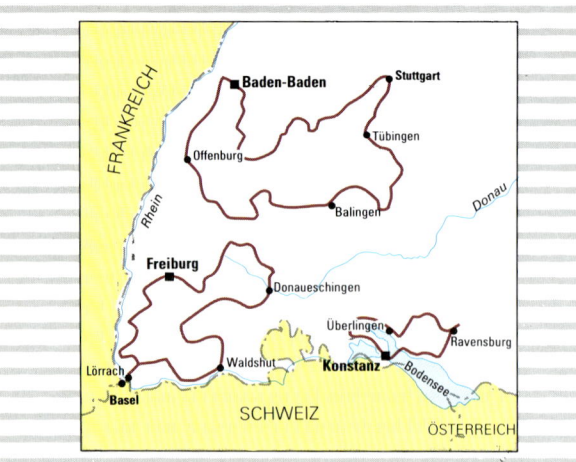

Panorama of Freiburg im Breisgau, capital of the Schwarzwald and site of a great European cathedral

Baden-Württemberg stretches across southwest Germany with the Rhine forming a natural border to the west and the south where it joins the Bodensee (Lake Constance). Germany occupies by far the largest proportion of the lake shores, but this geographical advantage over neighbouring Switzerland and Austria does not upset the harmony of this relaxed lakeside community. Lake steamers ply from country to country and a great deal of co-operation exists between the partners whose commerce, language and history has so much in common.

The Rhine flows past the southern reaches of the Black Forest region. Here it should be mentioned that the term 'black' is something of a misnomer, as the forest is both brilliantly green and extremely beautiful. There seems to be a parallel here with the 'Blue Danube', which rises near Donaueschingen. Poetic licence transforms this great river which is normally grey as it is fed by the molten waters from the alpine glaciers, though occasionally looked at from a certain angle, the river acts as a mirror and reflects the blue sky. The Black Forest also fails to live up to its name in winter when it is inevitably cloaked in deep snow which transforms the area into a popular winter sports location.

Traditional crafts such as clock-making and glass-blowing can still be seen in the Black Forest villages. The Deutsche Uhrenstrasse (German Clock Road) draws attention to the origins of the cuckoo-clock deep in the heart of the forest. Modern industry is largely restricted to tourism and the area around Bodensee and the Black Forest is not only spectacularly beautiful, but the woods and hills are well supplied with many enchanting small hotels and inns.

The Romans discovered the joy of spa life centuries ago, but the Black Forest's natural hot springs suffered a long period of neglect before their restorative powers came back into fashion again at the end of the last century. Europe's ruling monarchs and carriage-loads of the aristocracy enjoyed their summer vacations in these spas. Now they are open to all and still very popular.

Although the main attraction of the Black Forest region and Bodensee lies in their scenic beauty, there is no need to miss out on the sightseeing front with magnificent castle and other works of art standing testimony to the generations of gifted architects and artists of times gone by.

Tour 18

In ecological terms the Bodensee (Lake Constance) forms a reservoir for the Rhine. From the town of Konstanz, it is a pleasant drive along the south-western shores of the peninsula, which projects into the northern end of the lake, then southeast through a series of interesting lakeside towns. Where the lake reaches its full width, summer visitors could be forgiven for imagining they were by the Mediterranean, surrounded by vineyards on one side and the calm blue waters of the lake dotted with brightly coloured sailing boats on the other. A trip further inland leads through hilly countryside with plenty of stopping places and attractive scenery and views. A car ferry saves the long drive around the lake – regular lake steamer services provide reliable connections to all points around the shores. Ambitious travellers can visit three countries in a day with perfect ease by just hopping on and off the steamers.

Tour 19

This tour begins in historic Freiburg im Breisgau, one of Germany's greatest cultural centres. Striking out from Freiburg, the road runs through the Höllental (Valley of Hell), one of the

BADEN-WÜRTTEMBERG

best known valleys in the Black Forest, and then follows the Schwarzwälder Panoramastrasse (Black Forest Panoramic Road), both of which promise outstanding scenery. Donaueschingen marks the spot where the two primary tributaries of the Danube, the Breg and Brigach, unite to form one of Europe's major waterways. The might of the Danube is only evident much further on, when it is joined by rivers from the Alps. Small towns and magnificent scenery are the main feature of this tour as it proceeds along the Rhine, takes a turn on the Hochschwarzwald (High Black Forest), and stops off at a Roman spa before circling back by way of the evocative Hexental (Valley of the Witches).

Tour 20

The Romans were the first to stumble upon the charms of Baden-Baden, one of Germany's best known spas, and the starting point of this tour. Following a most attractive route through the Black Forest, the Mummelsee, near the Hornisgrinde mountain, is a popular stopping point about halfway along the outward journey. Approaching Stuttgart, it should be remembered that traffic is very heavy around the town. In spite of its industrial suburbs, the centre of the city has achieved a very pleasant atmosphere with traffic kept at bay by pedestrian precincts. From Stuttgart, the tour proceeds to two extraordinary castles with totally different concepts – fairy tale extravagance on the one hand, and a solid historical pedigree on the other. At Gengenbach the tour picks up the popular Badische Weinstrasse (Wine Route) and wends its way out of the western end of the Black Forest range into the vineyards and on to Baden-Baden.

The harbour at Meersburg on the northern shore of the Bodensee

1/2 days – 158km (97 miles)

LAKE & SHORES OF KONSTANZ

Konstanz • Insel Reichenau • Überlingen
Unteruhldingen • Salem • Heiligenberg • Wilhelmsdorf
Weingarten • Ravensburg • Friedrichshafen
Meersburg • Konstanz

Konstanz (Constance) is the largest town on Bodensee (Lake Constance). The *Altstadt* (Old Town) was fortunate to escape destruction during World War II, saved by its proximity to neutral Switzerland. It features lovely half-timbered houses, and the massive *Konzilgebäude*, a former warehouse, built in 1388 for the linen trade. The original Romanesque *Münster* (Minster) was started in 1052, and completed in 1089. Later generations, wanting to improve on the simplicity of the Romanesque style added more elaborate elements, such as the 14th-century Gothic chapels along the aisles, and the Renaissance vaulting in the nave together with the gilded choir.

Southeast of the *Rathaus* stands the *Haus zum Rosgarten*, the house of the medieval butchers guild, which now contains an interesting museum illustrating the history and culture of the whole Bodensee area.

RECOMMENDED WALK

1 *Insel Reichenau, Baden-Württemberg* Passing through Radolfzell, on the way from the island of Reichenau to Überlingen, stop off for a walk along the elegant lakeside promenade and, if time permits, try a visit to the 14th-century Gothic **Liebfrauenmünster**.

SCENIC ROUTES

From the island of Reichenau, there is a lovely drive along the shores of Lake Constance to Radolfzell. The first part of the road is called the **Swabian Poets Road**, and is followed by a Green Road.

Between Salem and Heiligenberg, the **Oberschwäbische Barockstrasse** (Upper Swabian Baroque Road) leads through some enchanting country.

ℹ️ Bahnhofplatz 13

*From Konstanz head northwest on the **B33** for Insel Reichenau, (9km/6 miles), which is reached by a causeway.*

Insel Reichenau, Baden-Württemberg

1 Reichenau is also known as the 'Garden Island', though vegetables are the main crop here, flourishing profitably in the rich soil and mild climate.

The first village over the causeway is **Oberzell**, which has one of the oldest Romanesque churches in Germany, dating back to about AD888. The interior is decorated with several famous wall frescos painted in the 10th and 11th centuries, which depict the *Miracles of Christ*. At **Mittelzell**, the 8th-century **Münster** (Minster) is dedicated to St Maria and St Markus. The original basilica, founded in AD724, is typically Romanesque in style, but the main parts of the monastery were built later, in the 10th and 11th centuries. Take time to inspect the treasures of the **Schatzkammer** (Treasury), such as the five Gothic shrines housing

The abbey church in Weingarten is a masterpiece of the baroque

religious relics, among them a 5th-century ivory goblet etched with details of the *Miracles of Christ*, and examples of 1,000-year-old stained glass.

The third church to visit is in **Niederzell**. Dedicated to St Peter and St Paul, the original Romanesque edifice was greatly altered and added to in the 15th century, but the highlight here is a series of Romanesque frescos uncovered during restoration in 1990.

*Leave the island via the causeway, take the **B33** northwest, then turn right on to the **B34** and drive round the northern end of the lake to meet the **B31** at Ludwigshafen. Take the **B31** southeast to Überlingen, 41km (26 miles).*

Überlingen, Baden-Württemberg

2 This part of the lake is actually called the Überlinger See, as the northern end of Lake Constance is divided by the Bodanruck peninsula, with Konstanz at its southernmost tip.

The city centre is formed by the **Münsterplatz**, with the **Altes Rathaus** and the **Münster** (Minster). The basilica is very large for a comparatively small town, but the site on which it was constructed originally held two churches. The present Gothic-style building consists of five naves, erected between 1350 and 1562, and it is topped by two spires, one smaller than the other, which contains the Osannaglocke bell. The fine **Altes Rathaus** (Old Town Hall), is in late Gothic style, and you can visit the **Ratsaal** (Council Chamber) with its High Gothic decorations, wooden panelling and figures representing the member states of the Holy Roman Empire, among others.

Northwest of the Münsterplatz, the **Franziskanerkirche** dates back to the 14th and 15th centuries. Facing across Union Square, the **Reichlin-Meldegg'sche Patrizierhaus** was originally the home of an important local family. It now houses the town's **Heimatmuseum** which uses a wide variety of interesting exhibits to explain the history of the town from its earliest origins.

ℹ️ Landungsplatz 7

Continue along the shore in a southeasterly direction for 7km (4 miles) to Unteruhldingen. Stop halfway to see the pilgrimage church at Kloster Birnau.

Unteruhldingen, Baden-Württemberg

3 A unique insight into the early life of Man is provided here on the shore of Bodensee at the **Freilichtmuseum Deutscher Vorzeit** (Museum of German Prehistory). The museum exhibits finds from local excavations and a re-creation of a lakeside village showing how the inhabitants would have lived in prehistoric times. Created in 1922 by the archaeologist Hans Reinerth, a visit is strongly recommended.

TOUR 18

[i] Fremdenverkehrsbetriebe Unteruhldingen-Mühlhofen

Turn away from the lake, heading northeast for about 7km (4 miles) to Salem.

Salem, Baden-Württemberg

4 Records of Salem's **Münster** date back to 1137. The abbey was created by the Cistercian order and was a substantial foundation, supporting 300 monks and novices within the walled precincts by the end of the 13th century. Although the foundation stone of the Münster was laid many years earlier, the abbey church was not consecrated until 1414, and is considered to have been the most important Gothic building in the region at its peak. The present monastery buildings date back to the 16th and 18th centuries and are largely baroque in style. A notable feature here is the wonderful Riepp-Organ, constructed in 1766. When the abbey was secularised it passed to the princes of Baden-Baden, and Prince Max of Baden founded a famous boarding school which still occupies part of the abbey complex. One renowned headmaster, Dr Kurt Hahn, later left Germany and founded Gordonstoun School in Scotland.

In 1700, part of the former Kloster (abbey) was rebuilt and renamed the **Schloss** (castle). Visitors will find the imposing **Kaisersaal** (Emperor's Hall) of particular interest.

[i] Leutkircher Strasse 1

Continue north for 7km (4 miles) to Heiligenberg.

Heiligenberg, Baden-Württemberg

5 Although the counts of Heiligenberg are supposed to have had a residence here even earlier, the first records of the present **castle** do not appear until 1276. There is a fabulous carved wooden ceiling adorning the **Rittersaal** (Knights' Hall), which occupies two floors of the south wing. The Renaissance carvings have been hailed as some of the finest examples of their kind in Germany. The castle chapel is also decorated with beautiful carvings, several of which date back to the 13th century, and its coloured glass paintings exude a marvellous glow, especially on a sunlit day.

[i] Rathaus

About 4.5km (2½ miles) north take a sharp right turn to Illmensee and drive via Pfrungen to Wilhelmsdorf.

FOR HISTORY BUFFS

1 *Insel Reichenau, Baden-Württemberg* A detour to Singen and the nearby ruins of the **Hohentwiel fortress** is recommended. Several parts of the fortress that are standing give a good idea of its size and magnificent position. The fortress was never conquered, but Napoleon felt compelled to have it destroyed between 1800 and 1801.

7 *Weingarten, Baden-Württemberg* Numerous Alemann graves were unearthed by archaeologists just outside Weingarten in the 1950s. These date back to the 6th to 8th centuries, and more information is provided by the **Alemannenmuseum**, which is housed in the Kornhaus, a former granary.

Colourful façade in Konstanz, a town with a very long history

BACK TO NATURE

Konstanz, Baden-Württemberg On the way to the island of Reichenau, just north of Konstanz, you will find the **Wollmatinger Ried Bird Sanctuary**. The most common inhabitants on these marshlands are waterfowl – waterproof boots are recommended.

10 *Meersburg, Baden-Württemberg* From Meersburg take a trip by lake steamer to **Mainau**, which belongs to the Swedish Bernadotte family. The island's famous **arboretum** contains hundreds of superb trees not normally seen so far north. Look out for banana trees, bougainvillaea and hibiscus among others, plus in spring the whole island is abloom with a multitude of brilliant, sweet-scented flowers.

FOR CHILDREN

Konstanz, Baden-Württemberg At **Allensbach**, about halfway between Konstanz and Radolfzell, the local **zoo** features a great variety of European wild animals, and there is a **Streichelzoo** (petting zoo) especially for children, with goats, donkeys and deer.

Wilhelmsdorf, Baden-Württemberg

6 The centre of the village is the square-shaped Saalplatz, formed by the intersection of the two roads, and dominated by the **church**. There is a small **museum** located in the oldest house in town, which is dedicated to the history of the village, and can be visited by appointment.

[i] Bürgermeisteramt

> *From Wilhelmsdorf head due south, bypassing Ravensburg, to Weingarten, 24km (15 miles).*

Weingarten, Baden-Württemberg

7 The present church in Weingarten was erected between 1715 and 1724 on the site of a former Romanesque basilica. Two spires, each 58m (190 feet) high, dominate the façade, but the interior is more interesting. One of Germany's largest baroque basilicas, the church was decorated and furnished by a distinguished collection of carefully selected artists. Cosmar Damian Asam contributed the ceiling frescos which, after more than 250 years, still shine as if they had been painted much more

Ravensburg, a town of medieval houses, towers and ramparts

recently. Another impressive sight is the massive organ by J Gabler, whose appearance is almost as imposing as the magnificent sound it produces.

[i] Münsterplatz 1

> *From Weingarten continue south on the **B30** for 4km (2 miles) to Ravensburg.*

Ravensburg, Baden-Württemberg

8 The historic town of Ravensburg grew up around its 11th-century **castle**, and served as the seat of the influential Welf dynasty. The castle enjoyed an advantageous military position, and the town's fortifications still present an imposing sight. The oblong Marienplatz forms the centre of the town. In the middle stands the 16th-century **Bläserturm**. Beautifully preserved medieval houses which belonged to the former **Patriziers**

The Altes Schloss in Meersburg, Germany's oldest inhabited castle

(patricians – the noble and wealthy citizens of the town) line Marienplatz and Marktplatz. **Drei König Haus** and **Rad Haus** are especially noteworthy.

Of particular historic interest for their commercial connections are the **Waaghaus** (Weighing Office), the elongated **Kornhaus** (Corn Exchange) and the **Lederhaus**, which was the leather workers' guildhouse, decorated with beautifully coloured frescos. The **Rathaus** (Town Hall), which was started in the second half of the 14th century and not finished until the 16th, has a 15th-century Lord Mayor's office which is well worth a visit. By far the most significant building in Ravensburg, and the emblem of the town, is the **Mehlsack** which translates to the 'bag of flour', so called because of its light colouring. A sort of spy post which allowed the town watchmen to keep an eye on neighbouring settlements, the 50m (164-foot) high tower still affords a terrific view, and on a clear day it is worth the effort of climbing up the 240 steps to see right over Bodensee to the Alps.

[i] Marienplatz 54

> *From Ravensburg turn southwest on the **B30** for Friedrichshafen, 19km (12 miles).*

Friedrichshafen, Baden-Württemberg

9 Back on the lakeshore, Friedrichshafen was not as fortunate as Konstanz in World War II, and suffered heavy bomb damage on account of its association with the German air industry. During World War I, the famous Zeppelin airships were deployed here, and in the 1920s and 1930s the Dornier flying boats were built here. The lake, whose calm waters had proved to be such an ideal base for the Zeppelins' floating hangers, was also a natural testing ground for the flying boats.

The **Bodenseemuseum** is housed in the northern wing of Friedrichshafen's **Rathaus**. It displays the works of painters and sculptors from the Bodensee area, and also devotes a section to the Zeppelin story.

A shore side promenade leads to the **Schloss Hofen**, once the residence of the kings of Württemberg. Its church, with two distinctive 55m (180-foot) high spires, can be seen from far away. The castle is now privately-owned by Duke Karl von Württemberg, and is not open to the public.

[i] Friedrichstrasse 18

> *From Friedrichshafen head northwest along the lakeshore for 20km (12 miles) to Meersburg.*

Meersburg, Baden-Württemberg

10 Meersburg celebrated its 1,000th birthday in 1988, though its origins are said to go back much further. In AD628, Dagobert, King of the Franks, is supposed to have laid the foundation stone of the **Altes Schloss** (Old Castle). Today, the Schloss, with its mighty Dagobert Tower, is

TOUR 18

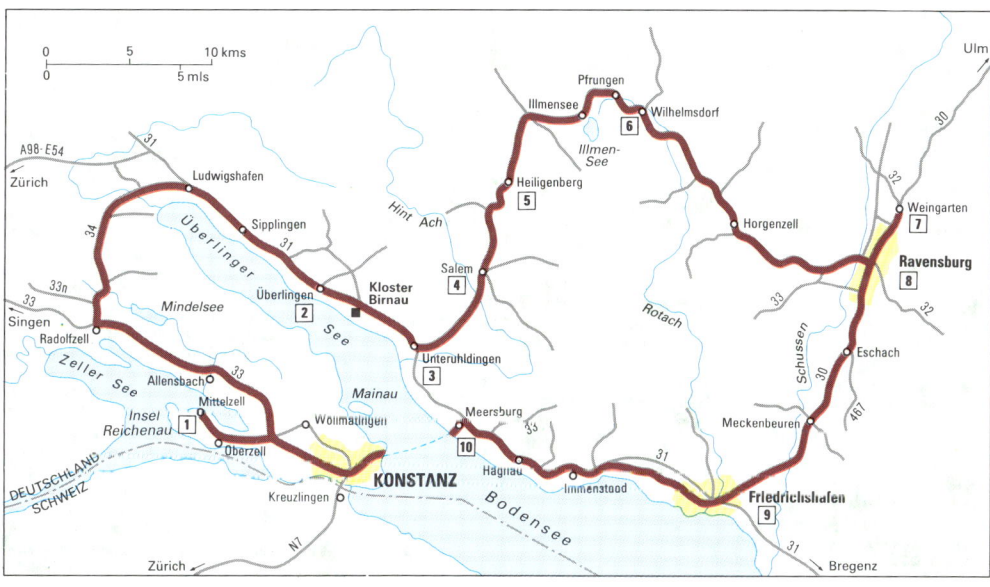

undoubtedly one of the oldest remaining German castles, really more a fortress than castle. It remains in private hands having been saved from demolition by Baron Joseph von Lassberg in the early 19th century. He made parts of the castle available to sympathetic artists, the most famous of these was his sister-in-law, the celebrated German poet Annette von Droste-Hülshoff (1797-1848). Her living quarters, the Knights' Hall, Minstrels' Gallery and dungeons can all be visited.

The **Neues Schloss**, opposite the original one, was built around 1750 as a residence for the Fürstbischofe (Prince-Bishops) of Konstanz. Balthasar Neumann and Franz Anton Bagnato both worked on the project and the grand double staircase is one of Neumann's masterpieces. Other features are the Spiegelsaal (Hall of Mirrors), which is used as a concert hall in summer; and the **Dornier Museum**, on the top floor, which exhibits items relating to the German aviation industry. Do not miss the **Weinbaumuseum**, with its enormous barrel with a capacity of 50,000 litres (11,000 gallons). An impressively large 1607 wine press is also on show.

[i] Kirchstrasse 4

From Meersburg take the car ferry back to Konstanz.

Konstanz – Insel Reichenau **9 (6)**
Insel Reichenau – Überlingen **41 (26)**
Überlingen – Unteruhldingen **7 (4)**
Unteruhldingen – Salem **7 (4)**
Salem – Heiligenberg **7 (4)**
Heiligenberg – Wilhelmsdorf **13 (8)**
Wilhelmsdorf – Weingarten **24 (15)**
Weingarten – Ravensburg **4 (2)**
Ravensburg – Friedrichshafen **19 (12)**
Friedrichshafen – Meersburg **20 (12)**
Meersburg – Konstanz **7 (4)**

SPECIAL TO...

7 *Weingarten, Baden-Württemberg* On the Friday after Ascension Day, Weingarten celebrates an historic ceremony involving the handing over of a relic of the Holy Blood of Christ, with a procession of horseback riders known as the '**Blutritt**'

10 *Meersburg, Baden-Württemberg* Summer visitors can enjoy a series of weekend concerts held in the Neues Schloss' Spiegelsaal (Hall of Mirrors). An international chamber music festival is held on Saturdays from June to September.

2/3 days – 344km (213 miles)

THE SOUTHERN BLACK FOREST

Freiburg im Breisgau • Furtwangen • Triberg • Villingen
Donaueschingen • Titisee • Todtnau • St Blasien
Waldshut • Bad Säckingen • Wehr • Lörrach • Kandern
Badenweiler • Sulzburg • Freiburg im Breisgau

Freiburg im Breisgau is without doubt the most important town in the southern part of the Black Forest. Its *Altstadt* (Old Town) district was razed to the ground in 1944, but meticulously rebuilt after the war using old plans and photographs. The outstanding *Münster* (Minster) is one of the finest examples of Gothic architecture in Germany. Do not miss the 14th-century glass paintings in the side naves and the high altar, a masterpiece which illustrates episodes from the *Life of Christ*.

The *Rathaus* (Town Hall) consist of two units which are linked together by a bridge across the street. The most outstanding non-ecclesiastical building on Münsterplatz is the red medieval *Kaufhaus*, with its arcades and a spire on each frontal end. Another attractive structure is the *Martinstor*, one of the old city gates.

FOR HISTORY BUFFS

3 *Villingen, Baden-Württemberg* The **Heimatmuseum** in Villingen exhibits an interesting collection of almost 1,500 timepieces of all shapes, sizes and descriptions, together with an informative history of 400 years of watches and clockmaking.

FOR CHILDREN

Freiburg, Baden-Württemberg
En route from Freiburg to Furtwangen, turn right at Kirchzarten and make a short detour (11km, 7 miles) to the **Berg-Wildpark Steinwasen**. The two 800m (2,623-foot) long summer toboggan runs are a huge favourite with young visitors.

5 *Titisee, Baden-Württemberg*
The **Black Forest Railway** makes a short trip from Titisee to Schluchsee rather more interesting. The **Schluchsee** is the largest lake in the region and offers plenty of opportunities for bathing and a variety of water sports.

[i] Rotteckring 14

Take the B31 southeast for 27km (17 miles), turn north at Hinterzarten and then drive 26km (16 miles) west on the B500 to Furtwangen.

Furtwangen, Baden-Württemberg

1 Furtwangen is the home of Germany's watchmaker's school, founded in the middle of the 19th century. Its first headmaster, Robert Gerwig, began to collect watches and clocks and the result of his labours, the **Deutsches Uhrenmuseum** (Horological Museum) now exhibits more than a thousand timepieces. A reconstructed workshop shows how clocks were made by hand and the finished products on display range from the first Black Forest clocks made in the 17th century, and driven by stone weights, to more elaborate clocks and, of course, the local speciality – cuckoo clocks. The Planetarium, an astronomical clock, driven by a pendulum, shows the movements of the sun and its planets.

The River Breg, one of the first tributaries of the mighty Danube, starts near 12th-century **St Martin's Chapel** in Furtwangen.

[i] Marktplatz 4

Take the B500 north for 17km (10½ miles) to Triberg.

The lively town of Freiburg

Triberg, Baden-Württemberg

2 Triberg's main attraction is its **Wasserfall** (waterfall), an easy half-hour walk from the main road. The water cascades 162m (531 feet) down over seven steps. On the Schönwald road, the pilgrimage church of **Maria in der Tanne** (Our Lady of the Fir Tree) was already a little chapel in 1645, with an altar painting of the Madonna reputed to work miracles. Later the painting was found fastened to a fir tree, which gave the church its name. It was one of the few buildings to survive a devastating fire in 1826, which completely destroyed Triberg. The present church was erected between 1699 and 1702, and a sculptor from nearby Villingen, Anton Joseph Schupp, designed the high altar with its famous Madonna.

[i] Luisenstrasse

From Triberg take the B33 east for 26km (16 miles) to Villingen.

Villingen, Baden-Württemberg

3 Villingen was founded by Duke Bertold III of the Zähringen dynasty, and much of the town's original defensive walls and the gate towers are still standing. In fact, the wall was so well built that it withstood two attacks by the Swedes in 1525 and 1625 and another by the French in 1703. In the centre of Villingen stands 12th-century **Münster Unser Lieben Frau** (Minster). Most of the original Romanesque architecture was replaced after a big fire in 1271.

Villingen's **Altes Rathaus** houses a museum displaying works of art dating back to the 13th century, and its former **Kloster** (abbey) was founded by the Franciscans in 1268. The **Franziskanermuseum** in the abbey exhibits archaeological finds from the tomb of a Celtic nobleman.

The twin city of Schwenningen was incorporated in 1972, providing industry and commerce to the newly formed double-barrelled metropolis of Villingen-Schwenningen.

[i] Rietstrasse 8

Take the B33/27 south for 17km (10½ miles) to Donaueschingen.

Donaueschingen, Baden-Württemberg

4 The rivers Breg and Brigach unite here and form the original source of the Danube. A circular pond in the Schlosspark marks the meeting-point. The baroque **Schloss** was founded in about 1723, but considerably altered in the 19th century. The interior is the most interesting part. Exquisite Renaissance, baroque and rococo furniture is exhibited in luxuriously appointed halls, their walls hung with elaborate Gobelin tapestries and paintings. Displayed in a gallery on Karlsplatz, the **Fürstenbergische Sammlungen** (Princes' Collections) contain paintings from the 15th- and 16th-century Swabian and Franconian schools.

[i] Karlstrasse 58

Take the B31 west to Titisee.

TOUR 19

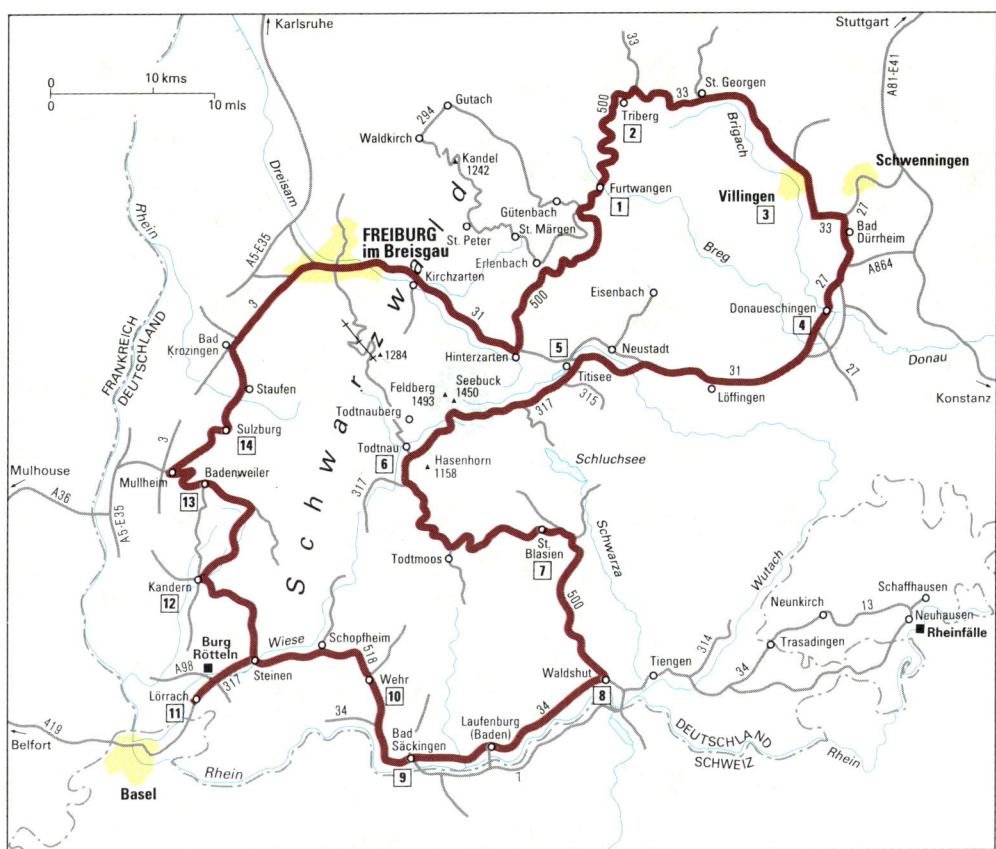

Titisee, Baden-Württemberg

5 Together with its sister town of Neustadt, Titisee is a well-situated centre in the southern Black Forest region. The picturesque lake provides all the usual recreational and water-sports facilities, and there are numerous hiking and driving excursions to be made using the town as a base.

i Kurverwaltung, Kurhaus

*From Titisee take the **B317** southwest for 21km (13 miles) to Todtnau.*

Todtnau, Baden Württemberg

6 Todtnau is surrounded by mountains on every side, all of which reach a height of over 1,000m (3,280 feet), and is officially classified as a health resort.

Situated between Todtnau and its neighbouring village of Todtnauberg, there is a large waterfall, where the water pelts down from a height of about 100m (328 feet) with a deafening noise. One of the nearby mountain peaks, the **Hasenhorn**, can be reached by chairlift, and it is well worth the trip for a great view over the southern Black Forest.

i M-Thoma Strasse 21

From Todtnau drive 3km (2 miles) south, turn left for Todtmoos, then east to St Blasien, 32km (20 miles).

St Blasien, Baden-Württemberg

7 Benedictine monks built the old **Kloster** (abbey) here between 1772 and 1783, though it is believed that previous buildings have stood on this site for over a thousand years. It is always a surprise to find a building of this size in a small village, and the dome of the abbey church is one of the largest in Europe. The interior of the dome is interesting as the architect cleverly created the illusion of the cupola being supported on 20 columns, whereas, in fact, it rests on another hidden structure which bears the full weight.

i Kurverwaltung, im Haus des Gastes

*Take the eastern exit from St Blasien in the direction of Häusern, then due south on the **B500** for Waldshut.*

The lake and town of Titisee are popular for summer breaks

BACK TO NATURE

6 *Todtnau, Baden-Württemberg* A 10-minute walk or short drive north of Todtnau leads to the **Hangloch Wasserfall** (waterfall). In the forest, look for birds such as Bonelli's warblers, nutcrackers, black woodpeckers and collared flycatchers.

SCENIC ROUTES

The main attraction of the **Schwarzwald** (Black Forest) is its scenery and there is an abundance of scenic drives. A circular trip from Furtwangen leads west via Gütenbach through the Simonswald forest and the Wilde Gutach Valley towards Gutach. Turn left, and after about 3km (2 miles) turn left again at Waldkirch. The road now climbs in serpentine bends to the Kandel mountain and on to St Peter. After numerous bends it reaches St Märgen and then changes direction from southeast in a sharp swing around to the northeast at Erlenbach and then due north to Furtwangen. The stretch of road between Waldkirch and Erlenbach is popularly known as the **Schwarzwälder Panoramastrasse** (Black Forest Panorama Road).

Waldshut, Baden-Württemberg

8 This small market town lies on the banks of the Rhein (Rhine) right by the Swiss border. The main street, Kaiserstrasse, boasts some fine examples of 16th-, 17th- and 18th-century architecture.

Although it means crossing into Switzerland, there is one excursion from here that should not be missed, the **Rheinfalle** (Rhine Falls) just outside Schaffhausen on the other side of the border. Europe's most powerful waterfall thunders down at an average rate of 700cu m (25,000 cubic feet) per second in a dazzling mist of spray and sound.

*From Waldshut drive west for 26km (16 miles) on the **B34** to Bad Säckingen.*

Bad Säckingen, Baden-Württemberg

9 As the 'Bad' suggests, Bad Säckingen is another natural spa with thermal springs recommended for the treatment of rheumatic pains. Its unique feature, however, is a 200m (655-foot) long, 400 year-old wooden pedestrian bridge over the Rhine, which links Germany with Switzerland. How many people must have looked longingly across to the freedom of neutral Switzerland, especially during World War II. It is a memorable crossing between the two countries. A happier story made Bad Säckingen famous, the epic romance of a young trumpeter and the daughter of the local lord of the manor. The episode occurred over 300 years ago, but it earned Bad Säckingen the nickname 'The Trumpet Capital', and in **Schloss Schönau**, a little palace in town, the legend is celebrated by a trumpet museum.

Do not miss the **Fridolinmünster** (St Fridolin's), the basilica of the former **kloster** (abbey) founded in the 13th century. Its two spires can be seen from many parts of the town.

i Waldshuter Strasse 20

*Continue on the **B34**, then take the **B518** for 10km (6 miles) to Wehr.*

Wehr, Baden-Württemberg

10 Two former fortresses, both of them in ruins, can be found near Wehr. The first, **Werach**, was probably built in the early Middle Ages to house and protect refugees from other war-torn areas. There is a fine view across the southern Wehrtal (valley) from a pavilion erected above the foundations of the old watch tower. The other fortress, **Bärenfels**, dates back to the 12th and 13th centuries.

At the amazing subterranean caves, the **Haseler Tropfsteinhöhle**, located 4km (2½ miles) north of Wehr, there is an interesting and professional presentation of life inside a mountain over the centuries.

i Hauptstrasse 31

*Take the **B518** northwest to join the **B317**, then head west for 21km (13 miles) to Lörrach.*

Lörrach, Baden-Württemberg

11 Four kilometres (2½ miles) north of Lörrach, **Burg Rötteln** was destroyed by the French when they invaded the area towards the latter end of the 17th century. It was one of the largest fortresses in southwest

The old wooden bridge across the Rhein at Bad Säckingen

Germany, and the origins of the complex can be traced back to the 12th century, when it was the seat of the Nobles of Rötteln. You can still identify the basic layout of the fortress, including the main tower which is still standing, and also the Romanesque keep.

The **Heimatmuseum** provides information on the history of Burg Rötteln and of Lörrach, and there are exhibits concerning the lifestyles of people through the ages.

[i] Verkehrsbüro, Bahnhofsplatz 6

*From Lörrach drive 5km (3 miles) east on the **B317**, then turn sharp left at Steinen and head northwards for 20km (12½ miles) to Kandern.*

Kandern, Baden-Württemberg

12 Kandern is a pleasant holiday resort with a small, but perfectly formed baroque palace, **Schloss Bürgeln**. It offers superb views and also includes a museum. Near by, the old **Sausenberg** fortress was another victim of French artillery in 1678. However, its tower is still standing, and affords a panoramic view over neighbouring Switzerland.

[i] Verkehrsamt, Hauptstrasse 18

Drive north via the Kandertal, then turn left to Badenweiler, 19km (12 miles).

Badenweiler, Baden-Württemberg

13 The Romans were the first to appreciate the potential of Badenweiler, and they built a baths complex around the natural spring in the 1st century AD, during the reign of Emperor Vespasian. After the with-

Waldshut has some of the character of towns in nearby Switzerland

drawal of the Roman garrison the spa fell into obscurity until 1784, when the baths were rediscovered, and careful excavations have revealed a great deal about the highly civilised lifestyle. Badenweiler now offers all the modern facilities for those seeking a cure.

Apart from the Roman baths, another historic ruin occupies a place in the modern **Kurpark**, the **Burgruine**, a ruined fortress which once belonged to the Zähringer dynasty.

[i] Ernst-Eisenlohrstrasse 4

Continue west to Mullheim, then turn right in a northeasterly direction to Sulzburg, 14km (9 miles).

Sulzburg, Baden-Württemberg

14 Sulzburg is renowned for its **Kloster**, a convent in this case. None of the original buildings are still standing, save the **Klosterkirche** (abbey church) which dates back to AD1000. The important segments of the church have been preserved over the centuries and can still be admired. In 1980 the government of Baden-Württemberg opened a **mining museum** in Sulzburg, which portrays the history of mining in the province.

*Continue north to join the main road (**B3**) leading north, the 'Badische Weinstrasse'. Follow this through the Hexental (Valley of the Witches) to Freiburg, 17km (10½ miles).*

Freiburg im Breisgau – Furtwangen 53 (33)
Furtwangen – Triberg 17 (10½)
Triberg – Villingen 26 (16)
Villingen – Donaueschingen 17 (10½)
Donaueschingen – Titisee 28 (17)
Titisee – Todtnau 21 (13)
Todtnau – St Blasien 32 (20)
St Blasien – Waldshut 23 (14)
Waldshut – Bad Säckingen 26 (16)
Bad Säckingen – Wehr 10 (6)
Wehr – Lörrach 21 (13)
Lörrach – Kandern 20 (12½)
Kandern – Badenweiler 19 (12)
Badenweiler – Sulzburg 14 (9)
Sulzburg – Freiburg im Breisgau 17 (10½)

SPECIAL TO...

6 *Todtnau, Baden-Württemberg* At Todtnau-Aftersteg you can visit the **Handglashütte** where hand-blown glass is still being made in the time-honoured fashion, using processes that have remained the same for centuries.

RECOMMENDED WALKS

Numerous walks are available in the area and the local information offices can provide the necessary details and maps. Usually the paths outside villages are marked on tree trunks.

In Triberg you can take a walk up to the pilgrimage church of **Maria in der Tanne** (Our Lady Mary of the Fir Tree).

Make a short detour from Sulzburg to Staufen, then take a walk up the Schlossberg to see the imposing ruins of the 12th-century fortress.

3 days – 445km (275 miles)

SPAS & THE NORTHERN BLACK FOREST

Baden-Baden • Freudenstadt • Herrenberg • Stuttgart
Tübingen • Reutlingen • Lichtenstein • Hechingen
Balingen • Alpirsbach • Gutach • Gengenbach
Offenburg • Baden-Baden

Herrenberg: half-timbered houses. This modest town is overshadowed by its great Gothic church tower

Baden-Baden is one of Europe's top spas, and its double-barrelled name not only distinguishes it from other Badens (spas), but it also denotes that this is the Baden of the province of Baden.

The actual spa, known as the *Caracalla Therme*, after its Roman patron, is today a luxuriously appointed complex with several pools. To enjoy Baden-Baden visitors must not be in a hurry, rather have plenty of time to linger and savour the atmosphere. There is plenty to do if you are interested in art and music. The *Kunsthalle* (Art Gallery) in the Lichtentaler Allee, the *Stadtmuseum* and *Brahmsmuseum* in the centre of the town speak for themselves, and there are seasonal concerts and ballet performances as well as horse racing.

i Augustplatz 8

*From Baden-Baden take the **B500/B28** (Schwarzwald Hochstrasse) south for 60km (37 miles) to Freudenstadt.*

Freudenstadt, Baden-Württemberg

1 Founded by Duke Friedrich von Württemberg as a silver mining town in 1599, Freudenstadt was flattened by allied bombs in 1945. The large square in the centre of town was part of the original plans drawn up by the duke, whose chessboard layout allowed all the houses around it and those in adjoining streets behind to be interconnected by passages.

The **Stadthaus** and **Post Office** are situated on the Marktplatz (Market Square), and the Protestant **parish church** takes up one corner. An interesting feature is the L-shaped nave which segregates men and women attending the same service.

On the opposite corner of the square, the **Rathaus** (Town Hall) tower affords superb views over the unique layout of the town and the surrounding countryside. Back at street level, take the time for a stroll through the charming shopping arcades built into the houses surrounding the square.

i Promenadenplatz 1

*Take the **B28** northeast for 52km (32 miles) to Herrenberg.*

Herrenberg, Baden-Württemberg

2 Herrenberg lies on the western border of the **Naturpark Schönbuch** and the 750-year-old **Schlossbergturm** (Castle Tower) gives a good view of the whole town, dominated by the **Stiftskirche's** mighty tower. The Gothic church, which was built between 1275 and 1294, features a late Gothic font, a 16th-century carved pulpit and a heavily decorated choir section dating from 1517.

i Marktplatz 5

*Follow the **B14** northeast for 39km (24 miles) to Stuttgart.*

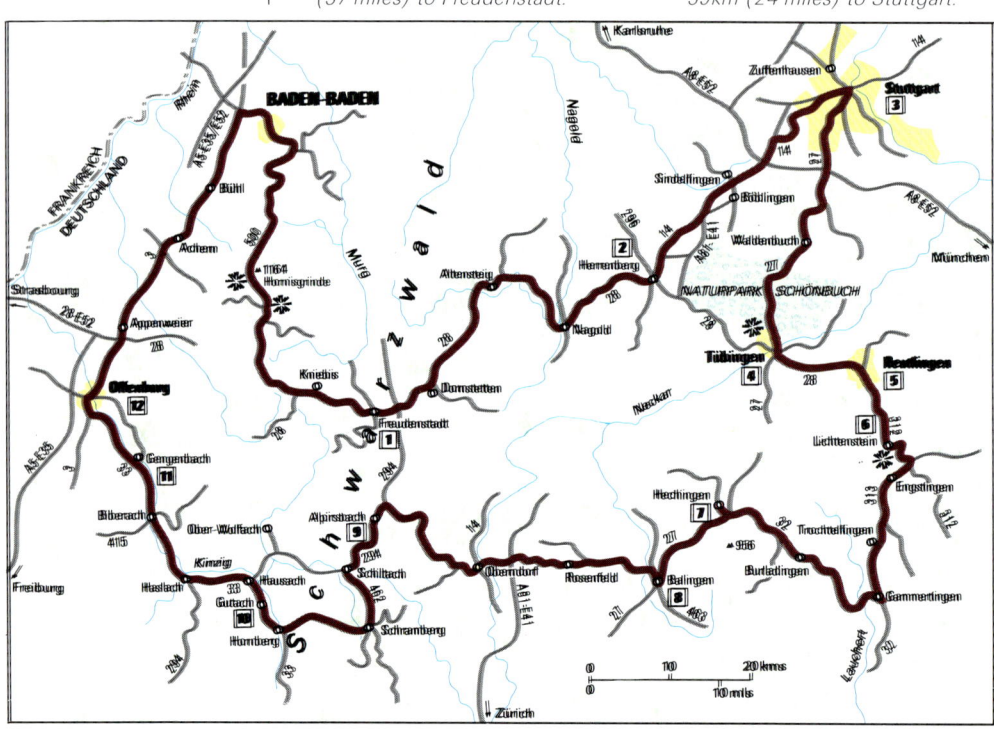

Stuttgart, Baden-Württemberg

3 Capital of the province of Baden-Württemberg, Stuttgart is situated at the bottom of a wide valley surrounded by hills, bordered to the northeast by the River Neckar and the adjoining town of Cannstatt.

Duke Liutolf set up a stud here in around 950. The town's name is derived from *Stute*, the German word for mare, and *Garten*, literally 'mare's garden'. The city's coat of arms bears a black horse.

The most impressive and important square in town is the **Schlossplatz** (Castle Square), across which the **Altes Schloss** (Old Castle) and the **Neues Schloss** (New Castle) face each other. The old castle is a massive Renaissance building, erected in the second half of the 16th century. The arcaded castle yard is particularly attractive and the castle houses the **Landesmuseum** collections of medieval art works, Württemberg's crown jewels, examples of historic costumes and archaeological finds. Adjoining the castle, **Schillerplatz** is notable for the historic buildings that surround it. There is the oldest church in Stuttgart, the **Stiftskirche**, which was founded in the 12th century; the **Fruchtkasten**, a wonderful medieval building of 1393; and the **Prinzenbau** (Dukes' Building), designed to contain the living quarters of the Erbprinz Friedrich Ludwig. At the centre of the square stands a monument to the poet Schiller.

Back on the Schlossplatz, the Neues Schloss was built along the lines of a French baroque castle between 1746 and 1807; it was all but destroyed in World War II. The façade was restored between 1959 and 1962, and the interior converted to house governmental offices as well as host receptions.

The west side of the Schlossplatz borders Stuttgart's main thoroughfare. A pedestrian zone, it is lined with all the best shops and businesses.

[i] Klett-Passage am Hauptbahnhof; Lautenschlagerstrasse 3

*From Stuttgart take the **B27** south, via Waldenbuch, to Tübingen, 40km (25 miles).*

Tübingen, Baden-Württemberg

4 There is a very good view of Tübingen's **Altstadt** (Old Town) from the Platanenallee on the right bank of the River Neckar. The Old Town rises steeply from the Neckar, sandwiched between the green knoll of the castle hill and the Osterberg's tower.

On **Holzmarkt** (Timber Market) the late Gothic **Stiftskirche** is a Protestant church dating from the 15th century. It houses several beautifully decorated tombs created for members of the House of Württemberg. When the great German poet Goethe visited the church, he was so impressed by the stained glass windows, he described them as 'items of supreme glory'.

The 15th-century **Rathaus** (Town Hall) is a really magnificent building on the market square. Its astronomical clock was added in 1511. The Neptune market fountain in front of the Rathaus was erected in 1615 and the whole market square is surrounded by marvellous medieval houses.

[i] an der Neckarbrücke (Eberhardsbrücke)

*Take the **B28** east for 13km (8 miles) to Reutlingen.*

Reutlingen, Baden-Württemberg

5 Reutlingen's **Tübinger Tor** (gate) is one of the old city gateways built in the 13th century. Its timber-framed upper storey was added in the 16th century to provide a better lookout and it somehow survived the great fire of 1726. Another landmark is the **Marienkirche**, a particularly beautiful

University students love to relax on Tübingen's quiet River Neckar

example of early Gothic style. The Holy Sepulchre in the choir section is late Gothic.

The main artery of the town is Wilhelmstrasse, a pedestrian precinct which is ideal for strolling along and admiring the interesting architecture. The **Nikolaikirche** overlooks a charming fountain erected by the tanners' and dyers' guild, while the mighty **Spendhaus**, built in 1518, now houses the town library and natural history museum.

[i] Listplatz 1

*From Reutlingen take the **B312** south for 12km (7 miles) to Lichtenstein.*

Lichtenstein, Baden-Württemberg

6 In the heart of the mountainous Swabian Jura, three villages joined together to form the town of Lichtenstein. In 1826, author Wilhelm Hauff published *Lichtenstein*, a novel about the town's old fortress which had been demolished in 1802. This novel inspired Count Wilhelm von Württemberg to make plans for a new castle to be built on the same spot,

---

FOR HISTORY BUFFS

5 *Reutlingen, Baden-Württemberg* Three beautiful 16th-century fountains can be admired in Reutlingen: the **Lindenbrunnen**, erected in 1544; the **Kirchbrunnen**, with a statue of Emperor Friedrich II, built in 1561; and the 1570 **Marktbrunnen**, adorned by a statue of Maximilian II.

SPECIAL TO...

3 *Stuttgart, Baden-Württemberg* A visit to the **Daimler Benz Museum** in Stuttgart-Untertürkheim is a must for motoring enthusiasts. Like Rolls and Royce, Daimler and Benz were – and the companies still are – pioneers in the development of motor vehicles. Exhibits range from the early days of motor transport right through to the most recent models, and modern demonstration techniques make this a fascinating visit.

Another famous manufacturer, **Porsche**, is based at Zuffenhausen, just north of Stuttgart. The business was started here in 1931, and all Porsche models are pure sports and high performance cars.

TOUR 20

General view of Herrenberg. The neighbouring Naturpark Schönbuch provides pleasant surroundings

SCENIC ROUTES

The **Schwarzwald Hochstrasse** (Black Forest High Road) from Baden-Baden to Freudenstadt skirts the rim of the hills and mountains and runs through magnificent scenery. There are numerous opportunities for scenic drives in the Black Forest region, not just on the Hochstrasse, but remember when planning a trip it can take rather longer to drive these winding roads than the actual distances would suggest.

RECOMMENDED WALKS

The Black Forest region is well organised and provides a staggering number of suggestions for walks, plus maps and information including the approximate duration of each route. Local information offices usually provide village maps and many offer to introduce visitors to the innovative **Wandern Ohne Gepäck** (hiking without luggage) concept. Certain villages and small hotels cooperate in the scheme by transporting your luggage from one stop to the next.

and so the present edifice took shape from 1840 to 1842. It looks like an image from a fairy tale and the design must have been influenced by Hauff's works.

Following a scramble up to the belvederes above the castle, there is an excellent detour to be made to the **Nebelhöhle** cave in nearby Unterhausen. The main part of the cave complex was discovered in 1920 and a 380m (1,246-foot) long walkway has been constructed for easy access. The view of the stalagmites and stalactites is superb and brilliantly enhanced by clever illuminations.

[i] Bürgermeisteramt, Rathausplatz 17

*From Lichtenstein take the **B313** south for 21km (13 miles) to Gammertingen, then the **B32** for 26km (16 miles) to Hechingen.*

Hechingen, Baden-Württemberg

7 From fairy tale castle to historic fortress, the imposing **Burg Hohenzollern**, seat of the kings of Prussia, perches on an 856m (2,808-foot) rocky outcrop. Plans for the old fortress were used for the new building, constructed between 1850 and 1867, but only the 15th-century Catholic **Chapel of St Michael** remains from the original site. The fortress treasury contains memorabilia of Friedrich der Grosse (the Great), decorations and insignia belonging to Wilhelm II, the crown of the Prussian kings and many works of art. On the **Schlossplatz** (Castle Square), the **Altes Schloss** (Old Castle), former seat of the dukes of Hechingen, now houses the local **Heimatmuseum**.

In 1976 the ruins of a Roman villa were discovered about 3km (1¾ miles) northwest of Hechingen. The excavated remains date back to the 1st to 3rd centuries AD and parts of the villa have been reconstructed.

[i] Marktplatz 1

*From Hechingen take the **B27** for 15km (9 miles) to Balingen.*

Balingen, Baden-Württemberg

8 Balingen's Protestant **parish church** is found in the market square. It was erected between 1443 and 1516, and the ceiling of the pulpit and the crucifix are the work of local sculptor Simon Schweitzer. Also of interest is the chapel in the cemetery which is decorated with late Gothic wall paintings. An attractive corner of town is the 'Little Venice' district, so named for the millstream which flows down past the old tanneries and remnants of the city wall.

The **Waagenmuseum** (Scales Museum) pays tribute to local priest M P Hahn, who invented a simple scale that could be used in the home, a precursor of the more modern appliances.

[i] Neue Strasse 33

From Balingen continue due west via Oberndorf for 46km (29 miles) to Alpirsbach.

Alpirsbach, Baden-Württemberg

9 The abbey church of the former Benedictine **Kloster Alpirsbach** dates back to the 12th century. The basilica, with its three naves, has undergone several enlargements and attempts at restoration, but has remained largely intact. South of the church are the cloister buildings where international orchestras perform in summer. The candlelit surroundings and excellent acoustics create an unforgettable atmosphere.

[i] Kurverwaltung, Haus des Gastes

*Take the **B294** south to Schiltach and continue on the **B462** to Schramberg. Turn right to Hornberg, then right again on the **B33** to Gutach, 39km (24 miles).*

Gutach, Baden-Württemberg

10 North of Gutach, sited on the Hausach road, the **Freilichtmuseum Vogtsbauernhof** is a fascinating open-air museum illustrating life in the Black Forest. Typical 16th- and 17th-century houses have been re-created with original furnishings and traditional artefacts and utensils to give the visitor a real insight into local lifestyles in former times. There are even old water-powered sawmills shown in full working order.

A monument to the 'Mourning Lady of Gutach' is a popular subject for snapshots. It portrays a grieving girl in front of a small rock, crying for those lost in the wars.

[i] Bürgermeisteramt

*Take the **B33** north, then west via Hausach for 29km (18 miles) to Gengenbach.*

Gengenbach, Baden-Württemberg

11 Gengenbach fulfils all ones expectations of a small, romantic German town. It has been placed under a preservation order and its timber-framed houses, gates and towers linked by sections of the old walls exude a timeless charm. There is a remarkable market place edged by the **Rathaus** (Town Hall) built in 1784, the **Kauf-und Kornhaus** of 1696 and numerous well-preserved 17th- to 18th-century patrician houses.

[i] Winzerhof

From Gengenbach continue northwest for 11km (7 miles) to Offenburg.

Offenburg, Baden-Württemberg

12 Offenburg lies on the outskirts of the Black Forest, between sloping vineyards and the plains of the Rhine Valley. The **Marktplatz** is the centre of the town, bordered by the **Rathaus** (Town Hall), which was rebuilt in 1741. Northwest of Marktplatz, the interior of the **Heilige Kreuzkirche** (Church of the Holy Cross) is dominated by an imposing high altar. Other historic sights include the **Fischmarkt** (Fish Market), **St Andreas' Kirche**, the **Löwenbrunnen** (Lion Fountain) and the **Hirschapotheke** (Pharmacy).

[i] Gärtnerstrasse 6 (west of Marktplatz)

*Return to Baden-Baden on the **B3**, 42km (26 miles).*

Baden-Baden – Freudenstadt **60 (37)**
Freudenstadt – Herrenberg **52 (32)**
Herrenberg – Stuttgart **39 (24)**
Stuttgart – Tübingen **40 (25)**
Tübingen – Reutlingen **13 (8)**
Reutlingen – Lichtenstein **12 (7)**
Lichtenstein – Hechingen **47 (29)**
Hechingen – Balingen **15 (9)**
Balingen – Alpirsbach **46 (29)**
Alpirsbach – Gutach **39 (24)**
Gutach – Gengenbach **29 (18)**
Gengenbach – Offenburg **11 (7)**
Offenburg – Baden-Baden **42 (26)**

Stuttgart: Schlossplatz with the huge baroque Neues Schloss

BACK TO NATURE

Almost anywhere in the Schwarzwald is a good habitat for birds. Look for woodpeckers, collared flycatchers, Bonelli's warblers and red kites. Plants include coralroot orchids and yellow wood violet.

FOR CHILDREN

12 Offenburg, Baden-Württemberg The **Europa Park** at **Rust** is one of the largest and most successful amusement parks in Europe. To get there, drive south from Offenburg on the **A5** in the direction of Lahr, then take the Ettenheim exit, or the **B3**, the Badische Weinstrasse, through the vineyards south to Ringshein and turn west to Rust. A trip on the suspended monorail around the grounds gives a good overall view of what is in store. Children will enjoy **Chocoland**, a so-called 'chocolate laboratory', where they can make their own chocolates. Other attractions include wild torrent rides, trips on the Swiss Bobsleigh, Acapulco 'death divers', high wire acts and dolphin and sealion performances.

THE FIVE RIVER VALLEYS

Rivers play an important part in this region, and the most prominent of all is the Rhine. Hilly woodlands and the lower lying vineyards put their pleasant mark on the countryside. This is the centre of the German wine growing area, and the famous labels of the Rhine and Mosel wines are internationally known by their distinctive flavour.

History has been made here since Roman times, but credit must be given to the Emperor Charlemagne who, in the 9th century, united the people of the former Roman provinces of Gaul and Germania and made Aachen (Aix-la-Chapelle) the capital of the Holy Roman Empire. Christianity then brought further cultural advancement and the most remarkable expressions of human creativity and effort may be seen in the magnificent cathedrals of this region.

Thanks to centuries of skirmishing and warring between medieval knights for power and wealth, the process that Charlemagne began at Aachen took 1,000 years to complete. One of the most famous aggressors of history, Napoleon Bonaparte, finally provided the impetus for the new empires of the 19th century.

The region has special appeal for those who want to be active on their vacation. There is an abundance of walks for serious hikers on offer, all well mapped out. The constant flow of the rivers provides the backdrop for tours here and visitors may choose to become part of the busy river traffic, or just enjoy it from afar. There is always something new round every bend in the mountain roads.

Nature also plays a big part in this area of Germany, with many nature parks and wild deer roaming about the forests. The evenings are something to look forward to, sitting on the banks of the Rhine or Mosel rivers watching the world go by, trying a sample of the delicious local produce. Touring in this part of Germany promises to be both interesting and enjoyable.

The former castle of Burg Stahleck at Bacharach, on the Rhine, is now a youth hostel

Tour 21
This tour starts in an area of large local coal deposits, but with a difference. Pleasant mountainous countryside and a zest for culture among the population make it a fascinating part of Germany. No wonder the French made several attempts to capture this area. The river has a deep green colour here, and it is all the more startling when one of the huge coal-carrying ships suddenly comes into view. A major cathedral town is visited and in the back yard of the church there is a familiar German wine label.

Tour 22
The starting point of this tour is difficult to leave as it is so full of historical interest. But a treat is in store – one of the most pleasant and enjoyable drives in Germany, right along the Mosel river and always surrounded by vineyards. An unconquered fortress offers an exciting visit until Koblenz is reached. Wine and the Rhine accompany the tour until it turns back into hiking country and the Mosel.

Tour 23
A world famous university town, Heidelberg, is at the start of this tour, but it then leaves the Neckar valley to take in some of the forests and attractive towns to the north. One of Germany's most treasured towns is next on the itinerary, saved from destruction under unusual circumstances. The tour then turns back to the long-awaited Neckar, with many pleasure boats plying up or downstream. Before returning there is a short interlude into the woods off the Neckar which provides an interesting diversion.

THE FIVE RIVER VALLEYS

Tour 24

Skyscrapers and finance put their stamp on the starting point of this tour. Then the route skirts along the 'Limes', the Roman border against the Germanic tribes. A famous spa and historic town in a beautiful setting are passed before the river is met again, further north. Ruins, castles and vineyards form the surroundings, and there are always ships on the Rhine. One of Germany's most elegant spas and a retreat from the business of the nearby financial world – Wiesbaden – is the last town before returning.

Tour 25

Perhaps the most magnificent of all Gothic churches was chosen to start this tour. Turning south, it takes in an eminent château and continues to what was once a sleepy little town on the Rhine, but made important through music and politics. The pleasant wooded countryside around make this a very attractive route to follow. Before returning to the start, the tour visits one of the oldest historical towns in Germany, the seat of the Holy Roman Empire chosen by Charlemagne.

Schwäbisch Hall is a treasury of fine medieval buildings, climbing steeply above the River Kocher

2/3 days – 438km (273 miles)

THE TRANQUIL SAAR VALLEY

Worms: part of the city wall. Home of emperors, Worms is prominent in legend and history

Saarbrücken • Merzig • Mettlach • Saarburg
Nonnweiler • Idar-Oberstein • Kaiserslautern • Worms
Bad Dürkheim • Neustadt-an-der-Weinstrasse
Pirmasens • Saarbrücken

Although Saarbrücken has a Celtic and Roman past, this 'bridge over the Saar' came into its own in the 19th century with the discovery and exploitation of its iron ore and coal deposits. *St Johann* is the hub of the town. The Catholic *basilica of St Johann* has been renovated over several centuries and the Protestant *Ludwigskirche* in Old Saarbrücken is an attractive baroque building. *Ludwigsplatz* is considered to be one of the finest of baroque squares, surrounded by palaces of the former aristocracy. The church was burned down during an air raid in 1944 but the outside has been painstakingly restored to its original design.

From the *Schlossplatz* walk to the *Alte Brücke* (old bridge) and stroll across to the other side of the river. Despite its industrial prestige, Saarbrücken has several theatres and museums as well as a school of music. There are also theatre and film festivals.

HISTORY BUFFS

5 *Idar-Oberstein, Rheinland-Pfalz* From Idar-Oberstein take the **B422** northwest to Katzenloch, then turn right to Kempfeld. Up on a rocky hill stands the ruin of the fortress **Wildenburg**, whose origins date back to the Celts. Parts have been reconstructed to demonstrate the original design.

[i] Rathausplatz

*From Saarbrücken take the **B51** northwest for 40km (25 miles) to Merzig.*

Merzig, Saarland

1 The **Stiftskirche** in Merzig can perhaps claim a record for the time it took to be built – started in the 12th century and only completely finished in the 19th. As a result it is a mixture of styles. Among the elaborate decorations inside is a crucifix from 1300, one of the best preserved items of this period. The **Rathaus** (town hall) was originally built between 1647 and 1650 as a hunting lodge for the Elector of Trier, but was remodelled several times to suit its new function.

[i] Zur Stadthalle 4

*From Merzig take the **B51** north for 5km (3¼ miles) to Mettlach.*

Mettlach, Saarland

2 Situated on the east side of the Saar river, Mettlach has many attractions. The former Benedictine **abbey**, built in the 18th century is in baroque style. Today it houses one of the largest ceramic factories in the world. Excavations around the building suggest an early Christian place of worship.

The modern town is dominated by ceramics and the **Keramische Museum** is housed in the restored **Schloss Ziegelberg**. One of the main attractions in the area is the **Saarschleife**, a loop in the Saar river, which can best be seen from the ruins of the **Burg** (fortress) **Montclair**, about 2km (1½ miles) west of Mettlach. The original fortress was built around the 9th century but existing remains are from a later 15th-century reconstruction. In the 16th century the fortress fell into gradual decay, and the rocks and cliffs now provide an ideal observation platform.

[i] Zum Grosswald 1

*From Mettlach continue north along the Saar via the **B51** for 21km (13 miles) to Saarburg.*

Saarburg, Rheinland-Pfalz

3 Saarburg is the centre for wine growing in the Saar valley. The town lies on both sides of the river and the Leukbach, a small stream with its noisy waterfall, flows through the middle. Marks on the houses still bear witness to the flooding of the Saar in former times.

Saarburg's other claim to fame is the casting of church bells, an industry here since the 17th century. The **foundry** is open to the public.

Also worth a visit are the ruins of the **Saarburg fortress** which gave the town its name, and the **church of St Marien** which has attracted many generations of pilgrims.

[i] Verkehrsamt, Graf-Siegfried Strasse 32

*From Saarburg take the **B407** east and turn right at Reinsfeld for the **B52** to Nonnweiler, 42km (26 miles).*

Nonnweiler, Saarland

4 Surrounded by woods, Nonnweiler prides itself on its healthy climate and offers many relaxing walks through the countryside, especially round its large man-made lake.

On the slopes of the **Dollberg** (mountain) in Otzenhausen, is the **Hunnenring**, a ringed wall up to 10m (33 feet) high in some places. It dates from the Celtic period and is estimated to be 2,000 years old.

[i] Rathaus, Kur-und Verkehrsamt, Trierstrasse 5

*Continue east to Nohfelden, turn right, then take the **B41** north to Idar-Oberstein.*

Idar-Oberstein, Rheinland-Pfalz

5 A most striking sight here is the **Felsenkirche** (church in the rock), built in a grotto in the rocks rising above the town. The church is in Gothic style and dates from 1482. A painted, winged altar of the 15th century has been incorporated into the building. Although it looks small when viewed from the Marktplatzbrücke, the church can hold 500 worshippers at a time.

The town is known for its precious stones and diamond industry. The **Deutsches Edelsteinmuseum** (precious stones museum) exhibits samples of precious stones found all over the world, in their raw and polished state. At the historic **Weiherschleife**, stones are polished in the old way, by water power – but this is more of a working museum. The industry now uses more modern methods. The **Heimatmuseum** also has interesting displays of raw materials, and fluorescent and precious stones.

Also recommended is a visit to the former copper mine at **Fischbach**, where green and turquoise coloured seams of copper contain deposits. The historic **Edelsteinmine** (precious stones mine) in the Steinkaulenberg is open to the public.

i Bahnhofstrasse 13

*From Idar-Oberstein continue on the **B41** northeast, then turn sharp right for the **B270** to Kaiserslautern, 62km (39 miles).*

Kaiserslautern, Rheinland-Pfalz

6 Kaiserslautern has great historic associations with the 12th-century Emperor, Friedrich Barbarossa (Redbeard). There are only a few remnants left of the old castle which are incorporated in the **Rathaus**. The **Stiftskirche** is an important church in early Gothic style and was built in the 13th and 14th centuries. An anteroom displays a monument erected in 1883 to commemorate the union of the Lutheran and Calvinist branches of Protestantism.

The **Fruchthalle**, formerly the fruit and vegetable market, was built in Renaissance style between 1843 and 1846 but now functions as a banqueting hall for official receptions. The **Pfalzgalerie** on the Museumplatz shows the work of local painters.

i Neues Rathaus

*From Kaiserslautern take the **B40** northeast to Marnheim, then turn right for the **B47** to Worms, 56km (35 miles).*

The old bridge still crosses the river in industrial Saarbrücken

---

SPECIAL TO...

5 *Idar-Oberstein, Rheinland-Pfalz* A well mapped-out circular route from Idar-Oberstein passes through a number of villages on the **Deutsche Edelsteinstrasse** (German Gems Road). There are about 60 traditional factories that transform raw stones from all over the world into gems. The sign of a cut diamond on the road shows directions to these places, and also denotes factories that can be visited. Lapidary seminars are offered and a master goldsmith arranges courses for those who wish to make their own jewellery.

TOUR 21

Balthasar Neumann's extravagant high altar in the Kaiserdom (imperial cathedral) in Worms

BACK TO NATURE

5 *Idar-Oberstein, Rheinland-Pfalz* Near Wildenburg is a memorable animal park with indigenous wildlife (deer, stags and wild boar). There are also enclosures housing animals from Asia and colourful birds (peacocks, wild geese, wild ducks and pheasants).

If you drive into the Idar mountains, be sure to keep your eyes open for birds such as red kites, sparrowhawks, hobbies, Bonelli's warblers and middle-spotted woodpeckers, which live in the forests, as do wild boar.

SCENIC ROUTES

The stretch from Merzig to Mettlach along the Saar river is very scenic. The following trips are also worth making: from Idar-Oberstein northwest into the Idar mountains, and a round trip taking the **B422** to Katzenloch, then northeast to Rhaunen, south to Kirn and back to Idar-Oberstein.

FOR CHILDREN

9 *Neustadt, Rheinland-Pfalz* Take the children to the **Hassloch Holiday Park**, about 9km (6 miles) east of Neustadt. Apart from the usual fun runs there are several special shows for entertainment: the waterski show, 'The Treasure of the Seven Seas', 'The Wonders of Radscha' and the 'Sun Tseng Hai Show'.

Worms, Rheinland-Pfalz

7 The curiously-named Worms is one of the oldest towns in Germany. Religion has played an important part in its turbulent history, and the number of churches testify to that. There was a bishopric here from the 4th century. The **Dom of St Peter and St Paul** is a Catholic cathedral known to be one of the finest constructions in late Romanesque style in the Rheinland. The high altar is by the famous Balthasar Neumann, and the late Gothic sandstone reliefs from the demolished cloisters are also worth noting. The Gothic **Liebfrauenkirche** (Church of Our Lady) stands amongst vineyards which produce the famous wine called Liebfraumilch. There is a monument to Luther on the Lutherplatz.

[i] Neumarkt 14

*From Worms join the **A61** west of town, drive due south to the exit west of Ludwigshafen and follow the **B37** via Maxdorf to the **B271** and Bad Dürkheim, 33km (20½ miles).*

Bad Dürkheim, Rheinland-Pfalz

8 This officially designated spa is in the middle of a major wine producing region. The warm spa waters are used to cure a variety of ailments. There is also a casino for those seeking financial cures.

The ruin of the **Kloster Limburg** was bought by the council in 1847 and the gardens were developed in the English style. Concerts and open-air performances take place here in the summer.

For those who enjoy wandering round ruins, try the **Burgruine Hardenburg**, 4km (2½ miles) west of the town. This building was first mentioned in 1093, but met with misfortune later. In 1692 it was blown up, and in 1794 burnt down.

[i] Mannheimer Strasse 24

*Continue south on the **B271** for 16km (10 miles) to Neustadt.*

Neustadt, Rheinland-Pfalz

9 The town's full name is Neustadt-an-der-Weinstrasse (Neustadt-on-the-wine-road), which gives a hint as to the major activity around here. As the centre of the largest German wine growing area, the town is also called the 'Wine Capital'. The centre has well-preserved houses with old interior courtyards. The **Stiftskirche** is 600 years old and still has the town watchman's apartment in the southern tower, occupied until only a few years ago. The church claims to have the largest church bell in the world, which is housed in the tower.

The **Hambacher Schloss** is noted for a meeting on 27 May, 1832, when 25,000 democratically orientated people supported a call from 34 citizens of Neustadt to demand German unity. It was here that the black, red and gold flag as a symbol of a united Germany was hoisted for the first time.

[i] Exterstrasse

*From Neustadt take the **B38** south towards Landau, then turn right for the **B10** west to Pirmasens, 58km (36 miles).*

TOUR 21

Pirmasens, Rheinland-Pfalz

10 The lively town centre is built around the wide **Schlossplatz** (castle square) which forms a well-designed pedestrian precinct. Shoe manufacture is the major industry here – the German college for shoe manufacture is also housed here.

Nearly all the historic buildings in the town were destroyed during World War II. Of interest, however, are the attractive dual staircases, the so-called **Ramba-Treppen**, which have water cascading down between them.

The Ramba-Treppen in Germany's footwear capital, Pirmasens

[i] Dankelsbachstrasse 19

*Take the **B10**, then the **B423** to Homburg. Turn left and return on the **B40** west to Saarbrücken, 65km (40 miles).*

Saarbrücken – Merzig **40 (25)**
Merzig – Mettlach **5 (3½)**
Mettlach – Saarburg **21 (13)**
Saarburg – Nonnweiler **42 (26)**
Nonnweiler – Idar-Oberstein **40 (25)**
Idar-Oberstein – Kaiserslautern **62 (39)**
Kaiserslautern – Worms **56 (35)**
Worms – Bad Dürkheim **33 (20½)**
Bad Dürkheim – Neustadt **16 (10)**
Neustadt – Pirmasens **58 (36)**
Pirmasens – Saarbrücken **65 (40)**

RECOMMENDED WALKS

9 Neustadt, Rheinland-Pfalz
There are pleasant walks to be had just off the **Deutsche Weinstrasse** (German Wine Road).

Stop at Annweiler, about halfway between Neustadt and Pirmasens and walk up to fortress **Trifels**, about 1km (½ mile). Here visitors can see the dungeon where King Richard the Lionheart of England was imprisoned in 1193. He was finally released after a huge ransom had been paid.

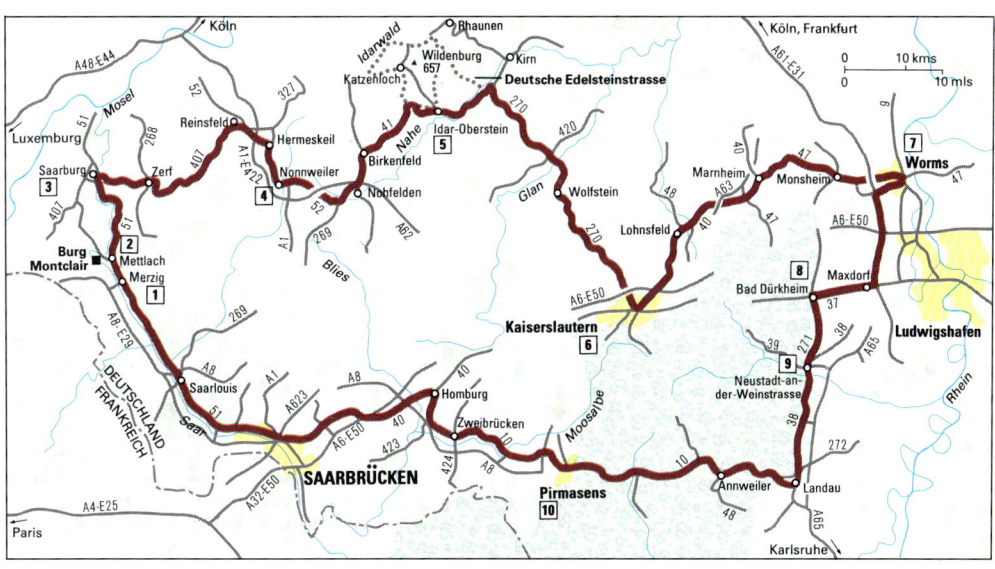

2/3 days – 432km (267 miles)

THE ENCHANTING MOSEL VALLEY

Trier • Bernkastel-Kues • Traben-Trarbach • Cochem
Burg Eltz • Koblenz • Boppard • St Goar • Bingen
Bad Kreuznach • Trier

Long before Rome was founded – legend says around 2050BC – there was a settlement at Trier. The city blossomed under the Romans, but throughout history it has been repeatedly destroyed by invading vandals. Despite such a turbulent past, Trier is one of the most remarkable cities in Europe. The Roman legacy is still in evidence – one of their city gates, the *Porta Nigra*, has been made the local emblem, a tribute to survival. The gate was actually a double one, and an inner courtyard enabled defenders to pour down molten lead on intruders in the approved fashion of the times. The 11th-century archbishop Poppa roofed over this courtyard, and created two churches in the Porta Nigra. Napoleon was responsible for the removal of most of the post-Roman additions to the gate.

The Constantine *Basilica*, large even by today's standards, is another Roman structure worth visiting, along with the baths and the amphitheatre, which had room for 25,000 spectators. The *Dom* (cathedral), dating from the 11th century, is built on the site of a Roman basilica.

SPECIAL TO...

1 *Bernkastel-Kues, Rheinland-Pfalz* En route from Bernkastel-Kues to Traben-Trarbach, branch off after crossing the Mosel past Zeltingen and drive for about 11km (6½ miles) to **Wittlich**. Every year in mid-August the town celebrates a festival called the **Saubrenner-Kirmes** (festival of the burnt sows). The story goes that one evening, when the town was under attack, the gatekeeper could not find the bolt to lock up the gate so he used a turnip in its place. A sow looking for food ate the turnip and thus opened the gate for the conquerors. As punishment, the citizens drove all the pigs to the marketplace and burnt them.

[i] An der Porta Nigra

*From Trier join the **B53** northeast for 60km (37½ miles) to Bernkastel-Kues.*

Bernkastel-Kues, Rheinland-Pfalz

1 The square of this picturesque town is surrounded by timber-framed houses, with the fountain of St Michael in its centre, and the **Rathaus** (town hall) which was built in 1608. Fascinating but not quite so picturesque are the iron chains of the **Pranger** (stocks), the public punishment of the Middle Ages, preserved here. The **parish church of St Michael** dates from the 14th century and contains interesting works by a local sculptor, H R Hoffman. Bernkastel-Kues has a **wine museum** and the Bernkastler wine is well-known.

South of Bernkastel stands the ruin of the **Landshut**, the second fortress to be built on the same site, in 1280.

[i] Gestade 5

*Continue on the **B53** for 26km (16 miles) to Traben-Trarbach.*

Grapes for the aromatic Mosel wine

Traben-Trarbach, Rheinland-Pfalz

2 A trip to the ruins of the fortress **Grevenburg** above Traben-Trarbach offers rewarding views over the town and the picturesque Mosel valley. Between the years 1520 and 1734 the fortress was besieged six times and then blown up, so it is small wonder that only a fragment of a wall with window holes is left.

The little town of **Zell**, on the other side of the river, should not be missed. It appears to be built into the landscape with vineyards all around it. The castle is open to visitors. Emperor Maximilian lived here at one time and it contains many treasures. Zeller Schwarze Katz (black cat) is a popular wine from the local grapes.

[i] Bahnstrasse 22

*Continue on the **B53**, then the **B49** for 52km (32 miles) to Cochem.*

Cochem, Rheinland-Pfalz

3 A real centre for tourism in the Mosel valley is Cochem, which also lies in an important wine-growing area. The former Reichsburg, now the **Burg** (castle), was rebuilt in 1874, using plans from 1576. It affords splendid views over the Mosel valley and its vineyards, which stretch from the river's edge up into the hills.

[i] Enderplatz

*From Cochem continue on the **B49/B416** and turn left at Moselkern for Burg Eltz.*

Bernkastel, backed by vineyards

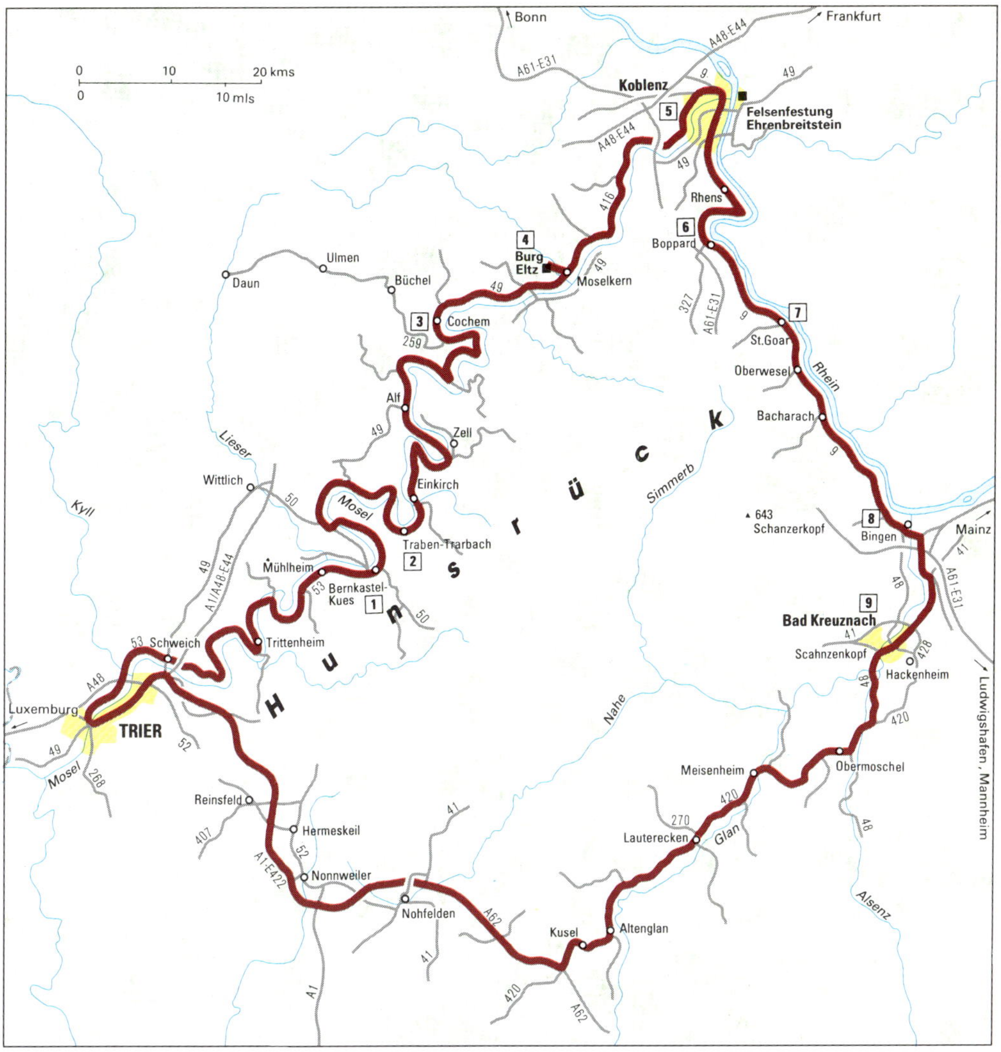

TOUR 22

FOR HISTORY BUFFS

1 *Bernkastel-Kues, Rheinland-Pfalz* **St Nikolaus-Hospital** in Kues dates back to a donation in 1447 by the scientist and philosopher Cardinal Nikolaus Krebs. He dedicated the hospital to 33 poor men of the village. He died in 1465 and in the hospital chapel lies his tombstone. Of special interest in the chapel are the high altar paintings which show the *Passion of Christ* and are the work of an artist from Cologne.

BACK TO NATURE

3 *Cochem, Rheinland-Pfalz* Take the **B259** south of Cochem uphill via Buchel to Ulmen for 21km (13 miles) and turn left for the **B257** to Daun. The area around Daun is called the **Vulkaneifel** (Volcanic Eifel) after the Eifel mountain range. The craters hereabouts were formed 10,000 years ago and have since filled with water. They are located south of Daun and are called **Maar**. Their depths range from 38 to 74m (75 to 242 feet) and some offer bathing, boat-hire and fishing. In some places you can still see bubbles of gas rising from the bottom of the craters.

Burg Eltz, Rheinland-Pfalz

4 High above the wine producing village of Moselkern stands the burg or fortress of Eltz, one of the most rewarding attractions in the area. Numerous oriels and towers and a superb position made this fortress unconquerable for centuries. Now, even cars find the ascent difficult. The road stops at the **Antonius chapel** and the last few hundred metres have to be covered on foot or by shuttle bus.

The knights of Eltz were called the Eisenköpfe (iron heads), a tribute to their stubborness as well as to the numerous skirmishes in which they took part. The guided tour around the fortress is accompanied by many entertaining stories and anecdotes.

i Moselkern: Heimat and Verkehrsverein

*From Burg Eltz return to Moselkern, then turn left on the **B416** for 35km (22 miles) to Koblenz.*

Koblenz, Rheinland-Pfalz

5 Where the Mosel enters the mighty Rhine lies Koblenz (Coblence). Its unique situation has made it a place of great importance from Roman times. Koblenz' name is derived from the Roman *castrum ad confluentes*, the 'camp at the confluence'. It is not known when the Romans actually began their outpost here, but it must have been before the reign of Emperor Tiberius (AD14–37).

After almost total wartime destruction, part of the old centre of Koblenz has been meticulously restored. The actual point of land where the Mosel and Rhine meets is called the **Deutsches Eck** (German Corner), marked by a monument to German unity.

The **Felsenfestung Ehrenbreitstein** (rock fortress) dominates the Rhine and Mosel and is supposedly the largest fortress in Europe. It is best reached by chair-lift. The view from the fortress' terrace is spectacular, down to Koblenz and in the distance to the Eifel and Hunsrück mountain ranges. The fortress was always a thorn in the flesh of the French and Napoleon destroyed it in 1801. It was subsequently rebuilt, but a clause in the Treaty of Versailles after World War I stated it must never again be used for military purposes. It now houses the **Rhine Museum**.

The former **Kurfürstliches Schloss** or Residenzschloss as it is also known, was once the seat of Prince Wilhelm von Preussen and until 1918 it was owned by the Prussian kings. It now belongs to the state and is used for administrative purposes.

Burg Stolzenfels, built in 1242, is a former royal castle now open to the public. It was destroyed by the French in 1688 and rebuilt after 1836. Its interior is worth seeing, especially the large **Rittersaal** (Knights' Hall) and the King's quarters.

i Pavillon am Hauptbahnhof

*From Koblenz take the **B9** south for 22km (13½ miles) to Boppard.*

Boppard is a popular start-point for round trips on the Rhine

SCENIC ROUTES

The drive from Trier through the Mosel valley is an enjoyable one but bear in mind that the many twists and turns of the road should dictate a careful speed. Allow ample time for the bends, but also stop to enjoy the views. The route from Koblenz to Bingen along the Rhine valley is full of dramatic scenery.

Boppard, Rheinland-Pfalz

6 At a bend in the Rhine lies Boppard, a very old settlement which the Celts called *Bandobriga*. Later the Romans erected fortifications here around AD400 and parts of the 8m (26-foot) high walls can still be seen. **St Severuskirche** (church of St Severus) is late Romanesque. The **Karmeliterkirche** is interesting; it has no tower which is very rare for a Gothic church. The **Alte Burg** (old castle), dating from the 14th century, now houses the local **Heimatmuseum**.

[i] Karmeliterstrasse 2

*Continue south on the **B9** for 15km (9 miles) to St Goar.*

St Goar, Rheinland-Pfalz

7 In the Middle Ages, many knights living in fortresses on narrow stretches of river supplemented their incomes by collecting tolls from passing ships – or just simply robbing them. They were the so-called **Raubritter** (robbing knights). One such fortress was 13th-century **Burg Rheinfels**, just before St Goar. This former royal castle is now open to the public.

The **Stiftskirche** in St Goar is a delightful mixture of styles. The church itself is 15th-century, the crypt is Romanesque and the marble tombs are from the 16th and 17th centuries.

[i] Heerstrasse 120

*From St Goar continue south on the **B9** for 34km (21 miles) to Bingen.*

Bingen, Rheinland-Pfalz

8 The Burg Klopp fortress which overlooks Bingen, was built on a Roman site with a deep well of 52m (170 feet), which probably goes back to the same period. The fortress was destroyed in 1689, and the remnants blown up in 1711, but between 1875 and 1879, it was totally rebuilt. The town has an interesting **museum** which contains prehistoric exhibits.

The pretty Rhine town of Bacharach lies downriver from Bingen

On an island in the river stands the **Mäuseturm** (Mice Tower). This stone construction dates from 1208 and replaced a wooden Roman tower erected in 8BC under the Roman military leader Drusus. Legend has it that when Bishop Hatto was thrown into the tower as a punishment for his cruelties, he was eaten alive by mice.

[i] Rheinkai 21

*From Bingen, continue due south on the **B9** for 13km (8 miles) to Bad Kreuznach.*

Bad Kreuznach, Rheinland-Pfalz

9 This sizeable spa lies on the River Nahe, and its thermal springs are used as the basis for well-organised treatments for rheumatism, gout and similar ailments. A unique feature in the town are the well-preserved **Brückenhäuser** (bridge houses). These date from the 15th century, and have been chosen as the town emblem. In the **Römerhalle Museum**, Roman mosaics and remains from the military camp are on view.

[i] Kur-und Salinenebetriebe, Kurfurstliches 23

*From Bad Kreuznach take the **B48**, then the **B420** south to Kusel. Join the **A62** and travel northwest towards Nonnweiler. Continue on the **A1/E422** north to exit Moseltal, then southwest to Trier on the **A602/B49**, 155km (96 miles).*

Trier – Bernkastel-Kues **60 (37½)**
Bernkastel-Kues – Traben-Trarbach **26 (16)**
Traben-Trarbach – Cochem **52 (32)**
Cochem – Burg Eltz **20 (12)**
Burg Eltz – Koblenz **35 (22)**
Koblenz – Boppard **22 (13½)**
Boppard – St Goar **15 (9)**
St Goar – Bingen **34 (21)**
Bingen – Bad Kreuznach **13 (8)**
Bad Kreuznach – Trier **155 (96)**

RECOMMENDED WALKS

9 *Bad Kreuznach, Rheinland-Pfalz* Drive to one of the **Wanderparkplätze**, car parks usually marked with a green 'W' and the starting point for a hike. From the Rotenfels car park there is a good brisk walk up to the Schanzenkopf.

After a short drive to Hackenheim, walk to the nearby recreation area of **Schloss Rheingrafenstein**.

FOR CHILDREN

Trier, Rheinland-Pfalz The **Museum of Toys** in the Nagelstrasse in Trier should amuse children, and probably arouse childhood nostalgia in adults too. Three floors contain a selection which includes metal toys, model railways, dolls' houses, cuddly toys and rocking horses.

THE ROMANTIC NECKAR

2 days – 417km (260 miles)

Heidelberg • Bensheim • Michelstadt • Miltenberg
Wertheim • Tauberbischofsheim • Bad Mergentheim
Rothenburg ob der Tauber • Schwäbisch Hall
Heilbronn • Heidelberg

Heidelberg is a charming and picturesque town. It is also ancient. 'Heidelberg Man', evidence of the earliest human life in Europe, is in fact a 500,000-year-old jawbone found near here.

More recently, Heidelberg was completely rebuilt in the 17th-century baroque style after Louis XIV all but destroyed the province. Visitors first approaching Heidelberg will immediately notice the ruined *Schloss* (castle), which was built in the typical local red Neckar sandstone over several centuries. In the cellars is the *Heidelberger Fass* (barrel), which was built in 1751 and holds over 220,000 litres (49,000 gallons).

The *Hexenturm* (witches' tower) is the only remnant of the 13th-century city wall. Heidelberg has an old tradition of printing and publishing and the university library has a collection of original manuscripts, documents and prints on show.

FOR HISTORY BUFFS

2 *Michelstadt, Hessen* Southeast of Michelstadt, in the village of **Würzberg**, remnants of two **Roman towers** can be seen and also an excavated Roman bath, now surrounded by woods.

FOR CHILDREN

2 *Michelstadt, Hessen* Take the children to see the **Spielzeugmuseum** in Michelstadt. Dolls' houses and toys from France and Mexico are on display, together with model farms, railways and dolls of all sizes.

[i] Am Hauptbahnhof

From Heidelberg take the B3 north for 33km (20 miles) to Bensheim.

Bensheim, Hessen

1 About 5km (3 miles) from the town, the former fortress **Auerbacher Schloss** is protected by an encircling wall and two high watch towers. Although the fortress is now really only a well-preserved ruin, it is a very popular spot in the area. Built in the 13th century on the slopes of the **Schlossberg** (castle mountain), it could at that time only be entered by drawbridge. It is now used as a state sanatorium for miners.
Landgrave Count Ludwig erected a small manor house, called the **Schlösschen**, near mineral springs between 1790 and 1795, and in the garden stands possibly the highest Mammut tree in Europe, 53m (173 feet) high and 5m (16 feet) thick.

[i] Beauner Platz

From Bensheim take the B47 northeast for 46km (29 miles) to Michelstadt.

The great castle of the Teutonic Knights at Bad Mergentheim

Michelstadt, Hessen

2 There are delightful medieval timber-framed buildings here, none so delightful as the fine **Rathaus** (town hall), built in 1484. Its two upper storeys are supported by columns, creating an open space at ground level. The second floor is built high into the roof, and two spires on oriels provide an attractive front. The **parish church** behind the Rathaus is in Gothic style and was built in the 15th to 16th centuries with a mighty elongated steeple. The Carolingian **Einhartbasilika** is interesting as it is a rare and well-preserved building dating from the 9th century.

[i] Marktplatz 1

Take the B47 east, turn north on the B469 towards the Main river near Weilbach, then turn sharp right to Miltenberg, 27km (17 miles).

Miltenberg, Bayern

3 A stop at **Amorbach** is worthwhile to see the **abbey church** and its organ. It has 5,000 pipes and 63 registers and is said to be the largest baroque organ in Europe.
In Miltenberg the market place exudes the unspoilt medieval atmosphere of the town. It is called the **Stadt in Holz** (town in timber) because of the well-preserved timber-framed houses which line the main street. The **Haus zum Riesen** (house of the giant) dates back to the 12th century. It was altered in 1590 and is supposed to be the oldest country inn in Germany. Boat trips on the River Main are available – and make a relaxing way to enjoy this pleasant area.

[i] Engelplatz 69

From Miltenberg drive north along the River Main for 32km (20 miles) to Wertheim.

Wertheim, Baden-Württemberg

4 Wertheim has retained the character of an old Franconian town. Tiny passageways between the timber-framed houses and many historic buildings all contribute to the charm of this old small town, which lies at the confluence of two rivers, the Main and the Tauber. In the market square are the **Engelsbrunnen** (angel's well) and the **Zobelhaus**, the narrowest house in the town. High above is the **Burg**, a ruined fortress which provides visitors with fine views over the old town.

[i] Fremdenverkehrsgesellschaft, Am Spitzen Turm

Drive south along the Tauber river, then south to Tauberbischofsheim, 31km (19 miles).

Tauberbischofsheim, Baden-Württemberg

5 The **Kurmainzisches Schloss** is a very attractive castle, completed in the 15th and 16th centuries. Uniquely asymmetrical and made up of separate units, it resembles a village rather more than a castle. The **Türmersturm** is a massive round tower of 13th-

Romantic Heidelberg, one of Germany's top tourist spots

century origin which gives superb views of the village below.

The **parish church of St Martin** was built in 1910 and displays work from the art school of the famous sculptor and woodcarver, Tilman Riemenschneider. Picturesque timber-framed houses in the **Hauptstrasse** (main street) and on the market square make for a relaxing and pleasant atmosphere.

[i] Verkehrsamt, Marktplatz 8

*Continue south on the **B290** for 17km (11 miles) to Bad Mergentheim.*

Bad Mergentheim, Baden-Württemberg

6 On the Deutschordensplatz stands the castle of the Order of the Teutonic Knights. It was the residence of the Grand Master from 1525 to 1809, when the order was dissolved. The buildings now standing were erected between 1565 and 1570. Today, part of the castle is a **museum** dedicated to the order, and in the castle's church are the tombs of former members.

The market square is dominated by the gabled **Rathaus** (town hall) which was built in 1564. In the middle of the square stands a fountain with a monument to Wolfgang Schutzbar, one of the members of the Order of Teutonic Knights, holding a flag and a shield.

In 1826 a shepherd discovered the natural springs which now offer cures for internal health problems.

[i] Marktplatz 3

*Leave Bad Mergentheim on the **B19** east to Igersheim. Turn right and continue east along the Tauber on the **Romantische Strasse** (Romantic Road) to Rothenburg, 48km (30 miles).*

Rothenburg ob der Tauber, Bayern

7 Few towns in Germany have been able to preserve their history and beauty as well as Rothenburg. It seems only once to have been in major trouble. This was in 1631 during the Thirty Years' War when the Imperial troops under General Tilly were about to destroy the conquered

BACK TO NATURE

2 *Michelstadt, Hessen* South of the village of Würzberg, near Michelstadt, visitors can watch the feeding of boar, which are kept in an enclosure in the woods. If you take a walk in the woods locally, you may also come across them living wild. Although normally shy – they are hunted – sows and families of striped piglets are occasionally seen by quiet strollers.

TOUR 23

SPECIAL TO...

8 *Schwäbisch Hall, Baden-Württemberg* Every year at Whitsun Schwäbisch Hall celebrates the town's saltmakers traditional **Kuchen- und Brunnenfest** (cake and fountain festival). Salt manufacturing here dates back to Celtic times and the town flourished as salt was a valuable commodity then.

SCENIC ROUTES

The following routes are especially noted for their scenic beauty, and will be enjoyed by visitors: from Bensheim through the nature park to Michelstadt, then on the Nibelungenstrasse to Miltenberg; from Wertheim along the Tauber valley to Tauberbischofsheim; and from Heilbronn through the Neckar valley.

town. But a brave ex-Mayor, Nusch, won a bet with the General by drinking 3¼ litres (5¾ pints) of wine in one go and thus saved the town. This occasion is commemorated in the centre of the town, where the former **Ratstrinkstube** (councillors' tavern), built in 1446, houses the clock which reminds the citizens and visitors of Nusch. The **Rathaus** is next door and shows an interesting combination of two main styles, older Gothic (between 1250 and 1400) and the later Renaissance, which includes the oriel. The view from the top of the tower is especially rewarding because of the attractive buildings in the town and the gentle Tauber valley beyond.

St Jacob's Kirche, a Gothic structure started in 1373, is worth visiting for its wonderful 'sacred blood' altar by Tilman Riemenschneider and some good stained glass. The old **Wehrgang** (watch path) is a passageway along the old city walls which

Part of Rothenburg's magnificently preserved medieval town walls

provides an interesting walk. The **Weisser Turm** (white tower), **Markusturm** and **Röderbogen** (Röder's arch) are all parts of the first city wall from the 12th century and are still standing. The **Klingenbastei** is also a covered walkway within the fortifications, dating back to 1587. The square tower once served as a water-tower. In the Burggasse there is a medieval **criminal museum** offering a grim insight into the processes of law and punishment in the Middle Ages. The fortifications encircle the **Burggarten**, a relaxing park entered by the **Burgtor**, a fortified medieval gate.

[i] Marktplatz 3

Drive southwest on the **Burgenstrasse** *(Castle Road) via Langenburg to Schwäbisch Hall, 50km (31 miles).*

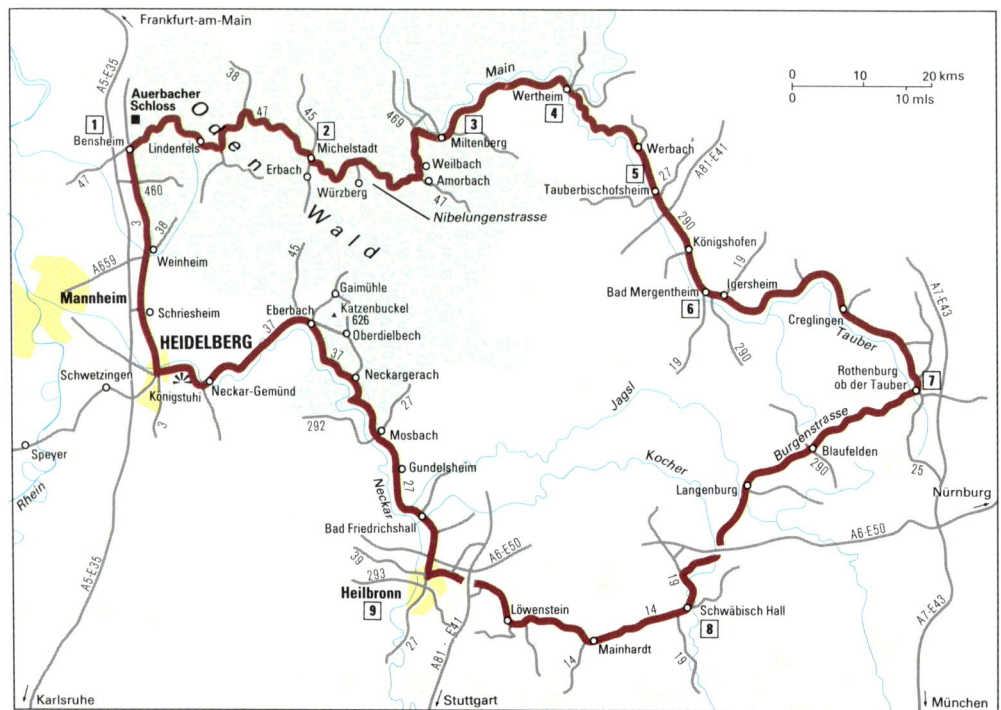

Schwäbisch Hall, Baden-Württemberg

8 The impressive **Benediktinerkloster Comburg** (Benedictine abbey) dominates the town. The prosperity, as well as the origins of its name, derived from salt. In medieval times salt was often used instead of money, and its merchants inevitably became prosperous. The medieval market place of this former Free Imperial City is claimed to be one of the most picturesque in Germany. It is surrounded by **St Michael's Church** and the baroque **Rathaus**. In the middle stands the **Fischbrunnen** (fish fountain) and the **pranger** (stocks).

Originally a fortress, Comburg was transformed into a **Kloster** (abbey) of the Order of St Benedict in 1079. The surrounding wall with the watch towers makes this complex resemble a fortified castle rather than an abbey. It is now a teachers' training college. Features of note inside include a Romanesque chandelier in the abbey church. This is called the **Radleuchter** (wheel-shaped chandelier), made of iron, copperplated and then gilded. It was made in 1130.

[i] Am Markt 9

Take the B14 then the B39 west for 51km (32 miles) to Heilbronn.

Heilbronn, Baden-Württemberg

9 Heilbronn is a very busy town which relies heavily on river traffic for commercial and leisure purposes. Wine is also an important product of the region. Unfortunately the old town was destroyed in 1944.

Schwäbisch Hall. The name means 'Swabian Place of Salt'

In the **Marktplatz** (market square) stands the **Rathaus**, which was constructed in Renaissance style and has a beautiful astronomical clock. Try to see the clock when it shows multiples of 4 (04.00, 08.00, 12.00, 16.00 etc) – it comes alive with a wonderful display of carved figures. The Gothic **St Kiliankirche** dates from the 13th century and has a remarkable 62m (203-foot) high tower, completed in 1529. The church has been selected as the emblem of the town. Opposite the church is the **well** (brunnen) which gave the town its name.

Before returning to Heidelberg, go north on the B27 then the B37, following the Neckar to **Speyer**, 82km (51 miles). Eight emperors and three empresses have been buried here in the majestic and inspiring **cathedral**, founded in AD1030. It is basically a Romanesque basilica, despite many alterations over the centuries, with four square-shaped towers and two domes. The **Krypta** (crypt), impressive in itself, provides the entrance to the tombs. The tomb of Rudolf von Habsburg, who died in 1291, is of special note.

[i] Rathaus, Verkehrsamt, Marktplatz, Heilbronn

Return to Heidelberg, 82km (51 miles).

Heidelberg – Bensheim 33 (20)
Bensheim – Michelstadt 46 (29)
Michelstadt – Miltenberg 27 (17)
Miltenberg – Wertheim 32 (20)
Wertheim – Tauberbischofsheim 31 (19)
Tauberbischofsheim – Bad Mergentheim 17 (11)
Bad Mergentheim – Rothenburg 48 (30)
Rothenburg – Schwäbisch Hall 50 (31)
Schwäbisch Hall – Heilbronn 51 (32)
Heilbronn – Heidelberg 82 (51)

RECOMMENDED WALKS

9 *Heilbronn, Baden-Württemberg* En route from Heilbronn to Heidelberg stop at **Neckargerach**, from where there is a remarkable walk through the **Margaretenschlucht** ravine. Also of interest is the **Gickels-Felsen** rock near by.

Turn right at Eberbach in the Neckar valley (en route to Heidelberg) for **Gaimühle**, then right again for **Waldkatzenbach**. Walk up to the **Katzenbuckel** mountain and enjoy the view from the observation tower. Return to Eberbach via Oberdielbach.

2 days – 393km (245 miles)

THE RIVER MAIN & EAST OF THE RHINE

Frankfurt-Am-Main • Hanau • Bad Homburg • Kronberg
Limburg • Königswinter • Bad Honnef • Lahnstein
St Goarshausen • Assmannshausen • Rüdesheim • Mainz
Wiesbaden • Frankfurt

Heavily bombed during the war, Frankfurt chose not to spend much on restoring old buildings, but instead to create an ultra-modern city, functional and efficient. The centre of Frankfurt is, however, a restored baroque-style building, the *Hauptwache*, once used to house the city's guards. Other old buildings include the *Römer*, founded in 1405, which has a medieval courtyard. Facing the Römer stands the *Justizbrunnen* (fountain of justice). A statue of the goddess Justicia, holding her scales, looks down towards the old town hall.

The great German poet, Goethe, was born here, and his house is open to the public. The *Eschenheimer Turm* (tower), built between 1426 and 1428, is one of the largest medieval defences. The *Dom* (cathedral) *of St Bartholomaus* was started here in 1290, and from 1562 the Holy Roman Emperors were crowned here.

The easy way up to the ruined Drachenfels fortress

[i] Im Hauptbannhof, Verkehrsamt Gutleutstrasse 7–9

From Frankfurt take the A66 east for 21km (13 miles) to Hanau.

Hanau, Hessen

1 Hanau is the beginning of the German 'Fairy Tale Road', and the birthplace of the Brothers Grimm. Apart from their universally known stories, the chief trade is gold – master goldsmiths have worked here for centuries. The Goldschmiedehaus (house of the goldsmiths) is an unusual timber-framed structure with a large gabled roof typical of this architectural style. The entrance is through an outside staircase to a raised ground floor, for security reasons. Inside, there are international exhibitions of jewellery from the past and present. It also houses the oldest German college for metalworking.

The Schloss Phillipsruhe (castle) near Hanau functions as a museum for works of art, and the entrance gate is a creation in wrought iron from Paris. There are many objects relating to Hanau porcelain manufacture, brought here by Dutch refugees from religious persecution.

Schloss Steinheim, built between the 13th and the 16th centuries with a mighty belfry, houses a museum exhibiting objects of pre- and early history, from the Stone Age to Roman times.

[i] Am Markt 14

Take the A66 west back towards Frankfurt and turn right for the A661 north to Bad Homburg, 35km (22 miles).

Bad Homburg, Hessen

2 Bad Homburg is a modern spa with a Roman history in the Taunus mountain range. The restored

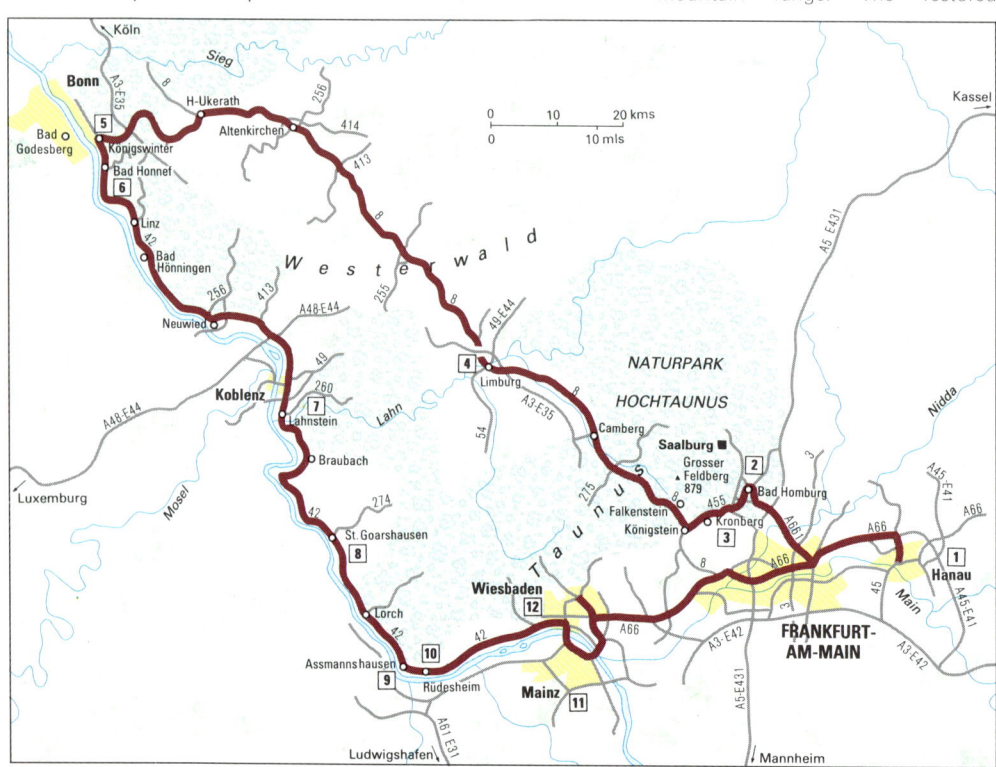

Römerkastell (Roman fort) at Saalburg is about 5km (3 miles) north and has been restored to its original design. It was part of the Roman Limes fortification line, and formed the northern frontier of the Roman Empire. The museum inside allows an interesting glimpse back to Roman times. The original fort was built in AD120, and could accommodate a contingent of 500 soldiers. The inside looks as though the Romans had just left it: catapults, armouries, shops, houses, temples and baths are all there.

The **Schloss** (castle) in its present form was built between 1680 and 1685 on the same spot as an older fortress. The medieval fortress is remembered only by one surviving tower, called the **Weisse Turm** (white tower). The castle was the residence of the Counts of Hesse-Homburg and later the summer residence of the Prussian Emperor Wilhelm II. The Schloss is open to the public, with valuable paintings and furniture from the 17th and 18th centuries. The **Schlosspark** is well cared for and has some exotic plants.

A curiosity to visit in the centre of Bad Homburg is the **Siamtemple**, donated by a Siamese king in gratitude for a successful cure at the spa. There is also a Russian chapel, and no less than seven health-giving springs in the attractively named Brunnenallee (Alley of Springs).

[i] Louisenstrasse 58

*Turn south to Oberursel and west to Kronberg on the **B455** 8km (5 miles).*

Kronberg, Hessen

3 On a rock in the middle of the town stands the **fortress** of the Knights of Kronberg, which dates from 1220. The town has been popular with painters because of its picturesque winding streets and timber-framed houses. In the 19th century the town became the home of the Kronberger school of artists, thus making its contribution to German art.

[i] Katharinenstrasse 7

*From Kronberg drive west to Königstein, and turn right for the **B8** to Limburg, 40km (25 miles).*

Limburg, Hessen

4 On the way to Limburg, the ruins of Falkenstein and Königstein make good stopping places. Königstein is also an interesting old town with the **Altes Rathaus** (old town hall) now housing the museum.

In the valley of the River Lahn, Limburg is an attractive medieval town with a **cathedral** dating from the 13th century, a masterpiece in late Romanesque style with seven towers. Inside, its original colours have been restored, and 13th-century frescos revealed. This restoration work was completed in 1973, and the visitor is given a unique flavour of a real medieval cathedral.

The **Domschatz** (treasury) is held in the bishop's residence and exhibits sacred works of art which also have great historic value. Special mention should be made of the **Staurothek**, a cross created by Byzantine craftsmen in the second half of the 10th century and the gem of the collection.

In the centre of the old town, around the fish market, there are many timber-framed houses, among them the **Rathaus** (town hall). Another building from 1296, claimed to be the oldest timber-framed house in Germany, is still lived in.

[i] Hospitalstrasse 2

*Head northwest on the **A8** for 68km (42 miles), then take the road leading west to Königswinter, 93km (58 miles) in total.*

Limburg's Romanesque cathedral towering over the town and river

Königswinter, Nordrhein-Westfalen

5 Königswinter lies on the banks of the Rhine, and one of the most popular ruins in this area is the fortress **Drachenfels**, which was destroyed in 1634. There are several ways of getting up there to enjoy the wide view over the Rhine valley and the countryside around: on foot, by donkey, by horse-drawn carriage or by cogwheel railway. The walk takes about half an hour, the railway eight minutes.

[i] Drachenfelsstrasse 3

*Take the **B42** south for 4km (2 miles) to Bad Honnef.*

Bad Honnef, Nordrhein-Westfalen

6 Bad Honnef offers mineral springs, a 30°C (86°F) swimming pool and a modern therapeutic institution. A visit is also recommended to the **parish church of St Johann**, which dates from the 12th century. In the section of town called Rhondorf there is a memorial to Konrad Adenauer, the well-known German statesman.

[i] Hauptstrasse 28a

*Continue on the **B42** for 51km (32 miles) to Lahnstein.*

FOR HISTORY BUFFS

2 *Bad Homburg, Hessen* In Bad Homburg there are mementoes of the famous men and women who visited this spa in its heyday. These include King Edward VII, Emperor Wilhelm II of Prussia, the Russian writer Dostoevsky and the last Tsarina of Russia, who, before her marriage, had been a Princess of Hessen.

BACK TO NATURE

Frankfurt, Hessen The **Enkheimer Marsh** near Frankfurt is an excellent spot for wildfowl, herons and waders, as are **Westerwald** and **Vogelsberg** lakes. In particular, look for greylag geese, black terns, bitterns, grey herons, redshank and pochard.

3 *Kronberg, Hessen* Hessen's oldest falconry can be visited on the **Grosser Feldberg**, north of Kronberg. Weather permitting, eagles and vultures can be observed in free flight.

FOR CHILDREN

3 *Kronberg, Hessen* The **Opel Zoo**, near Kronberg, has elephants, apes, giraffes, zebras and camels with other exotic and indigenous animals. Altogether over 950 species are kept here. Playing areas and a special petting zoo attract children. Camel riding is also on offer.

RECOMMENDED WALKS

3 *Kronberg, Hessen* A great number of hikes are offered from car parks around the Grosser Feldberg, north of Kronberg, through the **Naturpark Hochtaunus**.

10 *Rüdesheim, Hessen* Take the cable-car from Rüdesheim and ride over the vineyards to the hilltop. Very pleasant walks through the vineyards lead down to the valley and the town.

Lahnstein, Rheinland-Pfalz

7 Lahnstein lies on twin sites at the meeting of the rivers Lahn and Rhine. The left bank is called the Oberlahnstein, with Niederlahnstein opposite. Near **Oberlahnstein**, on a hill above the Rhine stands the fortified castle of **Burg Lahneck**, erected in the 13th century and typifying the charm of the Rhine valley. The interior furnishings and decorations are remarkable. There are attractive views from the castle down to the Rhine, but the best view of the castle and its setting can be obtained down below from the **Alte Lahnbrucke**.

In **Niederlahnstein**, there remains a few of the old manor houses which belonged to the aristocracy as well as the **Wirthaus an der Lahn** (Inn on the Lahn), which features in many German songs.

[i] Stadthallenpassage

From Lahnstein continue on the **B42** *south for 28km (17 miles) to St Goarshausen.*

St Goarshausen, Rheinland-Pfalz

8 This is also known as Loreleystadt (town of Loreley) because of its proximity to the famous rock known as the Loreley rock. Above the town stands the fortress **Katz**, crowning the rock on which it was built by the Counts of Katzenelnbogen. They controlled this area and the traffic on the Rhine through strategically sited fortresses, exacting what they believed were their 'dues' from passing ships. The fortress was built around the end of the 14th century and after its destruction rebuilt in 1806. It is not open to the public.

[i] Bahnhofstrasse 8

Continue on the **B42** *south for 25km (16 miles) to Assmannshausen.*

Assmannshausen, Hessen

9 The route passes the Loreley rock, 132m (433 feet) high. In German legend, various stories are told about this attractive Rhine maiden, who sits on her rock and lures passing ships to disaster.

There are not many districts in Germany which produce red wine, but Assmannshausen is known for its blue Burgundy grapes, which produce an excellent red. East of the town, in **Neiderwald**, stands a monument to German unity. The figure of *Germania* on top of the monument is 10m (33 feet) high with a 7m (22-foot) long sword in her hand.

Continue on the **B42** *south for 6km (4 miles) to Rüdesheim.*

Rüdesheim, Hessen

10 A wine centre on the banks of the Rhine, **Drosselgasse** in the centre is a popular meeting place with one tavern after another, and entertainment and music which go on until the early hours of the morning.

Taking the chairlift up above the Rhine from Assmannshausen

TOUR 24

The **Brömserburg**, a castle dating back to the 10th century, is now an important **wine museum**. The **Adlerturm** (eagle's tower) is a remnant of the town's 15th-century fortifications. It is only 20m (66 feet) high, but the walls are 1m (3 feet) thick. A cable-car from here travels up to the Niederwald monument.

[i] Rheinstrasse 16

Continue on the B42 towards Wiesbaden, turn right at Schierstein Kreuz for the A643 and turn left for Mainz after crossing the Rhine.

Mainz, Rheinland-Pfalz

11 The cathedral of Mainz is not far from the banks of the Rhine. The **St Martins Dom**, as it is called, belongs to a group of Romanesque cathedrals which show the mastery of German religious architecture in the Middle Ages. This enormous building project began in AD975. The western part of the cathedral is meant to symbolise the spiritual world, the eastern part the material world. After several fires the cathedral was finished in 1239 in its present form. Throughout the centuries it has been used for coronations and festive banquets, but it also housed soldiers during the Thirty Year Wars. Later it was used as a hospital for Napoleon's troops.

The **Kurfürstliche Schloss** (electoral palace) was finished in 1678 and now houses collections of the **Römisch-Germanisches Zentralmuseum** (Romano-German central museum). The history of Mainz goes back to a Roman stronghold called *Monguntiacum*, which was erected close to a former Celtic settlement.

[i] Bahnhofstrasse 15

From Mainz proceed to the ring road and drive north across the Rhine to Wiesbaden, 13km (8 miles).

St Goarshausen, overlooked by the 14th-century Katz castle

Wiesbaden, Hessen

12 On the right bank of the Rhine, between the foothills of the Taunus mountain range and the river, lies Wiesbaden, capital of the province of Hessen. The Romans first discovered the healing spring here, and called it *Aquae Mattiacorum*, after the Germanic tribe resident here. It probably became a Roman fort between AD41 and 50, was abandoned in 406 and taken over by the Franconians, who made it a local capital. The name of Wiesbaden is first recorded as Wisbada in AD829, which in German means the 'bath in the meadows'.

Its real prosperity grew in the 19th century, when the rich and famous of Europe rediscovered the hot springs and their healthful properties. The English had a special liking for the spa, even building their own church here in 1863. Wiesbaden was also the summer home of the Emperor Wilhelm II, and its popularity peaked around the turn of the century. The Wilhelmstrasse, the town's elegant main street, is a reminder of those affluent days.

[i] Ecke Wilhelm/Rheinstrasse 15

From Wiesbaden take the A66 for 40km (25 miles) back to Frankfurt am Main.

Frankfurt – Hanau 21 (13)
Hanau – Bad Homburg 35 (22)
Bad Homburg – Kronberg 8 (5)
Kronberg – Limburg 40 (25)
Limburg – Königswinter 95 (58)
Königswinter – Bad Honnef 4 (2)
Bad Honnef – Lahnstein 51 (32)
Lahnstein – St Goarshausen 28 (17)
St Goarshausen – Assmannshausen 25 (16)
Assmannshausen – Rüdesheim 6 (4)
Rüdesheim – Mainz 29 (18)
Mainz – Wiesbaden 13 (8)
Wiesbaden – Frankfurt 40 (25)

SPECIAL TO...

10 *Rüdesheim, Hessen* Close to the famous Drosselgasse in Rüdesheim, the historic **Brömserhof** houses a large collection of self-playing mechanical musical instruments.

SCENIC ROUTES

The route from Bad Homburg to Königswinter is particularly beautiful, while the delightful scenery from St Goarshausen along the Rhine is enhanced by the numerous castles and ruins on the hills, and the more graceful traffic of the river.

2 days – 305km (189 miles)

ALONG THE LEFT BANK OF THE RHINE

The house in Bonn where Ludwig van Beethoven was born, now a museum dedicated to the composer

Köln ● Brühl ● Bonn ● Bad Godesberg ● Remagen
Andernach ● Kloster Maria Laach ● Nürburgring
Bad Münstereifel ● Aachen ● Köln

Köln (Cologne) is the undisputed capital of the Rhineland. Founded by the Romans, it was an important medieval trading city and is now a major industrial and commercial centre. On the approach to the city, the skyline is dominated by the soaring twin spires of the *Dom* (cathedral), a classic example of Gothic church architecture, with 56 pillars supporting its massive roof. Building started in 1248, but the cathedral was only inaugurated in 1880. Altogether there are 14 churches within the ring road surrounding Köln's *Altstadt* (old town). Also of interest is the *Römisch-Germanisches Museum* (Roman-Germanic museum), which describes everyday Roman life. One exhibit is the Dionysos Mosaic, discovered in 1941 and illustrating the world of the god of wine. Roman and Barbarian ornaments in gold and enamel are among the other treasures in this fascinating museum.

FOR CHILDREN

1 *Brühl, Nordrhein-Westfalen* The **Phantasieland** amusement park at Brühl is open from April to October. The programme includes breathtaking rides through 'Hollywood' film sets and the Grand Canyon, and a trip on a monorail. Shows in 3-D, laser and the 'Western Saloon' are a few other examples of what is on offer. Allow about six hours for a visit.

4 *Remagen, Rheinland-Pfalz* En route from Remagen to Andernach, children can enjoy the **Märchenwald** at Bad Breisig. A fairy tale atmosphere prevails, with scale models and moving and speaking figures which add to the entertainment.

7 *Nürburgring, Rheinland-Pfalz* If you follow the **B257** about 20km (12 miles) north to Altenahr, you can take the children to the 500m (1,640-foot) long summer toboggan run. A draglift takes visitors up to the starting point.

[i] Unter Fettenhennen 19 (am Dom)

*From Köln take the **B51** south for 13km (8 miles) to Brühl.*

Brühl, Nordrhein-Westfalen

1 The castle of Brühl, called the **Augustusburg**, is a combined effort of three famous architects: Johann Conrad Schlaun, François Cuvilliés and Balthasar Neumann. The earlier castle had been blown up in 1689. Cuvilliés was responsible for the new rococo design of the castle, and Neumann designed the staircase, with pillars shaped in the form of male and female figures. The hall, with its ornate staircase, is now used for concerts and official receptions given by the Federal President. The gardens are laid out in formal French style.

[i] Uhlstrasse 3

*From Brühl drive east and join the **B9** south to Bonn, 19km (12 miles).*

Bonn, Nordrhein-Westfalen

2 Until the re-unification in October 1990, Bonn was the federal capital of the former West Germany. Although the focus of German politics is now shifting to Berlin, this elegant city has its own attractions. Before it became federal capital in May 1949, Bonn was a tranquil town on the Rhine, internationally known as the birthplace of the great composer Ludwig van Beethoven. The house where he was born in 1770 has been converted into a **museum**, displaying paintings from his time in Bonn and Vienna, his last piano, his string instruments and manuscripts. Beethoven lived in Bonn until he was 22, when he was drawn to the capital of music, Vienna.

The **Altes Rathaus** (old town hall) was built by the French architect Michel Leveilly in 1737. It has all the features of a French castle, including richly decorated façades and large windows. It is the official seat of the Mayor, and hosts many official receptions. The splendid **Münster** (minster) is 900 years old and was erected on an early Christian site during Roman times. It is a fine example of the 12th-century Rhenish-Romanesque transitional style, although the nave shows the advance of the Gothic influence which replaced it. The **Rheinisches Landesmuseum** exhibits collections from Roman and medieval times, as well as the head of a prehistoric man found in the village of Neandertal, 40km (24 miles) north of Cologne, and estimated to be 60,000 years old.

[i] Berliner Platz 2

Continue south for 7km (4 miles) to Bad Godesberg.

Bad Godesberg, Nordrhein-Westfalen

3 Its pleasant position on the Rhine has made this former spa a popular site for embassies and a residential area for diplomats and senior civil servants. The **Rheinpromenade** offers relaxing strolls along the river, and is especially attractive at sunset, surrounded by castles and ruins. The ruin of the **Godesburg**, blown up in 1583, offers wonderful views from the surviving tower. The ruin has been incorporated into a hotel.

[i] see Bonn

*From Bad Godesberg take the **B9** south for 14km (9 miles) to Remagen.*

Remagen, Rheinland-Pfalz

4 Remagen was originally a Celtic settlement and then a Roman fort. Of interest is the **parish church of St Peter and Paul**, rebuilt in late Romanesque style. Near the **Rathaus** (town hall) are reminders of the old Roman fort, known as *Ricomagus*.

The **bridge** at Remagen achieved fame in World War II. American soldiers captured it intact in March 1945, but it collapsed three days later under the weight of their military equipment, killing 18 soldiers. By the side of the Rhine, appropriately, is a **Friedensmuseum** (peace museum).

[i] Rathaus, Bachstrasse 2

*From Remagen continue on the **B9** for 22km (14 miles) to Andernach.*

TOUR 25

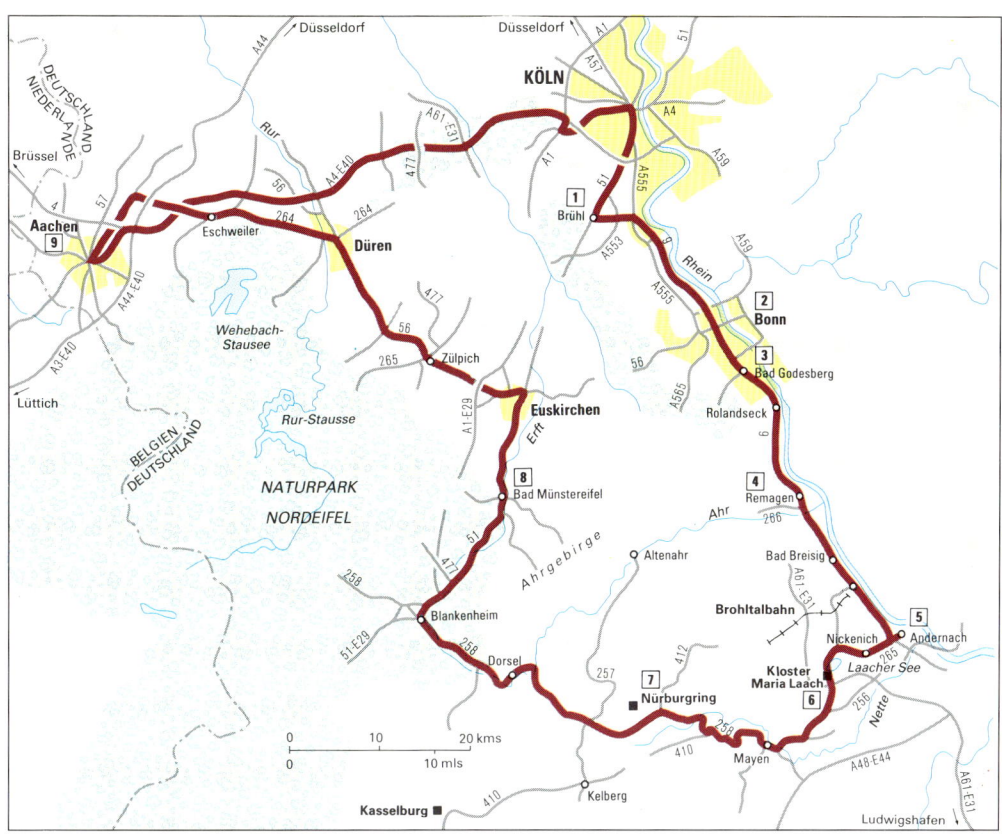

Andernach, Rheinland-Pfalz

5 Once a Roman fort, Andernach was still heavily fortified in medieval times and was the scene of many battles. The medieval gates are still intact. The **Runde Turm** (round tower) is a former watch-tower, 56m (184 feet) high, and solid enough to have survived an attempt to blow it up in 1689.

Köln's river frontage backed by the great Gothic cathedral. Its strategic position on the Rhine led to the city's early prosperity

i Laufstrasse 11

From Andernach go west via Nickenich for 13km (8 miles) to Kloster Maria Laach.

BACK TO NATURE

3 *Bad Godesberg, Nordrhein-Westfalen* At Rolandseck, south of Bad Godesberg, is a **deer park** with many species free to wander in natural, open surroundings.

7 *Nürburgring, Rheinland-Pfalz* From Nürburgring take the B257 south to Kelberg, then turn west on the B410 to Pelm/Gerolstein for the **Adler und Wolfspark** (eagle and wolf park), Kasselburg. The park is by the massive twin tower of the castle, easily seen from a distance. It features three daily attractions: the feeding of the wolves; a display of eagles, falcons and other birds in flight; and afterwards an acrobatic display by roller pigeons! All of these take place in the afternoon, weather permitting.

Between the displays, visitors can walk around the grounds and observe other animals, such as foxes and wild boar, in their enclosures, where great emphasis is given to the welfare and protection of the animals.

SCENIC ROUTES

The route along the Rhine from Bad Godesberg to Andernach is an exciting one, offering views of the river with a backdrop of mountains and hills, partly covered by vineyards stretching right down to the riverbanks.

The route from the Nürburgring to Bad Münstereifel leads through the attractive **Ahrgebirge** (Ahr mountain range), where beautiful forests reach up to the edge of the town walls.

TOUR 25

RECOMMENDED WALKS

7 *Nürburgring, Rheinland-Pfalz* Walks in the woods around the Kasselburg near Pelm/Gerolstein are very enjoyable. From Nürburgring, drive south on the **B257** to Kelberg, then west on the **B410**. The **Deutsche Wildstrasse** (German deer road) runs through the area and connects with numerous starting places for hikes. Detailed maps are available locally, and as hiking is very popular in Germany the information offices provide excellent advice.

Kloster Maria Laach, Rheinland-Pfalz

6 The Kloster Maria Laach is a Benedictine abbey on the south-western shores of Lake Laach. The well-preserved Romanesque basilica, with its six towers, is a notable building. It was donated by Heinrich II in 1093 and in the western part of the choir section is the colourful tomb of its founder. The church has three aisles, similar to the cathedrals of Mainz, Speyer and Worms. In accordance with Romanesque style, the interior looks bare and new stained glass windows had to be installed after World War II. The altar has a baldachin-style roof, and the oldest part of the church is the triple-aisled crypt. The churchyard is called **Das Paradies** (paradise) and in the middle stands the 'fountain of life'.

[i] Kloster

*Drive south to Mayen, turn right and take the **B258** west to Nürburgring, 33km (20 miles).*

Nürburgring, Rheinland-Pfalz

7 Nürburgring provides a change of diet from all the history of this area. One of the most famous motor-racing circuits in the world, it was built in the 1920s in the wooded countryside, where the first powerful motor cars were tested. The northern sector is over 20km (13 miles) long, but the new Grand Prix track which opened in 1984 is a mere 4.5km (3 miles). The German Grand Prix was recently transferred to Hockenheim, south of Heidelberg. On days when there is no racing or training going on, visitors may test their own cars on the circuit.

[i] Adenau, Kirchstrasse 15

*From Nürburgring take the **B258** northwest to Blankenheim, then turn right for the **B51** northeast to Bad Münstereifel, 48km (30 miles).*

The former grand prix motor racing track of Nürburgring

Bad Münstereifel, Nordrhein-Westfalen

8 Bad Münstereifel's old town is surrounded by a massive 13th-century wall, 1.5km (1 mile) long, with four gates and 18 watch-towers, and one of the best preserved medieval fortifications in Germany.

The restored Romanesque **abbey** dates back to the 10th century. A stroll round the **Marktplatz** reveals some interesting historical houses. Look out for the gabled **Windeckhaus** in a nearby street. Near the **Effelsberg** stands the radio telescope of the Max Planck Institute. This is one of the largest fully rotating telescopes in the world, with a disc of 100m (328 feet) in diameter.

[i] Langenhecke 2

> From Bad Münstereifel continue on the **B51** north towards Euskirchen, then turn left for the **B56** to Düren, and left again on the **B264** west to Aachen, 71km (44 miles).

Café in Aachen. Printen, sold here, is a speciality of the town – a type of gingerbread

Aachen, Nordrhein-Westfalen

9 The fall of the Roman Empire plunged Europe into chaos. The man who eventually united what is now basically Germany and France and ruled as King of the Franks was Charlemagne, and Aachen (Aix-la-Chapelle in French) was one of his centres of power. The **Dom** (cathedral) was a chapel founded by Charlemagne in 800. His throne and his crown are preserved here, and his tomb, the **Karlschrein**, is a beautifully ornate work of art. From 936 to 1531, 32 German emperors were crowned here, and each one followed the custom of making a donation to the cathedral. The result is one of the most valuable collections of art objects in Germany. A bust of Charlemagne, cast in gold and silver and encrusted with jewels, was donated by Charles IV in 1349. Outside the cathedral, the **Rathaus** (town hall) is a 14th-century building on the site of Charlemagne's palace. The frescos in the **Krönungsaal** depict his life, while the fountain in the market square is dedicated to the Emperor.

[i] Markt 39

> From Aachen take the **A4/E40** for 65km (40 miles) back to Köln.

Köln – Brühl **13 (8)**
Brühl – Bonn **19 (12)**
Bonn – Bad Godesberg **7 (4)**
Bad Godesberg – Remagen **14 (9)**
Remagen – Andernach **22 (14)**
Andernach – Maria Laach **13 (8)**
Maria Laach – Nürburgring **33 (20)**
Nürburgring – Bad Münstereifel **48 (30)**
Bad Münstereifel – Aachen **71 (44)**
Aachen – Köln **65 (40)**

HISTORY BUFFS

2 Bonn, Nordrhein-Westfalen
The **Schloss Poppelsdorf** in Bonn used to be the summer residence of the Electors of Cologne, who lived in Bonn after losing a battle against Cologne's burghers in the 13th century. It was originally designed in baroque style by the French architect de Cotte.

9 Aachen, Nordrhein-Westfalen The great chandelier in the **cathedral** at Aachen was installed there at the request of Emperor Friedrich Barbarossa. When it was hung, the mosaic on the ceiling was damaged, which is not altogether surprising: the chandelier is 4m (13 feet 9 inches) in diameter and the iron chain which suspends it from the ceiling is 27m (88 feet 6 inches) long. The chandelier has 16 turrets to symbolise Holy Jerusalem.

SPECIAL TO...

5 Andernach, Rheinland-Pfalz
Brohl-Lützing, just north of Andernach, is the terminus of a narrow gauge railway called the **Brohltalbahn**. The line, which passes through some very pleasant countryside, was built to transport phonolith, a rare volcanic mineral used for the manufacture of glass, to the port or main railway terminal on the Rhine. A timetable gives information about trains and special treats are available on Sundays and public holidays, when a steam engine pulls the carriages.

INDEX

References to captions are in *italic*.

A
Aachen 96, 117, *117*
Abenberg 57
Adler und Wolfspark 115
Ahrensburg 10
Ahrgebirge 115
Allensbach 86
Alpirsbach 95
Alsfeld 30, *31*, *40*, 42–3
Altdorf 54
Alte Saline 64
Amberg 54, *56*, 57
Amerang 63
Andernach 115, 117
Arnsberg 44–6
Arnsberger Wald 45, 46
Aschau 65
Assmannshausen 112, *112*
Augsburg 74

B
Bacharach *96–7*, 105
Bad Breisig 114
Bad Dürkheim 100
Bad Godesberg 114, 115
Bad Grund 35
Bad Harzburg 32, 33
Bad Hersfeld 43, *43*
Bad Homburg 110–11
Bad Honnef 111
Bad Kreuznach 105
Bad Lauterberg 33–4
Bad Mergentheim *106*, 107
Bad Münstereifel 117
Bad Reichenhall 64, *64*
Bad Säckingen 90, *90–1*
Bad Schandau 24
Bad Tölz 67, 69
Bad Wiessee 67
Baden-Baden *83*, 92
Baden-Württemberg 74–5, 81, 82–95, 106–7
  tour maps 75, 81, 87, 89, 92, 108
Badenweiler 91
Badische Weinstrasse (Wine Route) 83
Balingen 94
Baltic Sea coast 8
Bamberg 53, *53*
banks 5
Bastei 24, *25*
Bauer in der Au 67
Bauernhausmuseum 63
Bavaria 48–9
Bavarian Forest *58–9*, 60, 65
Bavarian Lakes 66–9
Bavarian Nature Park 58
Bavarian Swabia 48, 49, 74–7
Bayern 50–74, 75–8, 79–81, 106, 107–8
  tour maps 51, 55, 60, 63, 68, 71, 75, 81, 108
Bayreuth *50*, 50–2
Benediktbeuern 68–9
Bensheim 106
Berchtesgaden *4*, 64–5, *65*
Berg 70
Berlin 8, 9, *18*, 18–20, *19*, *20*
  tour map 19
Bernkastel-Kues 102, *102–3*, 103

Bilsteinhöhle 46
Bingen 105
Birgittenkloster 54
Black Forest (Schwarzwald) 82, 88–95
Blaubeuern 75
Bodensee (Lake Constance) *80–1*, 82, 84–7
Böhmerwald (Bohemian Forest) 54, 58, 59
Bonn 114, *114*, 117
Boppard *104*, 105
Brandenburg 21
Brandenburger Tor 18–19
Braunschweig 15
Breitachklamm 78, 79
Bremen 14, *14*
Brilon 47
Brodtener Steilufer 11
Brohltalbahn 117
Bruchhausen Steine 47
Brüder Grimm Museum 40
Brühl 114
Buddenbrookhaus 12
Bündheim 32
Burg Eltz 104
Burg Hohenzollern 94
Burg Lahneck 105
Burg Montclair 98
Burg Rotteln 90–1

C
car hire 6
Celle *8–9*, *16*, 16–17
Cham 58, *60*, 61
Checkpoint Charlie 21
Clausthal-Zellerfeld *32*, 35
Coburg 50, 51, *51*
Cochem 102, 103
Colditz 24, *24*
consulates 7
credit cards 4
currency 5
customs regulations 4

D
Daimler Benz Museum 93
Danube, River 49, 58, 82
Daun 103
Dechenhöhle 44, *44–5*
Deutsche Edelsteinstrasse (Gems Road) 99
Deutsche Ferienstrasse (Holiday Road) 14, 30, 35, 63
Deutsche Historische Strasse (Historical Road) 30
Deutsche Märchenstrasse (Fairy Tale Road) 30, 110
Deutsche Uhrenstrasse (Clock Road) 82
Deutsche Weinstrasse (Wine Road) 101
Deutsche Wildstrasse (Deer Road) 116
Die Bastei *9*
Dillingen 74, 77
Donaueschingen 83, 88
Donaustauf 60
Donauwörth 74
Drachenfels *110*, 111
Dresden 9, 22–3
Druggelter Kapelle 46

E
Ebrach 53
Eder Dam 40, *42*
Ehrenburg 50
Eichstätt 56–7
Einbeck 36–7
Einhornhöhle 34
Eisenach 28, *28*

Elbe–Lübeck Kanal 12
Elisabethkirche 41–2
Ellingen 57
emergency telephone numbers 4
Enkheimer Marsh 111
entry regulations 4
Erfurt *26*, 28, 29, *29*
Essing 60
Ettal 73
Ettendorf 64
Europa Park Rust 95
Eutin 12
Externsteine 38

F
Fellhornbahn 78
Felsenfestung Ehrenbreitstein 104
Felsenlabyrinth Luisenburg 52
Felsenmeer 44
Fernsehturm 20
Festung Rosenberg 50
Fischbach 99
Franconia 48, 50–3
Frankenberg 40–1, 42
Frankfurt 110, 111
Fraueninsel 62, *62–3*
Fraunhofer Glashütte 68–9
Freiburg im Breisgau 82, *82–3*, 88, *88*
Freudenberg 47
Freudenstadt 92
Friedrichroda 27
Friedrichshafen 86
Furtwangen 88
Füssen 79–80

G
Garmisch-Partenkirchen *49*, 70–1, 73, *73*
Gengenbach 95
Gera 27
Glashütte Süssmuth 43
Gmund 67
Goethehaus 26
Goslar *32*, 33
Gotha 28, 29
Göttingen 36, *36*
Graswarder nature reserve and bird sanctuary 13
Grosser Feldberg 111
Grosser Inselberg 27
Günzburg 74
Gutach 95

H
Habichtswald nature park 42
Hagen 44, *47*
Haina 41
Hamburg 10
Hameln (Hamelin) *36*, 38, *38*
Hanau 110
Hangloch Wasserfall 89
Hannover (Hanover) 14, 15, 16
Hansa Park 13
Harz mountains 30, 34, 35, *35*
Haseler Tropfsteinhöhle 90
health matters 4–5
Hechingen 94
Heide Park Soltau 16
Heidelberg 106, *107*
Heilbronn 109
Heiligenberg 85
Heiligenhafen 13
Heinrichschöhle 44
Hemfurth 43
Hermannsdenkmal 39
Herrenberg 92, *92*, 94
Herrenchiemsee 62
Herrenhausen Garten 14, *15*
Herzberg 34

INDEX

Hessen 7, 40–3, 106, 110–11, 112–13
  tour maps 41, 108, 110
Hildesheim 37, 37–8
Hintersee 64
Höchstädt 77
Hodenhagen 16
Hohenaschau 65
Höllental 82–3
Holsteinische Schweiz (Swiss Holstein) 11
Horn 38
Hunnenring 98

I

Iberger Tropfsteinhöhle 35
Idar-Oberstein 98, 99, 100
Immenstadt 78
Ingolstadt 61
Insel Reichenau 84, 85
Iserlohn 44
Isny 80–1

J

Jena 26–7
Johannes Kepler Museum 59

K

Kaiserslautern 99
Kallmünz 56
Kandern 91
Karl May Museum 23
Kassel 30, 40
Kasselburg 115
Kaufbeuren 48, 76, 76–7, 77
Kehlsteinhaus 64–5
Kelheim 59, 60
Kellerwald forest 42
Kempten 76–7
Kiel 13
Kiel Canal 13
Kipfenberg 56, 57
Kleine Walsertal (Österreich) 79
Kloster Bursfelde 39
Kloster Maria Laach 116
Kloster Seeon 62–3
Koblenz 104
Kochel 68
Köln (Cologne) 114, 115
Konig-Otto Tropfsteinhöhle 54
Königssee 65
Königstein (Hessen) 111
Königstein (Sachsen) 23–4
Königswinter 111
Konstanz 84, 85, 86
Kronach 50
Kronberg 111, 112
Kulturhöhlen 46
Kurfürstendamm 18

L

Lahnstein 112
Landsberg 77
Landshut 61
Lechfeld 77
Leipzig 22
Letmathe 44
Lichtenstein 93–4
Limburg 111, 111
Lindau 78, 80–1
local time 5
Loreley rock 112
Lörrach 90–1
Löwenburg 41
Lübbenau 21
Lübeck 10, 11, 12–13, 12–13
Lucas Cranach Haus 26
Lüneburger Heide 8, 14, 16, 17

M

Mainau 86
Mainz 113
maps (see also individual regions)
  Germany 6–7
Marburg/Lahn 41–2
Maria in der Tanne 88, 91
Marienglasgrotte 27
Mecklenburg—Vorpommern 11–12
  tour map 10
Meersburg 83, 86–7
Meissen 22, 22
Memmingen 75, 75–6
Merzig 98
Meschede 47
Mettlach 98
Michelstadt 106, 107
Miltenberg 106
Mittelzell 84
Mittenwald 70, 71, 72
Mon Plaisir Dolls' Museum 28
Moritzburg 23, 23
Mosel valley 102–5
motoring 6–7
Mühlhausen 28–9
München (Munich) 66, 66, 69, 70
Münden 39
Museum für Deutsche Volkskunde (German Folklore Museum) 20
Museumsinsel 20

N

Naturpark Diemelsee 42
Nebelhöhle 94
Neckar valley 96, 106–9
Neckargerach 109
Neunburg vorm Wald 56
Neuschwanstein 80
Neustadt 100, 101
Neidersachsen 14–17, 32, 33–8, 39
  tour maps 15, 33, 39
Niederzell 84
Nindorf Nature Park 17
Nonnweiler 98
Nordrhein-Westfalen 38–9, 44–7, 111, 114, 117
  tour maps 39, 45, 110, 115
Nordstemmen 38
Northeim 36
Nürburgring 114, 115, 116, 116
Nürnberg (Nuremberg) 48, 54, 57

O

Oberammergau 73, 73
Oberbayern 48
Oberpfälzer Wald 57
Oberstaufen 78
Oberstdorf 78, 79, 80
Oberzell 84
Oder-Stausee 34
Offenburg 95
Optisches Museum 26–7
Osterode 31, 34, 34
Osterseen 70, 71
Ottobeuren 76, 76
Ottofelsen 32

P

Paderborn 38–9
Passau 48, 58
Pergamon Museum 20
Pfaffenstein 24
Pfahl 56

Pirmasens 101, 101
post offices 5
Potsdam 21
Potsdamer Platz 19
Prien 62, 63, 64
Prunn 61
public holidays 6

R

Radebeul 23
Ramsbeck 47
Ratzeburg 10
Ravensburg 86, 86
Regen 58, 59, 61, 61
Regensburg 48, 58, 58–9
Reichstag 19
Reit im Winkl 65
Remagen 114
Rendsburg 13
Rennsteig forest nature trail 27
Reutlingen 93
Rheinfalle 90
Rheinland-Pfalz 98, 99–105, 112, 113, 114–16
  tour maps 101, 103, 110, 115
Rhine, River 5, 96
Richard Wagner Festspielhaus 52
Riedenburg 61
Rinderstall 39
Roemer-Pelizaeus Museum 38, 39
Rolandseck 115
Romantische Strasse (Romantic Road) 30
Römerkastell 111
Rosenheim 62, 62
Rossfeld Ringstrasse 65
Roth 57
Rothenburg ob der Tauber 107–8, 108
Rottach-Egern 66
Rüdesheim 112–13
Ruhpolding 65

S

Saarbrücken 98, 99
Saarburg 98
Saarland 98
  tour map 101
Sachsen 22–4
  tour map 25
Sachsen-Anhalt 32
  tour map 33
Safariland Stukenbrock 38
St Blasien 89
St Goar 105
St Goarshausen 112, 113
Salem 85
Sanssouci Castle 21, 21
Sauerland 30
Saxony 8
Scharzfeld 34
Schillerhaus 26
Schleswig-Holstein 10, 12–13
  tour map 10
Schliersee 66, 67
Schloss Cecilienhof 21
Schloss Charlottenburg 18
Schloss Elmau 71–2
Schloss Friedenstein 29
Schloss Hofen 86
Schloss Hohenschwangau 79, 80
Schloss Krottorf 47
Schloss Linderhof 72, 73
Schloss Neuhaus 38–9
Schluchsee 88
Schwäbisch Hall 97, 108, 109, 109
Schwarzwald Hochstrasse (Black Forest High Road) 94

INDEX

Schwarzwälder Panoramastrasse (Black Forest Panoramic Road) 83, 90
Schwenningen 88
Schwerin 11, *11*
Seebruck 62–3
Seeshaupt 70, 71
Semperoper (Opera House, Dresden) 23
Serengeti-Park 16
Siegen *44*, 45, *46*, 47
Siegessäule 18
Sierksdorf 13
Singen 85
Sosetalsperre (Sose Dam) 34
Sonthofen 78
Sorpesee 45–6
Speyer 109
Spreewald 21
Stadtforst Finsterbachtal Forest 41
Starnberg 48, 70, 73
Steigerwald nature park 53
Steingaden 80
Steinkirche 34
Stuttgart 83, 93, *95*
Sulzburg 91

T

Tauberbischofsheim 106–7
Tegernsee *66–7*, 67, 69
telephones 6
Thüringen 26–9
  tour map 26
Thüringer Wald 27, *27*
Thuringia 8
Titisee 88, 89, *89*
Todtnau 89, 91
tourist offices 4
Traben-Trarbach 102
Traunstein 64
Trausnitz Castle 61
Triberg 88, 91
Trier 102, 105
Trifels 101
Tübingen 93, *93*

U

Überlingen 84
Ulm *74*, 74–5
Unter den Linden 19–20
Unteruhldingen 84

V

Velburg 54
Villa Wahnfried 52
Villingen 88
Vogelpark Walsrode 16
Vohenstrauss 55–6
Volkswagenwerk 16
Völlinghausen 44
voltage 5
Vulkaneifel 103

W

Walchensee 68, *68*
Waldeck 40, 43
Waldshut 90, *91*
Walhalla 60
Wallgau 68
Wangen *78*, 80, 81
Wartburg Castle 28
Wasserburg 63
Wehr 90
Weiden 54, *55*
Weimar 26
Weingarten *84*, 85, 86, 87
Weinstube Vinzenz Richter 22
Weissenburg 57
Wernigerode 32, 33

Wertheim 106
Weserbergland 30
Wesertalstrasse 37
Wienhausen 16
Wiesbaden 97, 113
Wieskirche 80
Wilhelmsdorf 86
Wilhelmsthal 40, 43
Wilseder 17
Wismar 12, *13*
Wittlich 102
Wolfsburg 16
Wollmatinger Ried Bird Sanctuary 86
words and phrases 6
Worms *98*, 100, *100*
Würzberg 106
Würzburg *49*, 50, *52*

Z

Zeiss Planetarium 26
Zell 102
Zuffenhausen 93
Zugspitze 70–1
Zwinger Palace 22–3

ACKNOWLEDGEMENTS

The Automobile Association would like to thank the following photographers and library for their help in the preparation of this book.

A BAKER & D TRAVERSO took all the pictures not listed below (AA PHOTO LIBRARY).

SPECTRUM COLOUR LIBRARY Cover Neuschwanstein Castle.

Author's acknowledgements Adi Kraus thanks the following people and organisations for their help: Hans Wörndl, DER German Travel Service, London; Harald Henning, German National Tourist Office, London; and the Head Office of the German Tourist Offices (DZT) in Frankfurt/Main.